WOMEN IN THE WORKPLACE

WOMEN IN THE WORKPLACE

Edited by
PHYLLIS A. WALLACE
Alfred P. Sloan School of Management
Massachusetts Institute of Technology

⟨𝒜ℋ⟩ *Auburn House Publishing Company*
Boston, Massachusetts

Library of Congress Cataloging in Publication Data
Main entry under title:

Women in the workplace.

Includes index.
Contents: Increased labor force participation of women and affirmative
action / Phyllis A. Wallace—The MBA / Myra H. Strober—The apprenticeship model of organizational careers / Lotte Bailyn—[etc.]
1. Women—Employment—United States—Addresses, essays, lec-
tures. I. Wallace, Phyllis Ann.
HD6095.W6963   331.4'0973   81-12775
ISBN 0-86569-069-3   AACR2

Printed in the United States of America

ACKNOWLEDGMENTS

This volume is intended for everyone who is interested in the changing status of women workers. Several of the papers were presented before a large audience of representatives from the private sector who attended a symposium sponsored by the Industrial Liaison Program at MIT. The purpose of the Symposium was to relate current research to the more practical concerns of employers.

The individual authors have acknowledged the help of researchers, colleagues, and others who assisted them. I am especially grateful to Katharine Abraham and Annette LaMond for their review of selected chapters. Johanna Maeland's skillful editorial assistance certainly improved the text. The Industrial Relations Section at the Alfred P. Sloan School at MIT provided the funding required to prepare the manuscript for publication.

PHYLLIS A. WALLACE
Cambridge, Massachusetts

ABOUT THE EDITOR

Phyllis A. Wallace, Ph.D., is Professor of Management at the Alfred P. Sloan School of Management at MIT. She has been actively engaged as a researcher, teacher,,and consultant on problems concerning the development and management of human resources. Her publications include the following: *Pathways to Work: Unemployment Among Black Teenage Females* (Lexington Books, 1974); *Equal Employment Opportunity and the AT&T Case* (MIT Press, 1976); *Women, Minorities, and Employment Discrimination*, with Annette LaMond (Lexington Books, 1977); and *Black Women in the Labor Force* (MIT Press, 1980). Dr. Wallace serves on the Board of Directors of the State Street Bank and Trust Company (Boston), the Stop and Shop Companies (Boston), and Teachers Insurance and Annuity Association (TIAA), New York. In addition, she has served as a Commissioner of the U.S. Minimum Wage Study Commission and a public member of the President's Pay Advisory Committee.

LIST OF CONTRIBUTORS

Lotte Bailyn   Professor of Organizational Psychology and Management, Sloan School of Management, Massachusetts Institute of Technology

Anne Harlan   Associate Professor of Psychology, Wellesley College

Edith F. Lynton   Research Assistant, The Conference Board

Julianne M. Malveaux   Assistant Professor of Economics, San Francisco State University

Brigid O'Farrell   Research Associate, Wellesley College Center for Research on Women

Ruth G. Shaeffer   Senior Research Associate, The Conference Board

Myra H. Strober   Associate Professor, School of Education and Director of the Center for Research on Women, Stanford University

Phyllis A. Wallace   Professor of Management, Sloan School of Management, Massachusetts Institute of Technology

Carol L. Weiss   Research Associate, Wellesley College Center for Research on Women

CONTENTS

CHAPTER 7
Corporate Experiences in Improving Women's Job Opportunities
by Ruth Gilbert Shaeffer and Edith F. Lynton

INTRODUCTION

by Phyllis A. Wallace

The chapters in this book reflect the perspectives of social scientists from several disciplines and report their findings from research underway on women at work. Earlier versions of four of the papers (Bailyn, O'Farrell, Shaeffer, and Wallace) were presented to representatives from private sector employers who attended the symposium "Women in the Workplace: Management of Human Resources," which was sponsored by the Industrial Liaison Program at the Massachusetts Institute of Technology. Thus practitioners had an opportunity to respond to and comment on the issues that were highlighted. These revised papers and the others included in this book conclude that, although women are becoming an increasing share of the labor force, they continue to face poorer opportunities than men. Progress has been slow whether women are white collar or blue collar workers, or whether they are in traditional or nontraditional jobs.

The first chapter, "Increased Labor Force Participation of Women and Affirmative Action" by Phyllis Wallace, discusses the external legal environment of sex discrimination in employment. During the past sixteen years, various laws, regulations, and judicial decisions have helped to determine the rules of the workplace on issues that are important to working women. Guidelines on sex discrimination by the Equal Employment Opportunity Commission have induced employers and unions to scrutinize carefully and to modify, if need be, traditional policies on maternity benefits, retirement benefits, seniority and promotion, equal pay, and height and weight requirements. On balance, women workers have benefited from these actions. During the latter part of the 1970s, a shift occurred away from litigation to negotiated settlements (consent decrees) of some of the issues. The implementation of the American Telephone and Telegraph (AT&T) Consent Decree provided one of the models for such settlements.

Myra Strober's Chapter 2, "The MBA: Same Passport to Success for Women and Men?" reports on the job market experience of a sample of men and women MBAs from Stanford University's class of 1974. A follow-up study four years after graduation shows that women from this pool of highly talented young managers have not been as "successful" as their male counterparts. Although the women MBAs started with salaries equivalent to those of the males, four years later the female/male parity in salaries had eroded such that female salaries were 80 percent of the males'. The major reasons appear to be that women were more likely to have had discontinuous work experience (child care and home responsibilities) and did not work in those industries where the compensation was the highest. If other longitudinal studies of the upward mobility of women MBAs support this major finding of significant differences in compensation,* the implications will be far-reaching for employers, managerial women and men, and the management schools that produce the MBAs.

One question implicit in the Strober report of what employers can do to improve the work experience of highly talented managerial women is answered in Chapter 3 in Lotte Bailyn's "The Apprenticeship Model of Organizational Careers: A Response to Changes in the Relation Between Work and Family." Bailyn urges a reevaluation of organizational responses to changes in the interaction of work and family. Dual career families are at a disadvantage in pursuing high organizational positions that currently require extensive work orientation during the early years of the career. Alternatives to this career success model are examined, and the more flexible apprenticeship model of slower development of organizational careers is suggested. Such a model would better fit the new work/family patterns now emerging.

Anne Harlan and Carol Weiss in Chapter 4, "Sex Differences in Factors Affecting Managerial Career Advancement," discuss the findings from their study, which compares one hundred male and female managers (fifty each) in two large companies in the same labor market. In these companies women did not advance in management the way that men did. Harlan and Weiss analyze a number

---

* A longitudinal study of graduates from the master's program at the Sloan School of Management, MIT, is being conducted by Phyllis A. Wallace. A large sample of male and female graduates from the classes of 1975 to 1979 is being tracked over a five-year period.

of variables and conclude that, although strong similarities exist in both the individual characteristics and organizational experiences of men and women managers, the primary difference faced is the existence of sex bias. Subtle sex bias evident in the less critical feedback to women managers from their supervisors, stereotypic attitudes about women, and the need for women to prove themselves to a greater degree are the major barriers to the advancement of women managers. The approach of Harlan and Weiss strongly suggests that organizational strategies are needed to reduce the impact of sex bias.

A broad overview of women in white collar jobs is made by Julianne Malveaux in Chapter 5, "Moving Forward, Standing Still: Women in White Collar Jobs." The persistence of occupational segregation explains much of the lower earnings and higher unemployment that women workers experience. However, limited movement out of female-stratified jobs took place during the 1970s, especially among younger women. Except in the "typically female" occupations, males are distributed in broader industry groupings than women. Thus industrial segregation has a role in maintaining the earnings gap between men and women. Malveaux estimates the impact of the occupational and industrial distribution of men and women on wage differentials and finds that these distribution differences are responsible for a minimum of 15 percent of the earnings distribution differential.

Researchers on the labor market status of women tend to focus mainly on white collar jobs. Blue collar workers, however, represent nearly a third of the American work force, and women now make up almost a fifth of this category. In Chapter 6, "Women in Nontraditional Blue Collar Jobs in the 1980s: An Overview," Brigid O'Farrell examines the status of blue collar women workers. In the blue collar work world, women and men work in different occupation, industries, and jobs; skilled craft, high-paying jobs remain predominantly male. O'Farrell's case study of blue collar women workers at a large industrial facility illustrates her points. Women are a smaller proportion of the blue collar work force in nontraditional jobs because of barriers to recruitment, hiring, and problems on the job (hostility, training, health, and safety issues). The barriers for women in the blue collar work world are not present in white collar professions. Age limits for apprenticeship programs may exclude women from required training. Seniority systems and restrictive bidding procedures may constrain their mobility in internal labor markets. In many cases, joint action by unions and management is needed to reduce some of the organizational barriers for blue collar women. O'Farrell concludes that despite the complexities of early socialization, traditional attitudes and/or discrimination, women are interested in nontraditional blue collar jobs.

Ruth Shaeffer and Edith Lynton in Chapter 7 shift the focus of analysis to the role of large corporate employers in improving women's employment opportunities. Both the section on "Some Overall Perspectives on the Change Process" and the section "Some Experiences with Improving Women's Opportunities" emphasize organizational strategies. In 1976 The Conference Board, a business-oriented research agency, surveyed a number of companies and received responses from 265 large corporations that were willing to describe in considerable detail their approaches to improving the opportunities for women. Most of the information dealt with women as officials, managers, and professionals. These organizations reported that they did not rely on special programs, but utilized results-oriented management planning and control systems. Much of the success identified by corporations for improving women's opportunities in managerial and professional jobs was achieved by hiring inexperienced recent college graduates into entry-level jobs. The authors note that "very little is known about moving sizable numbers of women into higher managerial levels; thus far, only exceptional individual women have made it." Upgrading clerical workers and blue collar women to supervisory jobs has only recently become a major concern and meets considerable resistance within the firm.

Concluding comments by Phyllis Wallace are presented in the final chapter of the book.

Chapter 1

INCREASED LABOR FORCE PARTICIPATION OF WOMEN AND AFFIRMATIVE ACTION

by Phyllis A. Wallace

One of the major forces shaping the outcomes in the management of human resources has been the dramatic increase in the labor force participation of women. The labor force participation rate reflects the percentage of women in the total noninstitutional population, age 16 and over, who are either employed or seeking employment. At the present time more than half of all women work, and women comprise approximately 42 percent of all workers. Between 1950 and 1979 the labor force increased by 65 percent, and women accounted for more than three fifths of the net additions to this labor force. The number of women workers in the civilian labor force more than doubled during this period, increasing from 18.4 million to 43.4 million individuals.[1] The increased propensity of women to work for pay is attributed mainly to the changed labor market behavior of married women, who make up 56 percent of all women in the labor force.

The influx into the labor market of young wives (under 35), many with preschool children, has introduced a number of changes in the rules and norms of the workplace. Twenty-four million working wives, spouse present, account for 56 percent of all women workers, as compared with only 36 percent in 1940. The labor force participation rate for wives with children was 51.9 percent in March 1979, compared with 18.4 percent in 1950. One incentive for such wide-

1

spread labor force participation of wives may be the long-term growth in their real wages.

As the monetary rewards for working outside of the home have increased, more women enter and remain in the paid labor force. Nevertheless, most women received relatively low wages; the median, usual weekly earnings of women who were full-time wage and salary workers was 61 percent of men's weekly earnings. Median family income in 1978 for husband-wife families with both members working was $21,200 as compared with $17,200 for such families with the husband as the only worker.[2] Three fifths of all husband-wife families had two or more earners in the family.

Although the labor force participation of married women has increased significantly, the number of divorced, separated, and never-married women has risen rapidly. In 1979, nearly one out of every seven families was headed by a woman who was either widowed, divorced, separated, or never married, and 60 percent of these women were in the labor force. The median income in families maintained by women was half that of husband-wife families with the husband as the only earner ($8,500 as compared with $17,000), mainly due to the concentration of the former group in low-skill, low-paying occupations.[3]

Many women entrants into the labor market have been absorbed mostly into the rapidly expanding female jobs in the clerical and service categories where women represented at least 80 percent of all employees in an occupation. About three fourths of all women workers in 1973 were in fifty-seven occupations in which at least 100,000 women were employed. In seventeen of these occupations, women accounted for 90 percent or more of all employees, and in more than half of the occupations, women made up 75 percent or more of all employees.[4] (See Chapter 5 for a discussion of the occupational and industrial concentration of women.)

Although the occupational distribution of women during the past two decades has remained concentrated in a few traditionally female fields, the degree of concentration has been decreasing. More women have moved into nontraditional jobs for women, such as the skilled trades and legal, medical, engineering, and managerial professions. This shift in occupational distribution includes both upgrading in the female-intensive industries as well as entry into the predominantly male industries. (See Chapter 7 for a discussion of recent changes in female employment in higher-level occupations in the corporate sector.)

The dynamic increase in the labor force participation rates of women occurred during a period when economic theories of labor supply were being extended to focus on the optimal allocation of time between market and nonmarket activities. Within the context of the family, the labor supply of each member is determined by the wages of each individual as well as by the earnings of other family members.[5] In addition to the positive variation with wage rate changes for women, the increasing labor force participation of women is associated with the decline in fertility trends, increases in the educational attainment of women, and the significant increase in the number of female family heads. Also, during the latter part of the 1970s, the highly inflationary environment may have induced some women to seek paid work to maintain the family standard of living.

Analysis of trends in fertility, divorce rates, educational attainment of women, and wage growth suggests that women workers, especially wives, will continue to be a sizable portion of the work force. According to labor force projections of the U.S. Department of Labor, from 10.1 to 16.6 million additional women will be added to the work force between 1979 and 1990, as compared with an additional 4.3 to 8.7 million males.[6] These projections reflect three possible paths of growth: high growth, moderate growth, and low growth. The corresponding labor force participation rates in 1990 for women are projected to be 63.2 percent, 59.6 percent, and 56.4 percent, respectively.[7] Even as their labor force growth increases, shifts in the occupational distribution of women may be modest as younger women continue to enter the predominantly "female" fields.[8]

The changes in the composition and mix of workers have introduced changes in the rules of the workplace—that is, growing interest in part-time jobs (shorter hours and/or fewer weeks), flexible work schedules, and modifications in maternity leave and retirement benefits. Fifty-four percent of the 13 million persons working voluntarily on a part-time basis in 1977 were adult women. They represented one fifth of all women wage and salary workers in the nonagricultural sector and were employed mainly in retail trade and the service industries. Nearly three fourths of all the adult female part-timers were married.[9] About 10 percent of full-time women workers in nonfarm wage and salary jobs in May 1980 were on flexible schedules.[10]

Implementation of Employment Discrimination Regulations and Laws

Simultaneous with the changes in the labor supply of women workers, changes on the demand side of the market associated with the implementation of employment discrimination regulations and laws have improved job opportunities for women. Antidiscrimination laws enacted during the mid-1960s included women as well as minorities as protected groups. Employers, unions, and employment agencies were prohibited from discriminating on the basis of race, color, religion, sex, or national origin, in terms of recruitment, hiring, discharge, compensation, training, promotion, and terms and conditions or privileges of employment.[11] Title VII of the Civil Rights Act of 1964 and Executive Order 11246 established the guidelines for antidiscrimination practices and procedures.[12]

Initially, the primary focus was on racial discrimination, and it was not until 1969 that the Equal Employment Opportunity Commission (EEOC) resolved the conflict between state protective laws and Title VII of the Civil Rights Act of 1964. These special laws restricted the maximum number of hours worked, limited the amount of weight to be lifted, and prohibited night work.[13] Initially, EEOC treated the protective laws as bona fide occupational qualification (BFOQ) exceptions to Title VII—that is, sex discrimination in employment could be permitted where it was reasonably necessary to the normal operation of a business.

In August 1969 the EEOC revoked a portion of its *Guidelines on Discrimination Because of Sex* and inserted a new section stipulating that such (protective) laws and regulations conflict with and are superseded by Title VII of the Civil Rights Act of 1964. The 1969 Guidelines stated that since such protective laws did not take into account capacities, preferences, and abilities of individual females, they tended to discriminate rather than protect. Beneficial provisions of state labor laws, such as minimum wage, overtime pay, or rest periods, were not invalidated but in accordance with the 1972 Guidelines had to be extended to cover men in order not to violate Title VII.

Shortly after the amendment of Title VII in 1972 (Equal Employment Opportunity Act of 1972), a stringent set of guidelines on sex discrimination was issued by EEOC (see Appendix). This chapter examines the impact of judicial decisions and of administrative rulings of those sections of the 1972 Guidelines that deal with (1) height and weight requirements (BFOQ exceptions), (2) seniority systems, (3) equal pay, (4) retirement benefits, and (5) pregnancy. In 1980 sections on sexual harassment were added to the Guidelines. The interpretations of the Guidelines on sex discrimination and the implementation of the provisions of the antidiscrimination laws and regulations that are gender related have produced significant changes in the nature of the labor force participation of women. The Consent Decree by American Telegraph and Telephone Company (AT&T) signed in 1973 provides a case study of how several of these provisions contributed to upgrading the occupational status of women working for the largest private employer in the country. These external forces have not only shaped the work environment of women but of all workers.[14]

Height and Weight Requirements

Section 703(e) of Title VII permits bona fide occupational qualification (BFOQ) exceptions on the basis of religion, sex, or national origin, where reasonably necessary to the normal operation of a business. Beginning with the 1965 *Guidelines on Discrimination Because of Sex*, the EEOC has emphasized a narrow interpretation of the bona fide occupational qualification as to sex. Over the years questions have been raised about whether women are physically suited for some kinds of jobs because of arduous work requirements.

As early as 1969, in the *Weeks* v. *Southern Bell Telephone and Telegraph Company* case,[15] the Fifth Circuit Court invalidated a company-imposed weight-lifting limit of thirty pounds for females. It held that to rely on the BFOQ exception an employer had to prove "that all or substantially all women would be unable to perform safely and efficiently the duties of the job involved." A stricter standard of evaluating the individual ability to perform was introduced in 1971 in the *Rosenfeld* v. *Southern Pacific Company*. The work requirements for the position of agent-telegrapher entailed the heavy physical effort involved in climbing over and around box cars to adjust their vents, collapse their bunkers, and close and seal their doors. In addition, employees were required to lift various objects weighing more than twenty-five pounds and in some instances more than fifty pounds. The Ninth Circuit Court noted: "Equality of footing is established only if employees otherwise entitled to the position, whether male or female, are excluded only upon a showing of individual incapacity."[16]

In 1977 the Supreme Court found that Alabama's statutory minimum height and weight requirements for the position of correctional counselor (prison guard) violated Title VII (*Dothard* v. *Rawlinson*).[17] A 5'2" height requirement would exclude 33.3 percent of the women in the United States between the ages of 18 and 79, while excluding only 1.3 percent of men between the same ages. The 120-pound weight restriction would exclude 22.3 percent of the women and 2.4 percent of the men. When the height and weight restrictions were combined, Alabama's statutory standards would have excluded 41.1 percent of the female population, while excluding less than 1 percent of the male population. However, the majority of the Court concluded that the use of women as "guards" in contact positions in Alabama's maximum security male penitentiaries would pose a substantial security problem directly related to the sex of the prison guard. Therefore, being a male was a bona fide occupational qualification (BFOQ) for the job. Employer-imposed minimum height and weight requirements continue to be challenged in the courts as more women enter nontraditional jobs in the blue collar and service industries.

Seniority and Transfer

Two types of seniority usually operate in the American industrial setting. Benefit seniority computed on a plant or companywide basis determines an employee's rights to retirement, vacation pay, sick leave, and fringe benefits. Competitive-status seniority computed on a job classification or departmental basis determines layoff, recall, promotion, and transfer opportunities. The competitive-status seniority has been the focal point of employment discrimination cases. Many seniority systems had a disparate impact on female employees because they did not provide equal access to all job opportunities in a plant due to restricted movement across job ladders or because job assignments were initially discriminatory.[18]

Although the 1965 Guidelines on sex discrimination stated that employment practices were unlawful if jobs were classified as "male" or "female" or if separate lines of progression were maintained or separate seniority lists were based on sex, few remedies for sex-segregated lines of progression were designed. In the *Tippett* v. *Liggett and Myers Tobacco Company* case, a district court ruled in 1975 that female employees reassigned to jobs with lower permanent wage rates when they were recalled from layoff had no right to their higher-paying prelayoff jobs.[19] Bargaining unit jobs at the company's Durham facility prior to 1965 were divided along racial lines and between males and females. Within the sex seniority units, females could not transfer to jobs in the male unit, and males could not transfer to jobs in the female unit. These seniority classifications were later abolished under a new seniority system that was negotiated by all parties under the auspices of the federal government. As of June 1, 1967, all employees were eligible for all jobs and were assigned a permanent rate, and a single list based on a plantwide employment date seniority went into effect. Employees could advance under the new system in accordance with plantwide seniority within three lines of progression: making-machine line, packing-machine line, and nonoperating jobs.

The district court ruled that female employees were not affected adversely by being reassigned after recall from a lengthy layoff to a permanent rate of pay that was lower than rates assigned to white males with less seniority. Business necessity was the defense—"whether there exists an overriding legitimate business purpose such that the practice is necessary to the safe and efficient operation of the business." In the new seniority system, which had been established during the two-year layoff, the women were in nonoperating departments where promotion in lines of progression to permanent vacancies was based on plantwide seniority, and the white males were in machine lines of progression where promotion was a step-by-step process in which machine-operating skills could be systematically learned and applied as employees progressed to increasingly complex machines. The court found that retention of low-seniority white males in the machine-operating lines of progression was justified by business necessity.[20]

In 1977 the Supreme Court, in a major case on racial discrimination (*Teamsters*), determined that bona fide seniority systems established with no intent to discriminate are immune from the prohibitions of Title VII.[21] At the same time the Court ruled in *United Air Lines, Inc.* v. *Evans* that a female former flight attendant who had been forced to resign under the airline's "no marriage" rule could not challenge the failure to credit her with pre-rehire seniority on being rehired as a new employee. The company's seniority system was seen as neutral in its operation.[22] In recent years the seniority concerns for women workers have been raised either in the context of promotion and upgrading (see discussion on AT&T Consent Decree below) or of differentials in wage opportunities.[23]

Earnings Differential—Equal Pay

At the beginning of the decade of the 1980s the earnings of full-time women workers averaged about 62 percent of those of men. Although there was some variation by occupation, the overall ratio had widened slightly during the period of the most significant increases in the labor force participation of women. (See the discussion in Chapter 5 on the impact of occupational and industrial segregation.) There is considerable debate over how much of the sustained wage differential is attributable to productivity characteristics and how much to sex discrimination. Lloyd and Niemi have reviewed twenty-one important studies that decompose the male-female earnings gap by controlling for variables such as age, hours of work, marital status, work experience, continuity of work experience, education, turnover, absenteeism, and geographic region. In three fourths of the studies, the variables that might affect productivity explain less than half of the earnings differential.[24] Much of the unexplained residual has been attributed to wage discrimination.

Wage discrimination is prohibited by the Equal Pay Act of 1963 and Title VII of the Civil Rights Act of 1964. The Equal Pay Act was passed as an amendment to the Fair Labor Standards Act of 1938[25] and required employers to pay members of both sexes the same wages for equivalent work except when the differential was based on one of the following exceptions: (1) seniority system, (2) merit system, (3) a system that measures earnings by quantity or quality of production, (4) a differential based on any factor other than sex. Equal work was defined as jobs in the same establishment, the performance of which required equal skill, effort, and responsibility, and which were performed under similar working conditions. The legislative history of the Equal Pay Act and its judicial interpretations[26] indicate that the concept of equality embraces job content as well as the standards of skill, effort, responsibility, and working conditions.

Since women workers are concentrated heavily in occupations segregated by sex, the provisions of the Equal Pay Act dealing with equal work performed under similar working conditions may have limited impact. A further confusing definitional issue arose over whether equal pay for equal work should be replaced by equal pay for work of comparable worth—jobs that require comparable (not identical) skills, responsibility, and effort. However, Representative

Goodell, a sponsor of the Equal Pay Act bill, had substituted the term "equal work" for "comparable work," an approach that had been used by the War Labor Board during World War II. Goodell had stated: "Last year when the House changed the word 'comparable' to 'equal,' the clear intention was to narrow the whole concept. We went from 'comparable' to 'equal,' meaning that jobs involved should be virtually identical. . . ."[27] Also during the legislative debate on the Equal Pay Act, Representative Frelinghuysen noted that "[t]he jobs in dispute must be the same in *work content* [italics added], effort, skill, and responsibility requirements, and in working conditions. . . . [The Act] is not intended to compare unrelated jobs or jobs that have historically or normally been considered by the industry to be different."[28]

Shortly before the enactment of Title VII in 1964, Senator Bennett proposed an amendment providing that a compensation differential based on sex would not be unlawful if it was authorized by the Equal Pay Act. This amendment became Section 703(h) of Title VII:[11]

> *It shall not be an unlawful employment practice under this title for any employer to differentiate upon the basis of sex in determining the amount of the wages or compensation paid . . . if such differentiation is authorized . . . by the provisions of Section 6(d) of the Fair Labor Standards Act of 1938 as amended.*

It was not clear whether the Bennett Amendment dealt with the scope of the Equal Pay Act or the act's four exceptions. The former interpretation would have meant that Title VII's ban on discrimination in compensation on the basis of sex was constrained by the Equal Pay Act to jobs that were substantially equal in content and requiring equal skills, efforts, and responsibility within the same establishment. A violation of Title VII could be proven only if the Equal Pay Act was also violated.

The various guidelines for the EEOC appeared to support the view that the Bennett Amendment only referred to the four stated exceptions in the Equal Pay Act and that Title VII's prohibition was broader than that of the Equal Pay Act. Equal Pay Act case law established that a prima facie case for wage discrimination based on sex could be made under Title VII only if the Equal Pay Act standards were proven. However, recent decisions have held that Title VII is broader in scope than the Equal Pay Act, and that discriminatory compensation claims not based on a demand for equal pay can arise under Title VII.[29] The EEOC assumed jurisdiction over the Equal Pay Act on July 1, 1979, and published its final regulations on investigation, enforcement, and record keeping under the Equal Pay Act in January 1981.[30]

The *International Union of Electrical, Radio and Machine Workers (IUE)* v. *Westinghouse Electric Corp.* decision of the Third Circuit Court of Appeals[31] in August 1980 ruled that sex-based wage discrimination is prohibited under Title VII even when the jobs are different. The principle of equal pay for work of equal value (comparable value) holds that traditionally sex-segregated jobs pay lower wages to women and this amounts to intentional sex discrimination under Title VII. The lower wage rates were allegedly derived from a job classification and point system, rating knowledge, training, and responsibility that had been established almost forty years ago. Under this ruling, Title VII is extended beyond the more limited Equal Pay Act, and the Bennett Amendment incorporates only the four exceptions (seniority, merit, piece rate, and factor other than sex) into Title VII but does not otherwise limit Title VII to cases where employees are performing the same work. Judge Higginbotham stated:[32]

> The statutory issue here is whether Congress intended to permit Westinghouse to willfully discriminate against women in a way in which it could not discriminate against blacks or whites, Jews or Gentiles, Protestants or Catholics, Italians or Irishmen, or any other group protected by the Act.

This case was denied *certiorari* by the Supreme Court in June 1981.

At this writing the U.S. Supreme Court has affirmed a ruling of the Ninth Circuit Court of Appeals in *County of Washington* v. *Gunther* that sex-based discrimination charges under Title VII are not limited to claims of "equal pay for equal work."[33] A Title VII action was brought by four female jail matrons who alleged discrimination in their compensation as compared with the salaries of male guards. The women claimed that part of the differential in their pay was attributable to intentional sex discrimination since the county had set their pay scale at 70 percent as much as that of male officers—an amount that did not conform with the 95 percent that the county had derived from its own evaluation and survey of outside markets. The district court rejected this claim that was not based on the work standards of the Equal Pay Act, but the court of appeals reversed the decision.

The court of appeals held that even though the jobs of the female guards and the male guards were not equal under the Equal Pay Act definition, the women were not precluded from protesting sex-based wage discrimination under Title VII, provided their wage rate was not exempt under the Equal Pay Act's four affirmative defenses for wage differentials: seniority, merit, quantity or quality of production, or "any other factor other than sex."[34] The Supreme Court's majority ruled that the Bennett Amendment does not restrict Title VII's prohibition of sex-based wage discrimination to claims of equal pay for equal work.

This broader interpretation of discriminatory compensation practices will encourage those women workers in traditional female jobs who are paid less than men to seek various remedies. In the final analysis, the shifting of women workers out of the female-dominated occupations to the higher-paying jobs in the predominantly male occupations would tend to raise wages for women. An adjustment of wages in the predominantly female occupations (sex-segregated) may be difficult to achieve. Justice Brennan, who wrote the majority opinion, noted: "We do not decide in this case the precise contours of lawsuits challenging sex discrimination in compensation under Title VII."[35] In accordance with the court of appeals ruling, the case is now remanded to a district court for further evidence on wage discrimination.

The Court, however, did not examine the controversial issues of comparable pay in this case:[36]

We emphasize at the outset the narrowness of the question before us in this case. Respondents' claim is not based on the controversial concept of "comparable worth," under which plaintiffs might claim increased compensation on the basis of a comparison of the intrinsic worth or difficulty of their job with that of other jobs in the same organization or community.

Retirement Benefits

The EEOC guidelines on sex discrimination define fringe benefits as medical, hospital, accident, life insurance and retirement benefits, profit sharing and bonus plans, leave, and other terms and conditions and privileges of employment. Retirement benefits average less for women than for men because of the differentials in their life expectancies. Actuarial statistics used by insurance companies are based on average differences in life expectancies between men and women. The EEOC guidelines specified that monthly benefits for retirement plans must be equal for similarly situated men and women. The Supreme Court in *City of Los Angeles Department of Water and Power* v. *Manhart*[37] ruled that it is unlawful to require women employees to make a larger contribution to an employer-operated pension fund than similarly situated men. In order to equalize benefits, the Court noted that any individual's life expectancy was based on a number of factors of which sex is only one. Characteristics of a class may not be applied to individual members of that class.

In the *Manhart* decision the Supreme Court was presented with two administrative interpretations of sex-based discrimination in fringe benefits. The Court upheld the EEOC interpretation, which stated that it was an unlawful employment practice to differentiate in benefits on the basis of sex, and rejected the Labor Department's interpretation under the Equal Pay Act, which required only equal contributions made by employers to employee benefit plans. After the *Manhart* decision an employer was required to provide equal benefits under both Title VII and the Equal Pay Act. Before the Department of Labor was able to amend its regulations to accord with the *Manhart* decision, the EEOC assumed jurisdiction over the Equal Pay Act on July 1, 1979.[38]

The use of sex-segregated life expectancy tables to determine retirement benefits has been vigorously challenged by women in higher education. A number of institutions of higher education participating in a pension annuities and life insurance program sponsored by the Teachers Insurance and Annuity Association (TIAA) and College Retirement Equities Fund (CREF) have been named as codefendants in litigation involving these retirement contracts.[39] The size of the annuity benefits was based on separate male and female actuarial tables. In 1980 TIAA announced its intention to adopt a merged-gender (unisex) mortality table for future annuity purchases. Thus men and women retirees of the same age would receive equal monthly benefits for equal premiums paid. State and federal authorities are now arguing over the use of unisex tables, and several regulators of the insurance industry have ruled that unisex premium and mortality tables violate state insurance laws.[40] This dispute over the merged-gender pension plans may eventually be resolved in the Supreme Court.

Pregnancy

Guidelines on sex discrimination issued by the EEOC in 1965 and 1969 did not mention pregnancy or childbirth. Most of the pregnancy litigation prior to 1972 was initiated by public school teachers who challenged the rules of school boards on forced, unpaid maternity leave for fixed periods.[41] Title VII was amended to include educational institutions in 1972, and a third and more stringent set of guidelines by the EEOC specified the rights of pregnant workers to health or temporary disability insurance or sick leave benefits available to other employees [Section 1604.10(b)]: "Disabilities caused or contributed to by pregnancy, miscarriage, abortion, childbirth and recovery therefrom [are], for all job-related purposes, temporary disabilities. . . ." Section 1604.10(c) required that adequate leave be available for pregnant workers and permitted termination only if it was not sex-based and was justified by business necessity.

The U.S. Supreme Court reversed the lower courts in the *General Electric Company* v. *Gilbert* decision in 1976 and held that an exclusion of pregnancy-related disabilities from a disability benefits plan providing comprehensive coverage for nonoccupational sickness and accidents was not gender-based discrimination.[42] The Court further indicated that 1604.10(b) of the sex discrimination guidelines did not reflect congressional intent. In line with an earlier ruling on a disability plan for California state employees (*Geduldig* v. *Aiello*),[43] the majority opinion reiterated the earlier reasoning: "There is no risk from which men are protected and women are not . . . [and] no risks from which women are protected and men are not." The *Gilbert* decision was contrary to the EEOC's 1972 Guidelines and the holdings of seven federal appeals courts and eighteen federal district courts.[44]

This ruling prompted a major effort to amend Title VII by expanding sex discrimination to include discrimination based on pregnancy, childbirth, or related medical conditions. In October 1978 President Carter signed the Pregnancy Discrimination Act (PL 95–555), which amended Title VII of the Civil Rights Act of 1964 and reaffirmed, with minor modifications, EEOC's guidelines. Employers were required to modify fringe benefit and insurance programs to assure that pregnant workers were granted the same benefits as employees unable to work for other medical reasons. In addition, the amendment prohibits terminating or refusing to hire or promote a woman solely because she is pregnant and bars mandatory leaves for pregnant women arbitrarily set at a certain time in their pregnancy and not based on their inability to work.

The amendment also protects reinstatement rights of women on leave for pregnancy-related reasons, including credit for previous

service and accrued retirement benefits, and accumulated seniority. The only exception to the new law that women affected by
pregnancy, childbirth, or related medical conditions are to be
treated the same as other individuals covered by disability or health
programs is that employers are not required to pay for health insurance benefits for abortion, except where the life of the mother
would be endangered if the fetus were carried to term or where
medical complications have arisen from an abortion. Strong argu-
ments will continue to be made that since disability benefits are a
form of compensation, the effect of the new law "will be to confound
the social and economic picture for employee benefits."[45]

Sexual Harassment

Sexual harassment is now perceived to be a widespread problem in
the workplace. In 1979 the Committee on Post Office and Civil
Service of the House of Representatives had initiated an investigation into sexual harassment in the federal government. The Committee recommended that the EEOC be asked to improve their
processing of sexual harassment complaints and to train EEO officials in the handling of such complaints.[46] In November 1980 new
sex discrimination guidelines covering sexual harassment on the job
were adopted by the EEOC.[47] The guidelines had been issued in
March 1980 when it was clear that sexual harassment charges represented an increasing share of charges filed with the EEOC.[48] Sexual
harassment, defined as "unwelcome sexual advances, requests for
sexual favors and other verbal or physical conduct of a sexual nature," constitutes sex discrimination in violation of Section 703(a) of
Title VII: "It shall be an unlawful employment practice for an employer . . . to discriminate against any individual with respect to
[her] compensation, terms, conditions or privileges of employment,
because of such individual's . . . sex." The guidelines noted three
criteria for application of the definition: (1) where sexual conduct is
made a condition of an individual's employment, (2) where sexual
conduct is used as a basis for employment decisions affecting an
individual, and (3) where sexual conduct interferes with work performance or creates a hostile or offensive work environment.

Employers are liable under the guidelines for the misconduct of
supervisory employees or agents regardless of whether the conduct
was known to or authorized or forbidden by the employer. This
standard of employer liability was articulated in 1979 in the *Miller*

v. *Bank of America* case for the U.S. Court of Appeals for the Ninth Circuit.[49] The court held an employer to be liable for the sexually harassing acts of its supervisors even if the company had a policy of prohibiting such conduct and even if the victim did not formally notify the employer of the problem. Earlier court decisions had disagreed over whether sexual harassment constituted sex discrimination under Title VII and whether the employer was liable for an employee's actions.[50] The guidelines expanded the employer liability standards of the courts by including coworkers, nonemployees, and third parties. Also under the guidelines, employers are responsible for developing affirmative programs to prevent sexual misconduct, investigating all complaints alleging sexual harassment, and are required to undertake corrective action to remedy illegal activities.

In January 1981, in the case of *Bundy* v. *Jackson*, the U.S. Court of Appeals in Washington, D.C., ruled that sexual harassment is a violation of Title VII and that the victim was not required to prove that she resisted harassment and was penalized for the resistance. Employers are liable for sexual harassment in the workplace because it creates an offensive discriminatory environment by poisoning the atmosphere of employment.[51]

The *Harvard Business Review* in March-April 1981 reported on a survey of sexual harassment that was conducted among its subscribers (based on 1,846 replies from 7,408 surveyed):[52]

> *The major conclusions discussed include the following. Most people agree on what harassment is; but men and women disagree strongly on how frequently it occurs. The majority correlate the perceived seriousness of the behavior with the power of the person making the advance. Top management appears isolated from situations involving harassment. Many women, in particular, despair of having traditionally male-dominated management understand how much harassment humiliates and frustrates them, and they despair of having management's support in resisting it. Most people think that the EEOC guidelines—although reasonable in theory—will be difficult to implement because they are too vague.*

Consent Decrees

Consent decrees are negotiated settlements of disputes between employers and federal officials representing individuals protected under Title VII of the Civil Rights Act of 1964 or other antidiscrimination regulation. Unions are sometimes included if there is a collective bargaining agreement. The parties agree that during a specified number of years employers will undertake a major effort to achieve certain objectives for hiring, training, and promoting women and minorities. Job evaluation studies, (NBC Decree), modification of personal assessment techniques (Merrill Lynch Decree), or across-the-board adjustment in base salary rates (AT&T Decree) are typical of activities undertaken within the framework of multi-interest bargaining.

Federal district judges have final oversight responsibility for the affirmative action plans in the decrees, but progress may be monitored by representatives of the Women's Caucus who work with companies (*New York Times* and NBC Decrees) or other interested parties such as unions (Steel Decree). Recently, voluntary masters assigned to the court hear complaints, serve as mediators, and resolve disputes that may arise over interpretation of the terms of the agreement. What may be evolving is a mechanism, still somewhat crude, but based on the industrial relations procedures for resolution of conflicts in the workplace. Consent decrees in the telephone, newspaper publishing, airline, broadcasting, banking, and other financial services industries emphasized the reduction of the concentration of women in low-level, low-paying occupational groups. The AT&T 1973 Consent Decree served as a prototype for later negotiated settlements.

AT&T Consent Decree

The Consent Decree signed in January 1973 between the twenty-three operating companies of the American Telephone and Telegraph Company (AT&T) and the federal agencies responsible for employment discrimination regulations and laws (EEOC, Department of Labor, and Department of Justice) established a model for changing the internal labor market.[53] Considerable publicity has been devoted to the monetary settlements made, whether in back pay or adjustments in base pay scales. However, the AT&T Decree, which focused on the nonmanagerial work force, significantly restructured the internal labor market and enabled women to move into jobs that had not previously been available to them. Women workers gained in the nontraditional jobs.

The heart of the January 1973 Consent Decree, which lasted six years, was AT&T's Model Affirmative Action Plan, Upgrading and

Table 1-1   AAP Jobs for AT&T

AAP Job	Relevant Labor Pool
15 Service Workers	
14 Operators	Entry level (external
13 Office/Clerical Entry	labor market)
12 Office/Clerical Semiskilled	Jobs 13,14, 15
11 Office/Clerical Skilled	Job 12
10 Telephone Craft—Inside/	Jobs 11, 12, 13, 14, 15
Semiskilled	
9 Telephone Craft—Outside/	Jobs 15, 14, 11, 10, 8
Semiskilled	
8 General Services/Skilled	Job 15
7 Telephone Craft—Inside/Skilled	Jobs 10, 9, 8
6 Telephone Craft—Outside/Skilled	Jobs 9, 8
5 Sales Workers	Jobs 11, 10, 9, 8
4 Administrative Positions	
4A Admin. Management	Job 4B
4B Admin. Nonmanagement	Jobs 12, 11
3 First-Level Management	Jobs 11, 8, 7, 6, 5, 4A (some external labor market)
2 Second-Level Management	Job 3
1 Third-Level and Above Management	Job 2

SOURCE: Model Affirmative Action Program of the AT&T Consent Decree, January 1973.

Transfer Plan, and Job Briefs and Qualifications.[54] All jobs were classified into fifteen major categories known as Affirmative Action Program Jobs. These AAP Jobs comprised groups of jobs having similar content, opportunities, and wage rates. Then a utilization analysis was made to determine where deficiencies existed for women and minorities. Ultimate goals and intermediate targets for one-, two-, and three-year time frames were set for the establishments of each of the telephone operating companies. Under the modified seniority provisions of the Transfer Plan, women in nonmanagement and noncraft jobs could transfer to better-paying craft jobs on the basis of their operating company net credited service (seniority). The "affirmative action override" was used to promote women and minorities who met the basic qualifications requirements into vacancies where members of their group were not adequately represented. Thus, career ladders were publicized and relevant labor pools were redefined (see Table 1–1).

These internal labor market adjustments were designed by AT&T

management and negotiated with the federal government without the participation of the telephone unions, which represented more than 600,000 employees.[55] From 1973 through 1978, three telephone unions challenged in the courts the provisions of the Consent Decree. Immediately after the signing of the Consent Decree in 1973, the Communications Workers of America (CWA) challenged its implementation. CWA contended that the Consent Decree negated a bona fide seniority system and that the impact of the affirmative action override for AAP Jobs 15 through 5 (nonmanagerial work force) would be to undermine the seniority provisions of the contract. The Federal District Court of Eastern Pennsylvania denied CWA's motion to intervene as a plaintiff, but later CWA, the Telephone Coordinating Counsel of the International Brotherhood of Electrical Workers (TBEW), and the Alliance of Independent Unions were permitted to intervene as defendants.[56]

By January 1979 when the decree ended, management had developed a sophisticated model to track all of its employees (Goals 2); the unions had lost their legal battle over whether the affirmative action override undermined the seniority provisions of their collective bargaining contract, and the utilization of women had improved significantly (see Table 2–2). For example, prior to the Consent Decree, AAP Job category 10 (craft-inside, semiskilled) had been an entry-level job primarily for young males. In the restructured internal labor market of the decree, operators (AAP Job 14), office clerical (AAP Jobs 13, 12, and 11 differentiated by skill levels), and all predominantly female occupations served as the relevant labor pool from which vacancies in the craft jobs were filled.

Progress was uneven throughout the Bell System due to the severity of the 1974–1975 recession in some regions and to the introduction of technology, which displaced a number of women, especially telephone operators. The data in Table 1–2 show the occupational distribution of women in the Bell Telephone operating companies at two points: (1) two weeks before the 1973 Consent Decree was signed and (2) three and a half months before the expiration of the six-year decree. Although there was a decrease in the number of women in the system and a slight decline in their share of total employment, there was a noticeable shift away from the traditional female occupations (clerical, operator, administrative) into nontraditional jobs (management and crafts). The number of women who had reached middle management and above (general managers) had quadrupled, and women accounted for 59 percent of

Table 1-2 Employees in Bell Telephone Operating Companies, December 31, 1972 and September 30, 1978

AAP Job	Description	Total			Women	
		1972	1978	% Change	1972	1978
1	Middle management and above	15,780	17,711	12.2	338	1,374
2	Second-level management	43,138	52,415	21.5	4,830	11,078
3	Entry-level management	95,949	116,458	21.4	29,543	40,976
4	Administrative	32,716	32,468	−0.7	27,380	24,774
5	Salesworkers, nonmanagement	5,813	8,455	45.5	1,539	3,720
6	Skilled craft (outside)	65,107	70,884	8.9	38	1,928
7	Skilled craft (inside)	76,542	74,584	−2.6	2,619	8,830
8	General service (skilled)[a]	11,347	703	−93.8	540	176
9	Semiskilled craft (outside)	66,104	63,767	−3.6	206	3,386
10	Semiskilled craft (inside)	18,011	21,907	21.6	3,554	7,779
11	Clerical, skilled	82,392	104,065	26.3	77,633	91,206
12	Clerical, semiskilled	74,689	87,030	16.5	73,409	79,453
13	Clerical, entry level	45,140	34,890	−22.8	42,929	30,400
14	Telephone operators	148,622	104,134	−29.9	146,562	96,348
15	Service workers, entry level	12,365	10,296	−16.7	4,641	4,254
	Total	793,715	799,785	0.8	415,761	405,682
	Percentage of Total				52.4	50.7

SOURCE: Final Report to the Court of the AT&T Consent Decree, 1979.

[a] Later dropped from the classification.

the increase in all managerial jobs. The implementation of the upgrade and transfer segments of the decree was mainly responsible
for more than tripling the number of women in craft jobs. The
significant decline in operators was perhaps more associated with
the impact of the technology.

Fortune published a report on AT&T's equal employment efforts
just before the end of the Consent Decree, giving it a mixed assessment. Nevertheless, the article noted:[57]

> *This program is seen by management as having gratifyingly expanded
> the pool of people available to staff a company that has a large need
> for people. It may also have played a role in reducing turnover, which
> is down. It seems logical to note that AT&T should not have needed a
> consent decree to point the way to these benefits. The pool was always
> there; it was just, so to speak, not fished.*

Implications for the Management of Human Resources

With the increased participation of women in the labor force, employers should anticipate modifications in personnel procedures and
practices. Even if the largest proportion of the additional women
workers enters the traditional female occupations, their attitudes and
expectations of wages and salaries, fringe benefits, promotions, and
flexible working hours will accord with court rulings and administrative regulations of antidiscrimination agencies. Unlike women
workers of earlier decades, most of these women will be committed
to remaining in the labor market for a long time. As more women
are hired into nontraditional professional and managerial jobs, such
issues as dual career marriages, mentoring, training and development programs, and supervisory behavior may require more innovative treatment.

In addition to these direct effects on organizations, there may be
such unanticipated consequences as the decrease of labor force participation of males as wives contribute more to family income. As
the two-earner family becomes the labor market norm, major institutions must be prepared to accommodate these changes. The
development and implementation of a number of new and more
sensitive and responsive modes for the better integration of women
into the work force will eventually benefit *all* of the employees of an
organization. This is the challenge of the 1980s.

Endnotes

1. U.S., Department of Labor, Bureau of Labor Statistics, *Perspectives on Working Women: A Databook*, Bulletin 2080 (Washington, D.C.: U.S. Department of Labor, Bureau of Labor Statistics, 1980).
2. Ibid. and Paul Ryscavage, "More Wives in the Labor Force Have Husbands with Above-Average Incomes," *Monthly Labor Review* 102 (June 1979), pp. 40–42.
3. Bureau of Labor Statistics, *Perspectives on Working Women*; Beverly L. Johnson, "Women Who Head Families, 1970–77: Their Numbers Rose, Income Lagged," *Monthly Labor Review* 101 (February 1978), pp. 32–37; and Allyson Sherman Grossman, "Labor Force patterns of Single Women," *Monthly Labor Review* 102 (August 1979), pp. 46–49.
4. U.S. Department of Labor, Employment Standards Administration, Women's Bureau, *1975 Handbook on Women Workers*, Bulletin 297 (Washington, D.C.: U.S. Department of Labor, Employment Standards Administration, 1975), p. 92.
5. Cynthia B. Lloyd and Beth T. Niemi, "The Economics of Labor Supply: Work in the Market versus Work in the Home," in *The Economics of Sex Differentials* (New York: Columbia University Press, 1979).
6. Howard N. Fullerton, Jr., "The 1995 Labor Force: A First Look," *Monthly Labor Review* 103, 12 (December 1980), pp. 12–21; and Ralph E. Smith, ed., *The Subtle Revolution: Women at Work* (Washington, D.C.: The Urban Institute, 1979).
7. Fullerton, "The 1995 Labor Force," p. 15.
8. Leonard Lecht with Marc Matland and Richard Rosen, *Changes in Occupational Characteristics: Planning Ahead for the 1980s* (New York: The Conference Board, 1976).
9. Carol Leon and Robert Bednarzik, "A Profile of Women on Part-Time Schedules," *Monthly Labor Review* 101, 10 (1978), pp. 3–12.
10. U.S. Department of Labor, "10 Million Americans Work Flexible Schedules, 2 Million Work Full Time in 3 to 4½ Days," *News*, February 24, 1981.
11. 42 U.S.C., 2000e-2000e-17 as amended by Public Law 92-261 (March 24, 1972).
12. Executive Order 11246 as amended deals with federal contractors and federally assisted construction projects. For more than a decade the Equal Employment Opportunity Commission (EEOC) and the Office of Federal Contract Compliance Programs (OFCCP) in the U.S. Department of Labor, the agency with responsibility for implementing the executive order, had dual sets of guidelines. Since June 1978 the equal employment activities of the federal government have been restructured, and the EEOC has the primary responsibility. Only the Guidelines of the EEOC are examined in this report.
13. Barbara Allen Babcock, Anne E. Freedman, Eleanor Holmes Norton, and Susan C. Ross, "State Labor Laws and the BFOQ" in *Sex Discrimination and the Law* (Boston: Little, Brown & Company, 1975), Chapter Two, Section II B(3).
14. Phyllis A. Wallace, "The Impact of Equal Employment Opportunity Laws," in

Juanita Kreps, ed., *Women and the American Economy* (Englewood Cliffs, N.J.: Prentice-Hall, 1976).

15. 408 F.2d 288 (5th Cir. 1969); 1 FEP Cases 656.

16. 444 F.2d 1219 (9th Cir. 1971); 3 FEP Cases 604.

17. 433 U.S.C. 321 (1977); 15 FEP Cases 10.

18. James A. Craft, "Equal Opportunity and Seniority: Trends and Manpower Implications," *Labor Law Journal* 26, 12 (1975), pp. 750–58.

19. 402 F. Supp. 934 (1975); 11 FEP Cases 1294.

20. 11 FEP Cases 1304.

21. Teamsters v. U.S., 431 U.S.C. 324 (1977), 14 FEP Cases 1514.

22. 431 U.S.C. 553 (1977); 14 FEP Cases 1510.

23. Maryellen R. Kelley, "Seniority Systems and the Discriminatory Treatment of Experienced Women and Blacks in Blue Collar Jobs," unpublished article (Cambridge, Mass.: MIT Sloan School of Management, 1981); and Winn Newman, Section III—'The Prevalence Today of Sexually Segregated Job Patterns in the Electrical Equipment Manufacturing Industry,' in "Statements Before (the) EEOC Hearing on Job Segregation and Wage Discrimination under Title VII and (the) Equal Pay Act," *Daily Labor Report*, April 28, 1980.

24. Lloyd and Niemi, "Discrimination and the Dynamic Determinants of Wages and Unemployment," in *The Economics of Sex Differentials*.

25. 29 U.S.C., Sec. 206(d).

26. Angelo v. Bacharach Instrument Co., 555 F.2d 1164, 14 FEP Cases 1778 (3rd Cir. 1977); Brennan v. Prince William Hospital Corp., 503 F.2d 282, 9 FEP Cases 979 (4th Cir. 1974), *cert.* denied 420 U.S.C. 972, 11 FEP Cases 576 (1975); Schultz v. Wheaton Glass Co., 421 F.2d 259, 9 FEP Cases 502 (3rd Cir.), *cert.* denied 398 U.S.C. 905, 9 FEP Cases 1408 (1970); Corning Glass Works v. Brennan, 417 U.S.C. 188, 9 FEP Cases 919 (1974).

27. As cited in Angelo v. Bacharach Instrument Co., 14 FEP Cases 1786–87; also 108 Cong. Rec. 14771 (1962).

28. As cited in Angelo v. Bacharach Instrument Co., 1786.

29. Gunther v. County of Washington, 602 F.2d 882 (9th Cir. 1979), 20 FEP Cases 792; Fitzgerald v. Sirloin Stockade, Inc., 22 FEP Cases 262 (1980); EEOC v. Aetna Insurance Co., 616 F.2d 719 (1980), 22 FEP Cases 607.

30. "Final EEOC Recordkeeping and Administrative Regulations and Proposed Interpretative Regulations Under (the) Equal Pay Act," *Daily Labor Report*, January 9, 1981, pp. D1–D6.

31. 631 F.2d 1094, 23 FEP Cases 588 (1980).

32. 23 FEP Cases 590.

33. *The United States Law Week* 49 (June 9, 1981):4624.

34. 20 FEP Cases 798 (9th Cir. 1979).

35. *The United States Law Week* 49 (June 9, 1981):4629.

36. Ibid.

37. 435 U.S.C. 702, 17 FEP Cases 395 (1978).

38. See note 30 above.

39. EEOC v. Colby College and TIAA-CREF, 439 F. Supp. 631 (1977); reversed and remanded 598 F. Supp. 1139 (1978), 18 FEP Cases 1125; Peters v. Wayne State and TIAA-CREF, 476 F. Supp. 1343 (1979), 20 FEP Cases 162; Spirt v. LIU and TIAA-CREF, 475 F. Supp. 1298 (1979), 20 FEP Cases 1209.

40. New York Superintendent of Insurance and California statute prohibiting use of merged-gender mortality tables for individual annuity and life insurance contracts issued in that state after January 1, 1981.

41. LaFleur v. Cleveland Board of Education, 414 U.S.C. 632 (1974); Cohen v. Chesterfield County School Board, 474 F.2d 395 (4th Cir. 1973); Mitchell v. Board of Trustees, Pickens County School District (4th Cir. 1979), 19 FEP Cases 1711.

42. 429 U.S.C. 125 (1976), 13 FEP Cases 1657.

43. 417 U.S. 484 (1974).

44. Appeals decisions were as follows: Communications Workers of America v. AT&T, 10 FEP Cases 435 (1975); Wetzel v. Liberty Mutual Ins. Co., 9 FEP Cases 227 (1975); Gilbert v. General Electric Co., 10 FEP Cases 1201 (1975); Tyler v. Vickery, 11 FEP Cases (1975); Satty v. Nashville Gas Co., 11 FEP Cases 1 (1975); Hutchison v. Lake Oswego School District, 11 FEP Cases 161 (1975), Berg v. Richmond Unified School District (1975), 11 FEP Cases 1285; see also "Report of (the) House Labor Committee on H.R. 6075 to Prohibit Sex Discrimination Based on Pregnancy," in *Daily Labor Report*, March 16, 1978.

45. Patricia M. Lines, "Update: New Rights for Pregnant Employees," *Personnel Journal* (January 1979), p. 35.

46. Subcommittee on Investigations of the Committee on Post Office and Civil Services, House of Representatives, 96th Cong., 2d Sess., *Sexual Harassment in the Federal Government*, Committee Print No. 96-11 and 96-112 (Part II). See also U.S. Merit Systems and Protection Board, *Sexual Harassment in the Federal Workplace—Is It a Problem?* (March 1981).

47. Guidelines on Sexual Harassment (Guidelines on Discrimination Because of Sex), 29 CFR (November 10, 1980), Chapter XIV, Sec. 1604.11.

48. "EEOC Devises Rules Defining On-the-Job Sexual Harassment," *Wall Street Journal*, March 12, 1980.

49. 600 F.2d 211 (9th Cir. 1979), 20 FEP Cases 462.

50. Tompkins v. Public Service Electric and Gas. Co., 568 F.2d 1044 (3rd Cir. 1977), 16 FEP Cases 22; Garber v. Saxon Business Products, Inc., 552 F.2d 1032 (4th Cir. 1977), 15 FEP Cases 344; Barnes v. Costle, 561 F.2d 983 (D.C. Cir. 1977), 15 FEP Cases 345; and Kyriazi v. Western Electric Co., 461 F. Supp. 894 (D.N.J. 1978), 18 FEP Cases 924.

51. Bundy v. Jackson (D.C. Cir. 1981), 24 FEP Cases 1155.

52. Eliza G. C. Collins and Timothy B. Blodgett, "Sexual Harassment—Some See It—Some Won't," *Harvard Business Review* (March-April, 1981), pp. 76–95.

53. Phyllis A. Wallace, *Equal Employment Opportunity and the AT&T Case* (Cambridge, Mass.: The MIT Press, 1976), pp. 283–96.

54. Appendices A, B, and C of the AT&T Consent Decree.

55. A special task force of AT&T managers developed the Bell systemwide Model Affirmative Action Plan and the Transfer, Promotion and Upgrade Plan. These Plans were included in AT&T's personnel manual for nonrepresented employees in December 1971. In May 1972 the AAP was adopted, and in August 1972 the Transfer Plan was implemented. Although the General Services Administration, the federal contracting agency for the telephone company, approved both plans in September 1972, the Office of Federal Contract Compliance of the U.S. Department of Labor intervened. The version of the plans

modified as a result of negotiations represented the core of the January 1973 Consent Decree.

56. *Equal Employment Opportunity Commission* v. *AT&T Co.*, 419 F. Supp. 1022, 13 FEP Cases 392 (E.D. Pa. 1976).

57. Carol J. Loomis, "AT&T in the Throes of 'Equal Employment'" *Fortune* (Jan. 15, 1979), p. 57.

Chapter 2

THE MBA:
SAME PASSPORT TO SUCCESS
FOR WOMEN AND MEN?

by Myra H. Strober

In the early 1970s, as major sex-bias suits began to have noticeably unfavorable financial and public relations effects on several major corporations, many American companies became willing (in some cases even eager) to hire women for management positions. This new demand was rather quickly perceived by American schools of business, whose parent institutions were often themselves under legal or governmental pressure to improve the treatment of women. Before long, the number of women in MBA classes across the country rose meteorically. [1]

Stanford's MBA class of 1974, which entered in the fall of 1972, had thirty-four women, who represented 11 percent of the class. It was the first Stanford MBA class to have a sufficient number of women to compare to their male counterparts. In the late spring of 1974, a few weeks before graduation, Francine Gordon surveyed the women and men of the Stanford MBA Class of 1974; she obtained information concerning the jobs they were about to undertake, their work experience and background, and their long-term aspirations. These findings were presented and analyzed by Gordon

I wish to thank several people for their assistance: Marilyn Power, especially for help in designing the questionnaires, supervising the distribution and return of the surveys and coding; and Lanie Powers and Lynn W. Marples for computer work. In addition, this research is part of a larger set of alumni surveys at the Stanford Business School, and I wish to thank my colleagues, Carol Marchick, Seenu Srinivasin, Dick Wittink, Tom Harrell, and Charles Weinberg for their comments and suggestions.

and Strober in a 1978 article in the *Sloan Management Review*. The study found that the average starting salaries of the men and women were not significantly different statistically. However, it also found that the women's long-term salary and wealth aspirations were considerably below those of the men.[2]

This paper reports on a follow-up study that was carried out in the spring of 1978 to investigate job market experiences over a four-year period. The women MBAs of the Stanford class of 1974 are a pioneer cohort; thus, their job market experiences during the first four years of their career are of particular interest to those monitoring and studying the movement of women into occupations that formerly were all male. The primary purpose of the paper is to compare the jobs and salaries of the women MBAs with those of their male counterparts. In addition, we examine several factors closely related to jobs and salaries: the role of mentors, job satisfaction, aspirations and goals, and home-life patterns. In the paper's conclusion we discuss the question raised in our title: Is the MBA degree the same passport to success for women and men?

Survey Methodology

In the spring of 1978, addresses were obtained from the Stanford Business School alumni office for 283 graduates of the class of 1974. Thirty-two foreign members of the class (all men) who lived outside of the United States were excluded from the survey. Questionnaires were sent to 251 members of the class: 220 men and 31 women. Eight men were dropped from the sample when their surveys were returned by the post office because of incorrect addresses.

A second questionnaire was sent in the summer of 1978 to those who had not yet responded. In addition, 11 women who had not responded were phoned: We asked for their cooperation in the research, explaining that in view of the very small number of women in the '74 class, their participation was vital. Six of those who were phoned returned completed surveys. Finally, after surveys from the second mailing and the phone calls had been received, we sent postcards to all remaining nonrespondents asking them to provide answers to a few questions if they did not wish to complete the questionnaire. We received 176 completed questionnaires (a response rate of 72 percent), 26 from women (a response rate of 84 percent), and 150 from men (a response rate of 71 percent). Only 7 postcards were returned, too few to permit a comparison between respondents and nonrespondents.

Results

Jobs and Salaries

We found that four years after receiving the MBA, the men in our sample were earning a mean annual full-time salary of $27,787; the mean full-time annual salary for women was $25,657.[3] This difference was not significant at the 5 percent level. However, we did find a significant difference between men and women in their mean annual additional cash compensation (bonuses, commissions, etc.): $6,975 for men and $1,798 for women ($t = 2.16$; $p = .032$). Forty percent of the men earned additional cash compensation. Twenty-nine percent earned less than $5,000. Seven percent earned between $5,050 and $10,000, and 4 percent earned in excess of $10,000. Among the women, a higher percentage (56 percent) earned additional cash compensation, but the amounts earned were lower. Forty-three percent earned less than $5,000, and 13 percent earned between $6,000 and $10,000. None earned more than $10,000. When we added additional cash compensation to annual salary to obtain total annual salary, we found that women's mean annual total salary was $27,455, significantly different from men's mean annual total salary, $34,762 ($t = 2.21$; $p = .03$). The ratio of women's mean annual total salary to men's mean annual total salary was .79.

What accounts for these differences in total annual salary? We investigated five possible sources: (1) differences in work experience and training, (2) differences in ability (as measured by performance on standardized tests and school work), (3) differences in type of industry of employment, (4) differences in time spent out of town, and (5) differences in personal characteristics (sex and ethnic minority).

The first column of Table 2–1 lists the variables used in a regression to explain the annual total salary. In column 2 are the means of the variables for the regression sample (N = 144). The regression sample is smaller than the total sample because 32 respondents had missing data on their surveys. The regression coefficients and standard errors for each dependent variable are in column 3. Because

Table 2-1   Relationship of Various Factors to Annual Total Salary

Variable	Mean (Standard Deviation) of Variable	Coefficient (Standard Error) on Variable in Annual Total Salary Regression
Total annual salary (in dollars)	31,816 (11,353)	—
Months of experience prior to receiving MBA degree	16.0 (21.1)	−39.54 (40.15)
Months of experience since receiving MBA degree	32.8 (17.1)	−44.37 (50.05)
Attendance at executive program (Yes = 1)	.33	+1210.85 (1795.19)
Out of labor force for one month or more during four years (Yes = 1)	.097	−8879.18** (2894.71)
Total GMAT score	Confidential	−22.33 (13.39)
Number of units at business school in which H or P+ was earned	Confidential	+51.06 (52.29)
Employed in investment banking (Yes = 1)	.05	+14,143.94** (3,981.49)
Employed in real estate (Yes = 1)	.06	+8387.12** (3556.43)
Employed in public sector (Yes = 1)	.14	−1121.90 (2504.78)
Employed in commercial banking (Yes = 1)	.08	−3585.59 (3109.09)
No. days out of town per month	3.33 (3.23)	+939.55** (263.45)
Respondent is Hispanic (Yes = 1)	.06	−5673.25 (3745.41)
Respondent is black (Yes = 1)	.02	−6635.10 (5862.68)
Respondent is female (Yes = 1)	.13	−2875.55 (2589.32)
Constant	—	43,285.40

$N = 144$ $\bar{R}^2 = .30$ $F = 5.16$
** Significant at 1 percent level.

the number of women in our sample was so small, it was not possible to run separate regressions for women and men.

The women in the sample had about 7 months more work experience prior to the MBA degree than did the men (21.8 months versus 14.9 months). However, pre-MBA experience was not a significant determinant of total annual salary in our regression equation. Moreover, although women had spent fewer months with their current employers than had men, (27.7 versus 32.3), number of months with current employer also proved to be insignificantly related to salary in our regression.[4]

Since their graduation from Stanford, the same proportion of women and men had been in executive programs (.31 versus .33), and both sexes had spent the same number of median days (2.2) in such programs. In the regression, a dummy variable was created and set equal to 1 if the respondent spent time in an executive program since graduation from Stanford Business School. This variable was also not a significant determinant of total annual salary.

Because a great deal of research indicates that employees pay a penalty for noncontinuous work experience,[5] respondents were asked, "Since June 1974, how many months have you been out of the labor force (that is, without a job and not seeking work)?" Thirty-one percent of the women and 9 percent of the men had noncontinuous work experience. Among the women, 19 percent had been out of the work force for $\leq$ six months, and 12 percent had been out for one year or more. Among the men, 8 percent had been out for $\leq$ six months; 1 percent had been out for one year. As a rough measure of noncontinuous experience, a dummy variable was set equal to 1 for the respondents who had been out of the labor force for one month or more over the four-year period. In the regression sample, 10 percent of our respondents, 7 percent of the men and 26 percent of the women, were coded 1 on this dummy variable. This variable proved to have a highly significant negative effect on total annual salary. On the average, respondents who were out of the labor force during the four-year period suffered a reduction in income of almost $9,000 in 1978, other variables in the regression held constant.[6]

The two measures of ability we used were the total score on the standardized test for entry to business school and the number of units at the business school in which either an H or P+, equivalent to an A+ or an A, was earned. The values for these variables were *not* obtained from the survey, but rather from the Business School records. For our sample, women's average score on the total GMAT

was not statistically significantly different from men's total score.[7]
Men and women had, on the average, an equal number of business
school units with H or P+. In the regression, neither total GMAT
nor number of units in which either an H or P+ was earned were
significant determinants of total annual salary.

The most important determinants of total salary were the industries of employment. We entered dummy variables for four industries into our regression. The first two, investment banking and real
estate, were chosen for inclusion because they are widely known for
their high salaries. The two other industries in our regression were
the non-profit sector (including the government), examined because
non-profit and public sector salaries are often lower than those in
private industry, and commercial banking, examined because of the
widespread view that this industry has recently been particularly
hospitable to the employment and advancement of women.

The men and women in our sample were employed across twenty
industries: accounting, advertising, commercial banking, investment banking, communications, consulting, education, financial
management, government, health services, law firm, manufacturing, merchandising, military, petroleum/mining, real estate, research, transportation, highly diversified and "others." Their pattern
of employment strongly suggests the existence of industrial segregation by sex among MBAs. While manufacturing employed almost
one third of the men in our sample, it employed less than one fourth
of the women. On the other hand, while government employed
almost 20 percent of the women, it employed only 3 percent of the
men. Women were almost twice as likely to be in consulting as men
(9.5 percent versus 5 percent) and while investment banking, real
estate, and petroleum/mining each employed about 6 percent of the
men, none of these industries employed any women.

In the regression sample, 6 percent of men were employed in
investment banking; 7 percent of men were employed in real estate.
Employment in investment banking, all else in the regression held
constant, was associated with an additional $14,144 in total annual
salary; employment in real estate was associated with an additional
$8,387. Twenty-six percent of the women and 12 percent of the men
were employed in non-profit and public sector jobs, while 10 percent of the women and 8 percent of the men were employed in
commercial banking. However, employment in these industries
was not associated with a significantly higher or lower salary than
that earned in industries comprising the reference group.[8]

On the average, women and men spent the same number of days

per month on business out of town (4.0 for women; 3.1 for men). An additional day out of town per month significantly increased total annual salary, all else in the regression held constant, by about $940 per year.

Six percent of the men in our sample, but none of the women, are Hispanic; 2 percent of the men, but none of the women, are black. Neither of these dummy variables was significant in our regressions, possibly because the number of Hispanics and blacks was so small.

The sex dummy was also insignificant. However, this does not necessarily indicate an absence of discrimination against women MBAs. Taken as a whole, our results may be interpreted as follows: The women in our sample earn less than the men in part because they more frequently have noncontinuous work experience and in part because they are not represented in those industries that appear to be particularly lucrative. Their lack of representation in these industries may be due to the small size of our female sample, to employer discrimination, or to personal preferences, among the women. And, of course, such personal preferences may themselves be the result of past discrimination or fear of possible future discrimination.

Our regression equation explains only 30 percent of the variance in total annual salary. While this is a "respectable" finding, it nonetheless leaves 70 percent of the variance unexplained. We have also examined three other possible determinants of salary: hours worked, number of employees supervised, and "the total amount of company expenditures that you are permitted to approve at any one time without detailed review by your superiors." None of these variables was a significant determinant of total annual salary. However, comparison of their average values for the two sexes is illuminating.

The women and men in our sample both worked long hours; but women, on the average, worked significantly fewer hours than did men (50.0 versus 54.7; $t = 2.12$; $p = .04$). For managers, the relationship between hours worked and output produced is, of course, unclear. Some managers no doubt increase their output when they work additional hours; however, other managers may work longer hours because they are having difficulty completing their job in the course of the usual workweek.

Women and men did not differ significantly in the average number of employees they supervised (18.7 for women, 14.4 for men). Moreover, women and men were equally likely to hold line, as compared to staff, positions. Among the women, 39 percent held line positions and 48 percent staff positions; 13 percent indicated their jobs had both line and staff responsibilities. Among the men, 43 percent had line jobs, 47 percent staff jobs, and 10 percent, combined line-staff jobs.

However, we noted a clear sex difference in authority to approve expenditures. Forty-three percent of the men but only 13 percent of the women had the authority to approve expenditures in excess of $100 ($t = 2.23$; $p = .027$).

Mentors

To what extent can the difference in men and women's earnings be attributed to gender differences in mentor relationships? The popular literature, of course, has argued repeatedly that mentors are the key to success in business and the professions. Yet scholars have lamented that the notion of mentorship is poorly understood.[9] Just what do mentors do? How important is a mentor relationship? And do women and men have different mentor relationships?

We asked the women and men of the Stanford class of 1974: "In your current job, do you have a mentor (or mentors), that is, a person in a higher position in your company who is particularly helpful and supportive to your career?" We also asked: "If yes, please explain exactly how your mentor has been helpful." Fifty-two percent of the women and 46 percent of the men in our sample reported that they had a mentor; their explanations of how these mentors had been helpful were most enlightening and fall into three categories, listed here in order of frequency of mention.

The aspects of mentorship most often enounced were those associated with the *provision of general assistance:* "has helped me plot my career," "has given me the general benefit of his/her experience," "has encouraged me," "has given me a better perspective on the organization and its politics." The second type of help mentioned the *provision of specific assistance:* "hired me," "created jobs for me and gave me visibility," "got me more salary," "pushed my advancement," "gave me more authority," "gave me technical insights," "helped me finance projects," "gave me specific feedback." Finally, the third type of help was the *bestowing of protection:* "spoke up for me," "gave me protection," "stopped discrimination against me."[10]

A χ^2 test on the distribution of types of mentoring for women and men showed no significant differences between the two sexes. To the extent that one can measure mentoring in a survey, we find that the women in our sample seem to be getting just as much mentoring, and the same types of mentoring, as the men.

Moreover, the effects of mentoring are somewhat surprising. We find that having a mentor is not significantly correlated with total annual salary ($r = .02$ for women, .04 for men). Also, having a mentor has a small but significant *negative* association with job satisfaction for men ($r = -.18$). The correlation for women is $-.09$. Perhaps one of the functions of a mentor is, in fact, to create some dissatisfaction with the current job, thus motivating desire for promotion. Or, perhaps those whose accomplishments are achieved with the aid of a mentor are less satisfied than those whose accomplishments are achieved independently. More cynically, perhaps those who are more dissatisfied to begin with are more likely to seek mentors.

One of the questions we asked our respondents was whether they were serving as mentors. Of the men, 20 percent said they served as mentors and an additional 36 percent said they were mentors to some extent, "partially, in some ways." Among the women, an even higher percentage, 30 percent, said they were serving as a mentor and an additional 35 percent said they served "partially, in some ways."[11] Serving as a mentor was highly positively correlated with job satisfaction ($r = .31$ for women; $r = .34$ for men) but weakly correlated with total salary ($r = .12$ for women; $r = .10$ for men).

Job Satisfaction

Despite the fact that the women in our sample earned significantly less than the men, we found no significant sex differences in job satisfaction. On a scale of 1 to 7, 7 being most satisfactory, women rated their job satisfaction as 6.3, men as 5.9. Similarly, women and men were equally and highly satisfied with their careers to date (6.0 for women and 6.0 for men) and with "life in general" (6.0 for women and 5.9 for men). However, there was considerable variance in job, career, and life satisfaction.[12] With respect to job satisfaction, in the sample as a whole, 8 percent were very dissatisfied, dissatisfied, or mildly dissatisfied with their jobs; another 8 percent were neither satisfied nor dissatisfied; 16 percent were mildly satisfied; 37 percent were satisfied; and 39 percent were very satisfied. In order to investigate how much of a role being female and/or having a mentor or being a mentor played in determining

Table 2-2   Relationship of Various Factors to Job Satisfaction

Variable	Mean (Standard Deviation) of Variable	Coefficient (Standard Error) on Variable in Job Satisfaction Regression
Degree of job satisfaction (scale of 1–7, 7 being most satisfactory)	5.95 (1.22)	—
Total annual salary (in dollars)	31,698.67 (11,220.73)	.000023** (.00001)
Respondent is a mentor or a mentor in some ways (Yes = 1)	.57	.618** (.187)
No. hours of work per week	54.7 (9.7)	.025** (.0097)
Respondent is female (Yes = 1)	.13	.556** (.279)
Constant	—	3.41

$N = 147$ $\bar{R}^2 = .17$ $F = 8.73$
** Significant at 1 percent level

job satisfaction, we ran the regression reported in Table 2–2. In column 2 are the means and standard deviations of the variables used in the job satisfaction regression. In column 3 are the regression coefficients and their standard errors.

The variables significantly related to job satisfaction were as follows: total salary (every additional dollar of salary yields a .000023 increase in job satisfaction); a dummy variable equal to 1 if the respondent is a mentor or is a mentor "in some ways" (being a mentor adds .618 to the job satisfaction index); hours of work per week (working an additional hour per week adds .025 to the job satisfaction index); and being female (being female adds .556 to the job satisfaction index). Having a mentor was not significantly related to job satisfaction.

The regression explains only 17 percent of the variance in job satisfaction; it could be that in a more complete specification the sex dummy would not be significant. However, it is also possible that being female is significantly related to job satisfaction because the women MBAs, unlike the men, may have grown up expecting to hold jobs considerably less prestigious than those they hold now. Thus, the women may be particularly satisfied with their current situation. In this regard it is interesting that in a job satisfaction regression for males only (where of course there was no sex dummy variable) we found a significant coefficient on the dummy variable equal to 1 if the respondent's father held a nonprofessional or non-managerial position. This dummy variable, however, was not significant in the regression for both sexes. It may be that the occupational dummy variable plays the same role as the sex dummy variable: male respondents whose fathers were in nonprestigious jobs may find themselves particularly satisfied with their own high prestige positions.

Aspirations

In our earlier work, Gordon and I speculated that the sex differences we found in salary and wealth aspirations among newly graduated MBAs might well diminish over time as women became increasingly socialized to the work world and its values. It appears, however, that at least at the four-year point, the salary, job, and wealth aspirations of the men and women respondents remained disparate.

Values, goals, and expectations of our MBAs were ascertained through a variety of questions. First, respondents were asked to rate on a scale of 1 to 7, 7 being the most important, the importance of a variety of factors "in causing you to choose your present job." Women and men MBAs attributed the same degree of importance to the following factors: opportunity for promotion, variety, potential for impact on society, travel requirements, travel opportunities, opportunity for early responsibility, intellectual stimulation, job location and climate, flexibility of work hours, number of work hours, family considerations, image of firm, job provides useful experience or skills. A t-test indicated that women ranked salary as significantly less important than did men (4.1 versus 4.9; $t = 2.54$; $p = .01$), while they ranked the following as significantly more important than did men: independence (6.0 versus 5.2; $t = 3.12$; $p = .003$), compatibility with people (5.8 versus 5.0; $t = 3.12$; $p = .003$), and location for spouse (5.4 versus 3.7; $t = 2.78$; $p = .007$). For all other factors there were no statistically significant differences in ratings of importance.

Second, we asked respondents to rank the following ten values or goals in order of importance (items are listed in order of their average importance to women): to maximize personal development; to enjoy life; to obtain and share companionship with immediate family and friends; to have the opportunity for freedom of thought and action; to achieve a secure and stable position in work and financial situation; to become an influential leader; to contribute to the satisfaction of others; to become an authority on a special subject; to become well known, to obtain recognition, rewards, or high social status; and to earn a great deal of money and build up a large financial estate. It is important to note that, by and large, the rank order and mean rank of these goals for the two sexes were quite similar. However, men ranked the attainment of wealth significantly higher than did women. While the attainment of wealth was the least important of the goals for women, it ranked sixth in importance for men. On a scale of 1 to 10, where 1 is not important, the mean rank on this variable for men was 6.1, for women 7.4. ($t = 3.03$; $p = .003$).

Third, we asked the following questions about salary goals: "In 1978 United States dollars, *at the peak of your career*, what is the highest salary you *hope* to achieve and what is the highest salary you *expect* to achieve?" Men and women had quite different salary hopes and expectations. Women, on the average, hoped to achieve a salary at the peak of their careers equal to $115,205 in 1978 dollars. This figure contrasted with men's average hoped-for peak salary of $269,479 ($t = 2.15$; $p = .03$). The mean salary women expected at the peak of their career, in 1978 dollars, was $80,413; for men it was $202,437 ($t = 1.74$; $p = .08$).[13] At the time of the 1974 survey women's hoped-for salary and their expected salary at the peak of their career was about 60 percent of men's hoped-for and expected salary (see endnote 3). By 1978, women's hoped-for and expected salary was only about 40 percent of those of the men in their class. Relative to men, women's salary aspirations declined over the four-year period.

The fourth area we probed was job goals. We asked, "At the time of your highest expected salary, what do you expect your job title to be?" Half of the men expected to be an owner, partner, president, or chief executive officer (CEO). Only 24 percent of the women expected to achieve these job titles. Moreover, only 3 percent of the men but 24 percent of the women said they didn't know, or felt it wasn't important, what job title they expected to achieve.

Finally, we asked: "Do you feel that your present job is a satisfactory stepping stone toward your desired future position?" "What kinds of problems, if any, do you expect to face in achieving your career goals?" and "What are your strategies for overcoming these problems?" The vast majority of respondents felt that their present job was a satisfactory stepping stone to their desired future position. But despite the fact that women's job aspirations were lower than those of men, a lower percentage of women than of men were satisfied that their job was a satisfactory stepping stone to their desired future position (75 percent versus 91 percent).

The problems women and men reported they expected to face in achieving their career goals were quite different. A χ^2 test on the distribution of problems mentioned by men and women showed a significant difference ($\chi^2 = 63.5$, $p < .001$). The problems mentioned most frequently by women were discrimination and home-work conflict, including integrating own career with spouse's career. Women also mentioned organizational politics, managing, getting stuck, and gaining skills. Men, on the other hand, were rarely concerned with possible discrimination, and for them home-work conflict was a less salient problem than it was for women. For men, the most frequently mentioned problems (in order of frequency) were problems of managing, getting stuck, work-home conflict, gaining skills, becoming bored or frustrated, organizational politics, interpersonal problems, work requiring too much energy, gaining visibility, and gaining skills.

To overcome these problems women and men generally indicated that they would use similar strategies: work harder, get to know the right people, and learn the right ropes and skills. But several women mentioned two strategies not mentioned by any of the men: decrease expectations and work part-time.

Home Life Patterns

It has been alleged that one of the reasons why women earn less than men in market work is because women have greater home responsibilities. Do women MBAs have greater home responsibilities than their male classmates or have these pioneer women shed the more traditional female family chores?

The women and men in our sample were quite similar with respect to marital status. Sixty-five percent of the women and 69 percent of the men were married; 31 percent of the women and 28 percent of the men were single; and 4 percent of the women and 3 percent of the men were separated, divorced or widowed. However, only 41 percent of the men, as compared to 80 percent of the women, considered themselves to be part of a dual career couple. This despite the fact that most wives of men MBAs were employed:

only 11 percent of married men (and only 5 percent of the entire male sample) had wives who were full-time housewives. Moreover, although no man in our sample was married to a woman who earned an annual income of more than $30,000, about half of the married women in our sample had husbands whose annual incomes were above this figure.

With respect to household responsibilities, respondents were asked, "In your household, who is primarily responsible for housework?" The responses to this question were instructive. About half of the women reported that they had primary responsibility for housework, while almost half of the men reported that their wives took care of those responsibilities. Interestingly, about 20 percent of the men and 20 percent of the women indicated that in their households responsibility for housework was shared equally. An additional 8 percent of women and 8 percent of men noted some sharing (though not equal sharing) of housework responsibilities. Although 24 percent of the men had primary responsibility for housework (largely those who were single), none of the women MBAs were married to men who took primary responsibility for housework. Finally, women MBAs were much more likely than men MBAs to report that primary responsibility for housework was in the hands of hired help (20 percent versus 3 percent).

We find a similar picture on the issue of child-care responsibilities.[14] We asked, "In your household, who is primarily responsible for child care and/or arranging for child care?" Of those who had children (43 percent of the men and 35 percent of the women), 88 percent of women indicated that they had primary child-care responsibility; at the same time, 88 percent of the men said their wives took primary responsibility in this area. Three percent of the men took primary responsibility for child care, 2 percent shared this responsibility equally with their wives, and 7 percent took some responsibility, although less than that assumed by their wives. None of the women with children reported sharing child-care responsibilities with their husbands. However, one of the women (none of the men) noted that primary responsibility for child care rested with hired help.

Responses to the penultimate question about child care were additionally revealing. We asked, "If your child is sick (for example, having a high fever, vomiting) on a workday, what arrangement do you usually make for the child's care?" Half of the women said they stayed home; 81 percent of the men said their wives stayed home.

None of the women said their husbands usually stayed home, and none of the men said they usually stayed home. One of the women said she and her husband normally took turns staying home, and 12 percent of the men indicated they took turns with their wives in caring for sick children on workdays. Three women (38 percent of those with children) and 7 percent of the men said neither parent normally stayed home to care for a sick child, but rather other arrangements for care were made.

One of the problems faced by couples trying to combine two careers is finding two jobs in the same geographic location. In order to examine how widespread "commuting marriages" are among MBAs, we asked: "Do you and your spouse maintain separate residences in different cities for purposes of employment?" Four of the women (15 percent) but none of the men answered this question in the affirmative.

Conclusion

Although, on the average, the women MBAs of the Class of 1974 earned salaries equivalent to those of their male classmates when they graduated from Stanford, four years later the female-male parity in salaries had eroded.[15] Including bonuses and commissions in the calculation of salary, we found that in 1978 women MBAs' earnings were about 80 percent of those of their male counterparts. What were the causes of this emerging earnings differential? Several of the usual explanations for earnings differentials seem *not* to have been relevant for this sample. Our women and men MBAs were quite similar on a number of characteristics: ability (as measured by the GMAT and classroom performance at the Stanford Business School), number of job changes over the four years, number of days spent in executive programs, number of days per month spent out of town on business, number of employees supervised, presence in line as opposed to staff positions, having a mentor, and type of mentoring received. (There may, of course, be differences in quality of mentoring that our instrument was not sensitive enough to discern.) While women had somewhat more pre-MBA work experience than did men, they had spent fewer months with their current employer. However, neither of these variables was a significant predictor of salary in our regression.

On the other hand, women were more likely than men to have

had discontinuous work experience over the four-year period, and this, we found, was a powerful earnings depressant. As noted earlier, we did not investigate the causes of this discontinuous work experience. Clearly, future research should thoroughly explore this aspect of work history.

Women also were disadvantaged in their earnings because they were not employed in some of the particularly high-paying industries. Indeed, the distribution of men and women across industries was quite disparate. A larger sample will be required to determine the overall extent of the industrial segregation by sex found in our sample and a more careful probing of industry preferences of MBAs and job offer patterns by employers will be needed to examine its causes.

Returning to the issue of the salary differential by sex, three additional factors need to be reiterated. First, we found that the men in our sample had the authority to approve higher levels of expenditures than did the women. Although this variable was not significantly related to salary level, the fact that women and men lacked the same power to approve high-level expenditures suggests that women may have achieved a lower level of responsibility in their organizational hierarchies or were not employed in comparable organizations.

Second, women's family concerns and responsibilities probably affected their salary progress. It is likely that home responsibilities were a key factor in women's discontinuous work experience. Moreover, the fact that women were more likely than men to evaluate job offers with respect to their effects on spouse's location may have meant that women were more likely than men to accept jobs that were less satisfactory in other respects (for example, salary). Perhaps more importantly, the overwhelmingly different home and child-care responsibilities faced by our women and men respondents cannot help but affect such factors as hours of work, and job and salary aspirations. Although "companionship with immediate family . . ." was viewed as equally important by the women and men in our sample, the division of labor reported in the homes of our respondents made it clear that women invested considerably more time and energy in achieving this goal. None of this is meant to imply that the discrepancy between men and women's earnings is explainable solely by supply side forces; in a study such as this, it is really not possible to investigate adequately the role of the employer in producing a female-male earnings differential.

Finally, to the extent that wealth, salary, and job aspirations are predictive of future earnings, it seems unlikely that the development of salary inequality by sex over the last four years is likely to be quickly reversed. As in 1974, men continued to rank the attainment of wealth as a significantly more important goal than did women. With respect to salary, the ratio of women's to men's expected or hoped-for salary at the peak of their career *declined* over the four year period, from approximately .6 in 1974 to .4 in 1978. Moreover, while about half of the men in our sample aspired to become an owner, partner, president, or CEO at the peak of their career, only about one fourth of the women expected to achieve those job titles.

We come then to the question with which we began. Is the MBA degree the same passport to success for men and women? Clearly, the answer depends on one's definition of success. It is important to recall that, on average, the women and men in our sample reported equal job satisfaction. If success means job satisfaction, perhaps the answer to our question should be affirmative. However, if we equate success with earnings, as is the economist's wont, then clearly the answer to our question is "no" or, perhaps more optimistically, "not yet."

Some analysts, of course, will disagree with this assessment. They will argue that the absence of a significant negative coefficient on the female dummy variable in the salary regression equation reported in Table 2–1 "proves" that the degree *is* the same passport for the two sexes. But to look solely at that regression coefficient to answer our question is to look too narrowly. The two most important determinants of salary in our regression are the dummy variables representing employment in investment banking and real estate and the dummy variable representing discontinuous labor force participation. Perhaps no women were employed in those two high-paying industries because they did not choose to apply there for work. On the other hand, perhaps they applied but were not hired. In either case, the fact remains that women's passports were missing some critical visa stamps.

With regard to discontinuous labor force participation, again women and men were unequally represented in the dummy variable categories. Less than 10 percent of the men in our regression sample, but about one fourth of our women, had dropped out of the work force for one month or more during the four-year period. One might argue that the decision to drop out was a "choice" made by each respondent, that dropping out or not has no bearing on whether the MBA degree is the same passport for the two sexes. However, we do not know from our data whether some of the women who "chose" to drop out would in fact have preferred to take a maternity leave, or work part-time for a number of months, options which were perhaps vetoed by their employers. Nor do we know why employers exact such formidable financial penalties from MBAs for dropping out.

No assessment of "blame" for the unequal salaries earned by women and men is being made here. Noting that the MBA degree is not the same passport for men and women is not tantamount to claiming that there is employer discrimination against women MBAs. Indeed, as noted earlier, in a study of the supply side of the labor market it is not possible to adequately examine employer behavior, although researchers frequently try to do so. At the moment, all that can be said is that the MBA degree does not result in the same amount of financial success for women as it does for men, that women and men MBAs have different patterns of employment by industry, different patterns of employment continuity, different aspirations, and different home-life responsibilities. The role of possible employer discrimination in producing any or all of these outcomes awaits further study.

Endnotes

1. This implicit model of the increase in MBA students is (purposely) heavily demand oriented. Once business schools made it clear that they wished to accept women students, preexisting supply side barriers began to melt quickly and the number of applications from women soared.
2. The mean annual starting salary for women was $16,938; for men it was $17,000. The mean of the highest salary women *hoped* to earn was $81,471 (in 1974 dollars); for men it was $135,083. With respect to *expected* peak salary, women's mean was $44,222; men's $75,927 (all in 1974 dollars). See F. E. Gordon and M. H. Strober, "Initial Observations on a Pioneer Cohort: 1974 Women MBAs," *Sloan Management Review* 19,2 (Winter 1978), pp. 15–23.
3. The median annual salary for women was $26,950; for men, $28,004.
4. About half of the women and half of the men had not changed employers over the four-year period. The mean number of job changes over the period was .9 for women, .6 for men (not statistically significantly different). Women did, however, spend significantly less time with their first employer than did men (nineteen months versus twenty-four months). With respect to salary, we found no relationship between 1978 salary and being a job switcher or job stayer. Undoubtedly, some job switchers left their employer for a higher salary, while some left because they were unhappy and took a cut in salary.

5. See M. E. Corcoran, "Work Experience, Labor Force Withdrawals, and Women's Wages: Empirical Results Using the 1976 Panel of Income Dynamics," in C. Lloyd, E. Andrews, and C. Gilroy, eds., *Women in the Labor Market* (New York: Columbia University Press, 1979); J. E. Mincer and S. Polachek, "Family Investments in Human Capital: Earnings of Women," *Journal of Political Economy* 82 (March/April 1974), pp. 76–108; and S. H. Sandell and D. Shapiro, "The Theory of Human Capital and the Earnings of Women: A Re-examination of the Evidence," *Journal of Human Resources* 13 (Winter 1978), pp. 103–17. Corcoran did find, however, that the negative effects of withdrawal were more pronounced for women age 30 to 44 than for women in other age groups.

6. Unfortunately, we did not ask the reasons for absence from the labor force.

7. However, the women did score significantly lower on the quantitative part of the GMAT ($t = 4.09; p < .001$). On the verbal part of the GMAT, the scores were the same.

8. We also tested to see whether job type (marketing, finance, etc.) and geographic location were significant determinants of salary since Melvin Reder had found significant effects of both of these variables on the starting salaries of MBAs from the University of Chicago over the 1971–1974 period. See M. Reder, "Analysis of a Small Closely Observed Labor Market: Starting Salaries for University of Chicago MBAs" *Journal of Business* 51 (April 1978), pp. 263–97. We found that regressions including industry dummies explained a higher percentage of the variance in annual salary than did regressions including job-type dummies. The two sets of variables were, as might be expected, too highly correlated to include both in a single regression.

   In neither specification were job location dummies significant. Interestingly, men and women had similar, although not exactly the same, location patterns. About 45 percent of women (55 percent of men) were located in California; about 10 percent of both sexes were living in New York City. Women were more likely than men to be in Washington, D.C. (about 14 percent versus 4 percent).

9. For some of the popular literature see E. G. C. Collins and P. Scott, "Everyone Who Makes It Has a Mentor," *Harvard Business Review* 56,4 (1979), pp. 89–101. For some scholarly scepticism, see E. C. Shapiro, F. P. Haseltine, and M. P. Rowe, "Moving Up: Role Models, Mentors and the 'Patron System,'" *Sloan Management Review* 19 (Spring 1979), pp. 51–58; and J. Speizer, "Role Models, Mentors and Sponsors," *Signs: Journal of Women in Culture and Society*, forthcoming. A thoughtful discussion of mentoring may be found in J. G. Clawson, "Mentoring in Managerial Careers," in C. B. Derr, ed., *Work, Family and Career: New Frontiers in Theory and Research* (New York: Praeger, 1980).

10. R. M. Kanter in her study of a large business organization, *Men, Women and the Corporation*, (New York: Basic Books, 1977), argues that in addition to making introductions and providing training, sponsors also fight for the individual in question, help to bypass the hierarchy, and provide reflected power (pp. 181–82). Our categories of mentorship cut across Kanter's. Fighting for the individual is in part the bestowing of protection, but some fighting may also take place in the course of providing specific assistance, as when "pushing advancement" and "helping to finance projects." Similarly, bypassing the

hierarchy and providing reflected power may be part of giving visibility and/or creating jobs for a mentee.

11. In D. J. Levinson et al., *The Seasons of a Man's Life* (New York: Alfred Knopf, 1978), the authors suggest that to be a mentor one must usually be over 40. Our results squarely contradict that supposition. Only one man in our sample is over 40. The mean age of the women is 29.6 years, of the men, 30.5 years. On the other hand, the sense in which our respondents see themselves as mentors is not the same as the sense in which Levinson used the concept. In fact, what is termed mentoring by our respondents may be what Harlan and Weiss call "multiple helping relationships," which they distinguish sharply from mentorship. See A. Harlan and C. L. Weiss, "Career Opportunities for Women Managers" in C. B. Derr, ed., *Work, Family and the Career: New Frontiers in Theory and Research, op. cit.*

12. With respect to career satisfaction, 5 percent were dissatisfied or mildly dissatisfied, 1 percent were neither satisfied nor dissatisfied, 21 percent were mildly satisfied, 34 percent were satisfied, and 39 percent were very satisfied. Responses on degree of satisfaction with "life in general" were as follows: 5 percent either very dissatisfied, dissatisfied or mildly dissatisfied; 4 percent neither satisfied nor dissatisfied; 15 percent mildly satisfied; 41 percent satisfied; 35 percent very satisfied.

13. Looking at medians, we find little difference in the peak salary *hoped* for: $100,250 for women versus $100,941 for men. However, there remains quite a large difference in *expected* peak salary. The median for women was $60,000; for men, $99,643.

14. The reader is warned once again about the small number of women in our sample.

15. Absence of parity in earnings for men and women MBAs has also been found for MBAs in the Stanford classes of 1973 and 1975. See T. W. Harrell and M. S. Harrell, "Careers of Women, Minority and White Male MBAs," Stanford Graduate School of Business, Research Paper No. 558, 1981. L. T. Zappert and H. M. Weinstein, "Sex Differences in Adaptation to Work: Physical and Psychological Consequences," Paper presented to the Annual Meeting of the American Psychological Association, Montreal, Canada, August 1980, also found lack of parity in earnings for men and women MBAs from the classes of 1977 and 1978 of a large and prestigious graduate school of business.

Chapter 3

THE APPRENTICESHIP MODEL OF ORGANIZATIONAL CAREERS: A RESPONSE TO CHANGES IN THE RELATION BETWEEN WORK AND FAMILY

by Lotte Bailyn

Last year a student of mine brought me a wonderful cartoon. It shows a father walking with his young daughter, obviously engaged in a serious conversation. The caption reads, "But Daddy, I know all about the birds and the bees. What I want to know is how to become a corporation president!" Well, the father obviously is hard put to answer this question, and I can't blame him. The road to corporation president, as we now know it, is based on traditional family/work patterns, and it is not easy to say how a woman is supposed to travel it, or indeed a man who is married to such a woman rather than to one who plays the traditional "helpmeet" role.

This paper was presented to an Industrial Liaison Program Symposium on Women in the Workplace: Management of Human Resources, MIT, January 26, 1978. It has been published in a form directly geared to managers in L. Bailyn, "Taking Off for the Top: How Much Acceleration for Career Success?" *Management Review* 68 (1979); pp. 18–23; and some of its points have been elaborated in L. Bailyn, "The Slow-Burn Way to the Top: Some Thoughts on the Early Years of Organizational Careers," in C. Brooklyn Derr, ed., *Work, Family, and the Career: New Frontiers in Theory and Research* (New York: Praeger, 1980).

Changes in the Relation Between Work and Family

The increasing number of women going into organizational careers is putting pressure on traditional family/work patterns, both for them and the men to whom they are linked. Up to now adaptation to these pressures has been largely individual. But if current trends in the labor force participation of women continue, the time has come to consider organizational responses to these changes, and it is that problem I want primarily to consider.

The changes in the relation between work and family that are taking place today will, in my opinion, have far-reaching consequences for the way organizations manage their human resources. They are changes that result from two intersecting developments. I have already mentioned the first, the increased participation of women in the labor force, particularly women with families, at all levels of the occupational hierarchy. The second is less obvious, perhaps, but equally important: the changes taking place in traditional ways of thinking about women's and men's roles—in the home as well as in the workplace. It is an ideological change, most evident, perhaps, among those with higher education who are engaged in technical, professional, and managerial organizational roles, but beginning to permeate all parts of society. The simultaneous occurrence of both of these trends is forcing us into a reevaluation of organizational assumptions about work and careers that have long gone unquestioned. As such it will have consequences for the management not only of women workers but of all of an organization's employees.

When we think about promoting the equality of men and women in the workplace, a number of things are by now fairly clear. No longer do we blame the wage differential between the sexes on female deficiencies, whether biological or psychological. Nor are employers as likely as before to assume that female workers are a more or less homogeneous group and to generalize the performance of one particular woman to all women employees. I remember, for instance, five or six years ago at a seminar a lawyer remarking that his firm had already hired a woman, it had not worked out, and therefore the firm had decided that women do not make good lawyers. The remark went unchallenged. I don't think this would happen today.

We now are fully aware that female employees differ in abilities and motivations just as male workers do, and that there are very few jobs that cannot be equally well handled by the proper employee of either sex. But we also know that entering nontraditional jobs—jobs predominantly held by members of the other sex—is not always easy, and its success depends on a complex array of situational and individual factors. And, most important for my topic, we know that there can be no equality between women and men in the workplace if there is not a change in the traditional roles of men and women in the family.[18] As long as women continue to be expected to take the primary responsibility for the family, they will not be able, as easily as men, to meet the traditional requirements of jobs, especially jobs that culminate in the higher strata of our organizations. If nothing else, the example of the Soviet Union attests to this point. There, women's family roles are unchanged despite the fact that they are expected to participate fully in work. As a result, although there are many women doctors and engineers, top positions in these and other fields are primarily held by men.

Any change in family roles, however, will have far-reaching implications for organizational careers as we now know them. The traditional male employee moving up in an organization has always lived in a world of work and family. But by delegating the responsibility for the family to his wife, he personally has experienced little conflict in this combination. As a matter of fact, since success in his work has been seen as necessary for the well-being of the whole family, organizational requirements for overtime, travel, and relocation have been seen as necessary evils to be fully supported by the wife. This division of labor and these assumptions result in what has been called the two-person career,[16] two people, in their different ways, enhancing one career. Organizations, of course, have been implicitly aware of this situation: most would much prefer to have a married man in a top position, for he has a support system in his personal as well as in his occupational life. Women have never had such double support systems, as is evident by the often repeated lament of the career woman that all she needs is a wife. Rather, the "best" that most career-oriented women can do is not to have a family at all.

By no other change, therefore, than the labor force participation of his wife, a man's ability to meet traditional organizational requirements will be somewhat diminished. And if he also believes in the ideology of equality, which gives equal weight to his wife's career and necessitates his active involvement in the family, then his organizational position may change dramatically.

Young men are not unaware of this dilemma. We know that many express an almost classic ambivalence during their college years between the commitment to equality and the sense of concern, even of deprivation, when they compare their situations to those with more traditional expectations.[15] The concern increases as they enter the work world and see themselves competing for jobs from what they feel—and with some justification according to today's rules—to be a "disadvantaged" position. Ironically, since highly competent people tend to marry each other, these dilemmas are most prevalent among employees with the highest potential since these are the employees on whom both sets of demands are likely to be the greatest.

Women entering these jobs face the same issues, of course, as well as others that stem from their minority position on these career paths. Compared to men with traditional family support systems, they are doubly deprived. Many are choosing to deal with the issues by staying single, and many married couples trying to establish two careers are deciding not to have children during this period or are demanding and taking advantage of new and different child-care facilities. The cohort in which these innovations are frequent enough to be studied systematically is not yet old enough to assess the consequences of these early decisions on the experiences of the later stages of life. We have enough information to be pretty sure that children will not be adversely affected by new arrangements for their care.[10,11] We are less certain, though, about how the dynamics of personality development will change in response to full father involvement in infant care and to androgynous or sex-blind childhood socialization. Nor do we know whether the regret at childlessness seen by psychiatrists in today's middle-aged women will also hit the part of this cohort who have decided to simplify the demands of top organizational careers by not having children. And we are only beginning to understand the consequences of delayed child bearing.[1]

There is no doubt, however, that women and men from dual career families are at a disadvantage today in pursuing high organizational positions.* They are faced with choices that men in top positions have previously not had to make. Personally, of course,

---

* As I have discussed elsewhere,[2] there are different patterns possible for dual career families which will affect these outcomes to a certain extent. But only a completely differentiated division of work and family responsibilities can provide for one partner the career advantages that now accrue to men in traditional families.

such choices may lead to more integrated lives, but in terms *strictly* of organizational success, the difficulties are apparent.

You may think that such a bleak picture is not quite fair, since everyone can cite exceptions either from personal knowledge or from the media. Some women *have* reached high positions, some dual career couples *are* successful, and some *do* have children. But as of now these exceptions are limited to people of unusual ability, energy, and health. They represent the individual adaptations of a small highly selective minority: individual solutions against a back-drop of high-level organizational careers as traditionally viewed. As such, they put a great burden on the individuals pursuing these careers and therefore will never be applicable to the large number whom we now expect to fit into these new patterns. It is important, therefore, to confront this traditional view of the organizational career and to seek organizational solutions for some of these dilemmas.

Challenge/Success Model

What is this traditional view of the organizational career? It fits into what one might call the challenge/success model. An employee enters an organization with a bachelor's degree or MBA and after an initial period of orientation starts his first real assignment—his first job with that organization. It is an important period in the new employee's life: much of the rest of the career in that organization rests on what happens during this early period. If the new employee has a challenging first job and lives up to all its requirements, his chances of being successful are much improved. If he fails, and even if he performs effectively but isn't given a sufficiently challenging job, the chances of success are less.[6] So, according to this model, the early career is crucial. It is a period of both excitement and strain. In pursuing a series of new and challenging jobs, the young recruit learns to know himself as an organizational employee—to identify his particular areas of competence and interest—and, by learning how his organization works, can begin to mesh these with the available career paths in that organization. The organization, in turn, learns to evaluate the employee—Is he high potential? Is this a candidate who will be able to fill crucial managerial roles?—and sets a career track for the employee in line with this early evaluation. If all goes well, a high-potential employee will find himself, as he enters the period of mid-career, in a key managerial role, possibly in line for succession to top management. To reach this position, he will have worked in many parts of the company, both functionally and geographically, and performed effectively in all. Of course, derailments are possible on the fast track: sometimes a developmental assignment is seen as a dead-end assignment or a promotion is viewed as being kicked upstairs. Then performance may falter, evaluations may change, and new routes may be established in mid-journey.

You may wonder why I use the pronoun "he" in this description. I do so because the challenge/success model is geared to traditional work/family patterns in which "he" really is the one who has the career. And although I have drawn a very general, somewhat stereotyped picture, I suspect it is not far from the truth in many organizations. It also highlights the areas of conflict between the requirements of organizational careers as traditionally viewed and new patterns of work/family interaction. This is not to say that conflicts between work and family have never occurred before. Of course they have, but they were not questioned, not seen as such. Rather they were experienced as individual problems to be adapted to as well as possible: sometimes dramatically by a radical career change (a second career) or divorce; most often incrementally by small adjustments here and there, a process that does not necessarily guarantee a satisfactory outcome. I am reminded here of the economic argument that a host of small decisions may sometimes yield an outcome exactly opposite to the one that would have been wanted had the large choice been available. For example, many small decisions to take a car (or plane) rather than a train may lead to the elimination of railroad service to a community which, had the choice been available, would have gladly contributed to the railroad in order to assure its continued availability.[14] Similarly, small individual adjustments on work/family issues may lead to outcomes that are far from optimal for either the individual or the employing organization.

The point I want to make is that in the challenge/success model a tremendous premium is placed on extremely high orientation to work during the early career years. The value of such an orientation, moreover, is seemingly supported by career research which shows that later success depends on it, by psychological research which has identified youth as the most creative period in one's life, and by the speed with which formal learning (that absorbed in colleges and universities) becomes obsolete. It is a model of the organizational career that has a curve of work involvement that is very high at the beginning but remains very high primarily for those most high-potential employees who eventually succeed to the top positions. For the bulk of an organization's employees, in contrast, it tends to drop slowly throughout the course of the career. At mid-career the curve may have reached the disenchantment stage, which is then falsely seen as a separate organizational problem rather than as a problem that follows logically from an organizational career based on the challenge/success model.

The demand the challenge/success model makes for extensive work orientation during the early career years is critically important because this is the same period during which one is expected to establish a family. It is the period in a family when children are being born—a period of high demand for someone's time and attention. As long as these two sets of demands can be met by different people—as in the traditional family pattern—the model is viable. But this solution is not possible for women entering these career paths, nor for men in dual career families. For this reason it is important to consider alternative models for organizational careers that will better fit the new work/family patterns we now see evolving—particularly those of women and of men in dual career families.

Apprenticeship Model

The model I would like to consider here I have termed the *apprenticeship model.** It consists of a career path in which there is a fairly long period of continued learning and training during the early career with assignments of slowly increasing challenge building up to top involvement only at a later period. It is a model in which the work involvement curve starts low and gradually increases with time —quite different, therefore, from the challenge/success model. For the family the advantages of careers based on such a model are obvious. Without the excessive work demands in these early

---

* By using this term I mean to draw attention only to the timetable aspects, not the legal aspects, associated with apprenticeship for skilled crafts.

years, young people can establish their family lives at the same time as their careers are being established, and in more equitable ways. But what about the work career—will it not suffer?

To answer this question we must go back to those supports of the challenge/success model that I have already mentioned: the correlation of early challenge with future success, the creativity of youth, and the short half-life of formal knowledge. In doing so I will not be able to quote fully established research results. Indeed, these questions are terribly difficult to probe systematically since it is almost impossible in a period of rapid social change such as has recently occurred in this whole area, to separate developmental from cohort effects—to distinguish between what happens to people as they develop and get older from what is happening historically to the world in which they grew up and now live in. For this same reason, also, this is an area where we cannot reliably use our own experience to guide our thinking about younger people—neither our children nor our subordinates. But it is nonetheless important, I believe, to confront these accepted supports for the challenge/success model and see if alternative explanations of these would-be "facts"—more in line with other models—are not possible.

The correlation between early job challenge, high work involvement, and organizational success is seemingly very strong. It reflects the contingent realities of organizational career progression: a highly involved and work-oriented employee is seen as a go-getter. He is therefore given more challenging assignments, which engage him even further and thus mark him for rapid promotion. Such success, then, reinforces his involvement, and an upward spiral begins. This outcome is seemingly so obvious that it is difficult to question it. I would like to point out, however, that it depends quite a bit on the interpretation given to the initially high work involvement. If, for example, instead of seeing it as a positive indicator of effective performance, it were seen as a sign of disorganization, the scenario might be different.

The role that such interpretations play was brought out vividly by the study of an undergraduate student a few years ago. She was interested in employer discrimination against women and therefore prepared two vitas, identical except for sex, which she presented to prospective employers of computer programmers. In each case the applicant had had two years of college, then took off a year to work as a programmer, then came back to college to get a degree in computer science, and was now applying for a computer programmer job. The most interesting finding in my opinion related to the way this history was interpreted by the prospective employers. They were pleased with the young man's resume. It showed a determination to finish his college education, even if it required taking a year off. Not so for the young woman, who was accused of changing her mind and of not knowing what her educational or career interests really were.[8]

In another context we have seen a shift in interpretation of frequent job changes. What used to be viewed as a sign of personal instability in an executive, is now taken as indicative of personal drive and breadth of experience.[13] The point is that a young employee whose involvement builds up slowly while meeting the demands of a young family might well be seen as accumulating valuable experience in preparation for crucial organizational tasks at a later stage in life rather than as a poor prospect. I am not suggesting that there aren't problems here, but only that research results that seemingly buttress the challenge/success model are based on a series of shared assumptions that are now being questioned and need not necessarily hold true.

I would also like to point out that the "slow" period in the apprenticeship model is not devoid of work involvements, nor does it last forever. If we think of a period of five to seven years as necessary to establish a fixed career path in the traditional model,[20] then the equivalent period in the apprenticeship model might be twice as long—perhaps ten to fourteen years—certainly not enough time to turn an energetic young employee into a decrepit dodderer. Further, it is important to note that many women in top positions today have successfully, though probably unintentionally, pursued a career based on the apprenticeship model.

Nonetheless, the apprenticeship model does imply that employees in the early career stages will be older, so it is important to confront the second seeming support for the traditional model, the relation between creativity and youth. Again, I have no definitive answer. But it now seems likely that the correlation between creativity and youth may be as much a function of the length of time one has been engaged in a particular activity as it is of chronological age. Since most often new activities are started when young, it is hard to separate age from length of time on an activity. Evidence from second careers, however, or careers started late in life (as with women entering the occupational world only when their children are grown), indicates that a similar initial period of high creativity may occur no matter what age the activity is embarked upon. Further, in many fields there seems to be a period of high creativity relatively late in the career: one that is more integrative, perhaps, than strictly original, but which advances a field as much or more as do earlier creative peaks.[12,17]

Finally, regarding the obsolescence of formal knowledge, two comments are relevant. First, we know that the acquisition of knowledge is much easier when connected to specific tasks that require that knowledge. Hence the effective performance of organizational tasks is probably as much or more dependent on on-the-job training as it is on formal learning. Second, if the early career period is less demanding, it is easier to include in it the continuing pursuit of formal knowledge. Since this is a time when people are more accustomed to "book" learning than in the more usual periods when continuing education is tried, the goal of "lifelong learning" may be reached more easily this way.

All these points indicate that the apprenticeship model differs from the challenge/success model in putting less of a premium on the advantages of youth and more on the importance of accumulated experience. It is based on a sense of organizational careers that develop more slowly than we are used to and build to a variety of differentiated roles in later life, among which the training of the next generation of "apprentices" would necessarily play a large role.[5] It would lessen, therefore, the problem of long career plateaus and the accompanying sense of failure and decrements in performance that these characteristically produce. Maybe it would ease the mid-career crisis.

I do not want to give the impression, though, that the apprenticeship model should now replace the challenge/success model for all employees. On the contrary, the most general implication of what I have been trying to say is that we need more differentiation of career paths within an organization. We need multiple models so that career paths can have sufficient flexibility to accommodate the much greater variety of life styles now emerging.*

---

* Two other models come to mind. The first is the *two-career* model, in which a person pursues two different careers in one lifetime: one started right after school, one at mid-career.[19] Such a model does not undo the difficulties of the challenge/success model in the early years, but does alleviate the mid-career plateauing problems often associated with that model. Another possible model is the *paternalistic* one, in which an organization guarantees a person lifetime employment. It shares with the apprenticeship model the possibility of a slow career buildup and the necessity to optimize the usefulness of older employees. It represents, however, an organizationwide (or broader) policy. The apprenticeship model is meant, in contrast, to define career paths that are only one among many possible ones in an organization. As such it is likely to include, and in fact may require, movement between organizations.

Managing Multiple Models

Managing the pluralism that results from multiple career paths is a challenging task, both for organizations and for their employees. This is easy to see if one considers two young employees, one of whom is more attuned to the challenge/success model, the other to the apprenticeship model. Unless this discrepancy is handled intelligently, we are back to the same disadvantageous position for the apprenticeship employee that dual career men are currently becoming concerned about. It is the awareness of alternative models, I believe, that can help in this situation—can help both the employee and the organization managing that employee's career. The differences are invidious only in the short run. With a longer-range view it is clear that the apprenticeship model defines a different career curve, one that rises more slowly but eventually may end up at the same point, though at a later stage in life. During the early years, however, it is essential that both the employee and the organization be aware of these differences so that they do not interpret the slower initial rise as failure, as a sign of low potential. Thus the management of employees following both of these models will require a long-range view, one that encompasses a total career. It will require also a new understanding of age and of what happens to people as they grow older. It will necessitate breaking down age stereotypes and undoing age discrimination.

In addition to this more long-range view of careers, the inclusion in an organization of career paths based on the apprenticeship model will also require a new understanding of organizational commitment. An organization has a right to demand commitment from an employee—commitment in the sense of taking responsibility for assigned tasks. But it cannot prescribe the form that this commitment must take. Neither amount of time spent at work nor an exclusive orientation to the work situation is a legitimate sign of responsible commitment for employees whose careers follow the apprenticeship model. Employees can be fully committed and perform effectively, even when working part-time. As a matter of fact, recent evidence from time use studies[7] shows that many part-time workers are more committed to their work—make more of an effort and take more responsibility—than those who are working what we now call full time. And though many employers feel that time put in is crucial because responsibility cannot be shared, we know from the experience of job sharing that mechanisms assuring continuity of responsibility are quickly evolved by the participants.[21] And in activities that require around-the-clock monitoring (as in the care of very sick patients, for instance), responsibility has always been shared.

So, a long-range view of career and a new understanding of commitment are some of the changes that would be necessary if organizations are to manage effectively a work force that follows different career paths based on different models. There is one more change I would like to mention: a different perspective on mobility, in the sense of geographic relocation and interorganizational moves. The right location and the right organization will be even more important for employees who are inclined to the apprenticeship model because their choices are not determined solely by criteria relating to their work. Companies are already aware of the difficulties that may arise from moving their personnel. Some organizations have had the experience of employees declining assignments that require geographical relocation and evidence exists of a not insignificant decrement in performance after a move. Similarly, there is research evidence that a company's most valued employees are not necessarily its organizationally most loyal ones.[9] With the acceptance of more varied career paths, there will, I think, be more movement between organizations. But as long as employees move in as well as out, organizations need not suffer, and might, in fact, benefit.

What I have been saying is that changes in the interaction of work and family and in people's optimal work/family patterns have led them toward a new view of careers: toward new notions of success and new integrations between work and the rest of their lives. Those new concerns do not mean, however, that these new kinds of employees are ineffective or unproductive. But they may become so if they are forced into traditional paths based on the challenge/success model of organizational careers. It is crucial, therefore, that new and more flexible career paths be made available based on alternative models, and that organizations adopt a longer-range perspective on careers, come to a new understanding of organizational commitment, and rethink their currently accepted views on employee mobility.

These very general notions are based on the requirements of the apprenticeship model—one alternative model of organizational careers that I have tried to describe. As all models, it represents a way of thinking and can only guide, rather than define, policies and procedures necessary to implement it. I would like to suggest, however, a few specific organizational policies that seem particularly suitable to this model:

1. Cafeteria benefits, which give employees a choice among benefits.
2. Flexible time schedules and the availability of part-time positions, job sharing, and time off as possible benefit choices.
3. A consideration of personal needs in setting working conditions (e.g. making child care available, giving paternal as well as maternal leave, rethinking nepotism rules, reconsidering mandatory changes in working shifts and expectations for being on-call).

These policies imply an acceptance of the relevance for work of personal needs (other than illness), and a multiple, complex view of the individual employee.

An immediate objection to these suggestions might be their cost. True, some increased costs are associated with all of these policies. But what about the costs of dissatisfied workers, of promising young employees caught in an impossible dilemma between the demands of their employing organizations and their families? The fact that these costs are difficult to quantify does not mean that their effect on organizational performance is minimal. On the contrary, it may well be that the benefits gained from more flexible policies will far outweigh their costs.

To conclude, let me reiterate one basic point that underlies everything I have been saying. The changes in work/family patterns we have been observing over the past years have far-reaching implications for the management of human resources in organizations. In particular, the entrance of women into all levels of organizational positions has ramifications well beyond those problems that can be dealt with by affirmative action staffs geared to the unique issues of women. Its effects are much more fundamental because they also directly involve the career responses of the men to which these working women are linked, and thus necessitate a rethinking of career requirements and career paths for *all* of an organization's employees.

Endnotes

1. See, for example, A. Alden, "Delayed Childbearing: Issues and Implications" (unpublished doctoral thesis, Harvard University Graduate School of Education, 1981).

2. L. Bailyn, "Accommodation of Work to Family," in R. Rapoport and R. N. Rapoport, eds., *Working Couples* (London: Routledge and Kegan Paul, 1978).

3. L. Bailyn, "Taking Off for the Top: How Much Acceleration for Career Success?" *Management Review* 68, 1 (1979), pp. 18–23.

4. L. Bailyn, "The Slow-Burn Way to the Top: Some Thoughts on the Early Years of Organizational Careers," in C. B. Derr, ed., *Work, Family, and the Career: New Frontiers in Theory and Research* (New York: Praeger, 1980).

5. L. Bailyn in collaboration with E. H. Schein, *Living with Technology: Issues at Mid-Career* (Cambridge, Mass.: MIT Press, 1980).

6. See, for example, D. W. Bray, R. J. Campbell, and D. L. Grant, *Formative Years in Business: A Long-term AT&T Study of Managerial Lives* (New York: Wiley, 1974).

7. G. Duncan and F. Stafford, quoted in *ISR Newsletter*, Summer 1977.

8. J. Ellensen, Personal communication, 1974.

9. E. Getchell, "Factors Affecting Employee Loyalty" (unpublished master's thesis, MIT, 1975).

10. L. W. Hoffman and F. I. Nye, *Working Mothers* (San Francisco: Jossey-Bass, 1974).

11. M. C. Howell, "Effects of Maternal Employment on the Child," *Pediatrics* 52 (1973), pp. 327–43.

12. E. Jaques, "Death and the Mid-Life Crisis," *International Journal of Psychoanalysis* 46 (1965), pp. 502–14.

13. E. E. Jennings, *Routes to the Executive Suite* (New York: McGraw-Hill, 1971). Quoted in D. T. Hall, *Careers in Organizations* (Pacific Palisades: Goodyear, 1976), pp. 5–6.

14. A. E. Kahn, "The Tyranny of Small Decisions: Market Failures, Imperfections, and the Limits of Economics," *Kyklos* 19 (1966), pp. 23–47.

15. M. Komarovsky, "Cultural Contradictions and Sex Roles: The Masculine Case," *American Journal of Sociology* 78 (1973), pp. 873–84.

16. H. Papanek, "Men, Women and Work: Reflections on the Two-Person Career," *American Journal of Sociology* 78 (1973), pp. 857–72.

17. D. C. Pelz and F. M. Andrews, *Scientists in Organizations: Productive Climates for Research and Development* (New York: Wiley, 1966).

18. C. Safilios-Rothschild, "Dual Linkages Between the Occupational and Family Systems: A Macrosociological Analysis," *Signs* 1 (1976), pp. 51–60.

19. S. B. Sarason, *Work, Aging, and Social Change: Professionals and the One Life–One Career Imperative* (New York: Free Press, 1977).

20. E. H. Schein, *Career Dynamics: Matching Individual and Organizational Needs* (Reading, Mass.: Addison-Wesley, 1978).

21. A. Wood and D. R. Gardner, "An Impressionistic Evaluation of Job-Sharing" (unpublished paper, 1976).

Chapter 4

SEX DIFFERENCES IN FACTORS AFFECTING MANAGERIAL CAREER ADVANCEMENT

by Anne Harlan and Carol L. Weiss

Between the years 1970 and 1975, the increase in the number of women in managerial positions amounted to some 202,000 individuals. According to The Conference Board (1978), this figure represented an increase from 13 percent in 1970 to 17 percent in 1975. These statistics are indicative of the last fifteen years, which have brought expanded career opportunities to women in corporate life. Whereas traditionally women have held predominantly clerical and service jobs, now more women are functioning in managerial and professional roles.

Even with this influx of women into management, problems still exist. Management remains a heavily male-dominated occupation, with women comprising 15 percent of entry-level managers, but only 5 percent of middle management and 1 percent of top manage-

We gratefully acknowledge the support of this research by the following organizations: American Can Company Foundation, Atlantic Richfield Company, Business and Professional Women's Foundation, Center for Research on Women, Wellesley College, Digital Equipment Corporation, William H. Donner Foundation, General Electric Company Foundation, General Mills Foundation, International Paper Company Foundation, Kellogg Company, Kimberly-Clark Foundation, Inc., Lever Brothers Company Foundation, Polaroid Corporation Foundation, Helena Rubinstein Foundation, Safeway Stores, Inc., Stop & Shop Companies, Inc., and Time, Inc. Special thanks also go to Joseph Pleck and Susan Calechman for their many substantive contributions to this research.

ment (*Business Week*, Nov. 24, 1975). The proportion of women in middle- and top-level management has remained relatively constant from preceding decades.

Description of Study

The data above, taken together, suggest that while more women are entering management, women do not advance in management the way men do. This chapter describes some of the preliminary analysis of data from a two-and-a-half-year study on male and female managerial advancement patterns. We were interested in examining four primary areas:

1. *Differences between men and women managers' psychological and personal background characteristics shown in past studies to predict managerial success.* Many such characteristics could have been studied, including socialization patterns, childhood and adolescence periods of development, and role models. However, we chose to examine particular psychological and background characteristics that were pertinent to performance of managerial functions, including motivational patterns, education, goals and aspirations, as well as age, marital, and parenting statuses.

2. *Differences between men and women managers' organizational experiences shown in past studies to predict success.* The variables we chose for study included the amount and types of power, formal, and informal training, and feedback and evaluations received by managers. These organizational experiences have been identified in past studies as predicting success.

3. *The extent and nature of sex bias in organizations today.* Our interests lay beyond merely examining stereotypic attitudes. We also gathered data on occupational segregation in hiring and promotion, behavioral manifestations of sex bias in supervisory activities, and sexual harassment from supervisors and colleagues.

4. *The effects of differing proportions of women in management on women managers' organizational experiences.* The proportion of women to men has been seen as a key factor by Kanter in determining the degree of sex bias women experi-

ence on the job.[34] We investigated the effects of different proportions of women in management on performance pressures felt by the women and on sex stereotyping. In addition, we examined the effects of different proportions on the amount of advancement opportunity both women and men perceived.

Research Sites

The research was conducted in two large companies, both under one corporate umbrella. Each company was a separate entity, having its own president and top management team. There was almost no movement of personnel from one company to the other. Both organizations were located in the same geographic region and were in the retail industry. We purposely chose the retail industry because it was most often seen as being a favorable industry for women. Therefore, we thought any barriers that emerged for women in that industry were likely to be less severe than the difficulties facing women in other industries. This choice carried with it the possibility that we might not discover some problems that are faced by women in nonretail industries. However, we believed that barriers occurring even in the industry thought to be most favorable to women would be highly generalizable to other companies and industries.

The two organizations differed on the proportion of women holding managerial positions. In the past five years both companies had made an effort to increase the proportion of women in management, resulting in women in one company comprising 19 percent of management and women in the other company comprising 6 percent of the management population. For the purpose of discussion, we will refer to the organization in which women comprised 19 percent of all management positions as Company 19; the other organization in which women comprised only 6 percent of management will be referred to as Company 6. These two companies, therefore, were at different points in the process of bringing women into managerial positions.

We thought this dimension was an especially important element to study for two basic reasons. First of all, difficulties facing women managers in companies where women have seldom been part of management are likely to differ from difficulties faced by women in other companies where a substantial proportion of managerial-level positions have been filled by women. Second, the organization itself may face different problems in attracting and utilizing women in management as the proportion of women increases. For example, we would predict that problems of recruitment, development, and retainment would be encountered most often in organizations having low proportions of women managers. As the number of women managers increases, we would expect to see the problems confronting the company shift to issues of equal utilization and opportunity.

A second feature that differentiated the two companies under study is the growth pattern exhibited over the last five-year period. Company 19 had been in a growth period characterized by increased sales volume and greater market penetration. Company 6 had been in a declining period, marked by store closings and decreased sales. We believe it is especially important to examine the effects of company growth rate on employee career advancement opportunity. A slow growth rate or decline would present unique problems for companies that feel an urgency and responsibility to advance women to higher-level positions but at the same time are facing a decline in the number of higher-level positions available.

Though it is especially difficult to disentangle outcomes due to differing proportions of women in management from those due to company growth patterns, we have attempted to overcome this problem through our interviewing procedure. In our questionnaire to the managerial sample, as well as their supervisors, we asked a series of questions to determine the amount of opportunity for advancement. Special probes were used to determine the extent to which individual perceptions were shaped by the economic environment and by other forces. Through these data, we have gained some insight regarding the individual effects of company growth and differing proportions of women in management.

Research Sample

Our sample was composed of fifty managers from each organization—twenty-five males and twenty-five females matched on level of management, responsibility, and functional area. In these two companies positions were designated by functions and grade levels. Managerial or exempt positions in both companies ranged from grade 10 through grade 18. Forty-eight percent of our sample fell in the three lower-management grades (10–12), and 52 percent were in the four middle-management grades (13–16). In addition to the sample, a few extra managers from each company were recruited to allow for possible attrition. The sample selected represented a cross section of management and encompassed all functional areas, age categories, success categories, and experience levels.

Methods of Data Collection

All data have been collected from our sample of one hundred managers. The data collection consisted of administration of a battery of psychological instruments and a two- to three-hour taped interview with each participant, based on a semistructured interview questionnaire. In the interview we asked for career history, difficulties encountered, career plans and goals, and perceptions of the company. The psychological instruments included Miner's Sentence Completion Scale, the Achievement and Dominance Scales from the California Psychological Inventory, a version of the Thematic Apperception Test, Rosenberg's Self-Esteem Scale, a measure of organizational climate, and a career history questionnaire. Participants were given individual feedback on their own psychological data and will meet later to discuss implications of the organization-wide research data for management career development.

In addition, from the supervisors of our sample we collected data through a one-and-a-half hour interview, which tapped perceptions about the supervisee's career path, skill level, and promotability, as well as perceptions of the supervisor's own career. Also included were a series of questions about organizational procedures and dynamics. Furthermore, each supervisor was asked to evaluate the supervisee's level of ability on sixteen skill dimensions, which form the core of the company performance appraisal system. Finally, each supervisor completed an instrument designed to reveal underlying attitudes toward women holding managerial positions, the Attitude Toward Women as Managers Scale (ATWAM).

Goals

The philosophy that has guided our data analysis has been that the careers of managers are determined by a combination of factors. Quite important are the personal characteristics of the manager—the personality, needs and motives, skills and experience, education, and training. Yet in order to determine whether a person will succeed or fail, the organization into which one enters must be taken into account as well. Certain organizations will value some skills over others, require different patterns of interactions, have different structures necessitating different patterns of communication, and have different policies and procedures. To adequately understand career success, we believe the focus should be on understanding the individual in the context of the organization.

This study attempts to map out the dimensions that are especially important to managerial success for women as well as men. By taking this approach, we think organizations can become more aware of where to look for possible career blockages that are partly the result of the organization's structure or process. Likewise, individual managers can become more aware of how their own personal characteristics "fit" within a given organizational environment and can begin to take more responsibility for their own career development.

We have begun analysis of all the data collected. Though more in-depth analyses will be undertaken in the coming months, some of the preliminary analyses have yielded intriguing results.

Comparison of Men and Women Managers on Measures of Psychological and Personal Background

In our assessment of psychological and personal background characteristics, we examined the personal attributes of the manager such as motivations, needs, career goals, and educational background. There are ways in which organizations can impact some of these personal characteristics, but under normal circumstances, organizations would be under no obligation to attempt to change personal characteristics.

Personal Background

Age. Age has been shown to have a curvilinear relationship with opportunity for advancement.[66] One's opportunities appear to increase as age increases until approximately middle age, at which point opportunities begin to decline. Because of the historical trend for women to leave the labor force upon marriage and return at some later point,[18] we predicted the women holding managerial positions would be older than their male colleagues. If this prediction proved accurate, age might act as a subtle barrier against women's advancement.

Results from each company showed that women managers were slightly older than men managers, although these differences were not statistically significant. At Company 6, the range of ages went from 24 to 59 years of age. The mean age of female respondents was 36.7 years; of male respondents, 32.9 years. For Company 19, the age range extended from 23 to 63 years. Women averaged 39 years of age while men averaged 36.9 years. This age difference between women and men appears to reflect the somewhat later age at which women entered full-time employment. No differences were found between women and men in years of full-time employment with the companies.

Education. Educational level attained has been widely used as a means of determining a person's potential for career success. Stein suggested education was one of the ways an employee was categorized and subsequently located within the organization.[72] A recent survey of selection procedures showed 49 percent of companies surveyed used educational criteria in the selection of professional and managerial staff.[28]

Despite its widespread use, there is little evidence to suggest educational level attained has any relationship to later job performance.[8,21,56] However, education does have great impact on career advancement opportunity and salary.[15,78]

Stein noted women were likely to enter the organization holding lesser educational credentials than men and as a result tended to be excluded from certain positions.[72] We predicted that men in our sample would have attained higher levels of education than the women.

Results from Company 6 revealed that men had attained slightly higher levels of education, although these differences were not statistically significant. In that organization, we found 52 percent of the male managers had graduated from college, compared with 42 percent of the women. Approximately 22 percent of the men had some graduate education as did 17 percent of the women.

In Company 19, however, significant differences clearly emerged between the men and women. In that sample, 55 percent of the males were college graduates, whereas only 10 percent of the women had achieved this level of education. In addition, 30 percent of the men had taken part in graduate-level education, but none of the women had begun graduate study. The predominant major for both men and women was business administration.

Marital and Parenting Statuses.   Marital and parenting statuses have been found to be related to career success in quite complex ways. For men, marriage and family have been seen as indications of stability and maturity, as well as a sign that traditional values and norms were being upheld.[34] In addition, marriage has proved helpful to many male managers' careers because of the roles taken on by their wives. Such roles have included providing emotional support, aiding in time management, providing social contacts, and entertaining important organizational members and clients.[34,70,80,81]

For women managers, marital and parenting statuses have shown no clear-cut relationship to success. Recent surveys, however, have shown women managers were only a third to half as likely as male managers to be married, and less likely to have children.[9,27] In this sample, we expected more men than women would have married. Likewise, we expected a higher incidence of children for male managers. For those women managers who also were parents, we predicted their children would fall into an older age range and thus need less parental attention and time.

We found no statistically significant differences between men and women in our sample on the dimensions of marital or parenting status. In fact, most of the sample, both men and women, were married. However, there was a trend for more men than women to be married. In Company 6, 78 percent of the men were married as compared with 57 percent of the women. In Company 19, 68 percent of the men were married in contrast to 58 percent of the women.

Similarly, there was a trend for men to have a greater likelihood of being parents. For Company 6 women, only 36 percent were parents compared to 68 percent of the men. In Company 19, 53 percent of the women managers had children as did 60 percent of the male managers. Of those women who were mothers, only one in the entire sample had a child under six years of age. In contrast, over one third of the men managers from the sample had at least one child under six years of age.

Needs and Motives

Men and women in our sample were compared on a variety of personality characteristics, including needs for achievement, affiliation and power, dominance, motivation to manage, and self-esteem. The results are described below and illustrated in Figure 4–1.

Need for Achievement. The achievement motive has been defined as a disposition or behavioral tendency to strive for excellence or success. A number of studies have shown that managers manifest higher achievement needs and rate accomplishment as more important in their jobs than most other occupational groups.[48,63,75,77] Past studies have found some sex differences in achievement needs as well. However, rather than women showing differences in absolute level of need to achieve, the context in which achievement needs are measured has been seen as critical. In one study, women's need for achievement was found to be higher than that of men in noncompetitive situations, whereas under competitive conditions men's achievement needs were higher than those of women.[47]

Because of its importance in differentiating managers from other populations, need to achieve was measured in three separate ways. First we used the traditional projective test, which required the manager to write a story to a picture. These stories were then scored using a system developed by McClelland. In addition, managers were asked to complete two scales from the California Psychological Inventory. The first scale identified interest and motivation to achieve in settings where autonomy and independence were positive behaviors. The second scale identified interest and motivation to achieve in settings where cooperation and conformance were positive behaviors. In none of these cases, however, did we predict any differences between men and women's scores in measuring need to achieve.

Data from both companies showed no differences between men and women on two of the three measures, with women managers scoring lower than men on measure of achievement through conformance. Such a pattern suggests that the women who are attracted to management are high in need to achieve and are especially likely to enjoy an environment where they are given substantial autonomy and independence.

Need for Affiliation. Need for affiliation was defined as the need to draw near, please, or win affection from others. This need has often been considered an indication of dependence and need for approval. As such, it is generally perceived as being a counterindication of managerial success. Many studies have shown women in general to have greater needs for affiliation than do men.[46,54] These affiliation needs may become particularly important if they are as

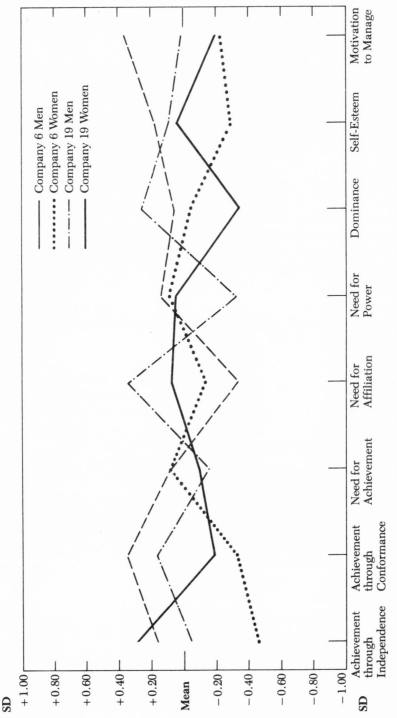

Figure 4-1 Comparsion of Men and Women in Two Companies on Personality Measures (average z scores)

high or higher than achievement needs. In such a situation, desire to be close or affiliate with others may begin to conflict with achievement activities, with the result that achievement activities are suppressed. Horner spoke of a variant of this phenomenon, calling it "fear of success." She suggested that many women sought to avoid success because of a perception that social rejection would follow success.[32]

Because of the strength of data supporting the differences between men and women in the general population on need for affiliation, we predicted that women managers, as well, would show higher levels of this need than would their male colleagues. Though we made no prediction about whether need for affiliation would exceed need for achievement in women, we examined the data for such a relationship. If such a pattern were found, it would be a strong indication of potential conflict between the two needs.

Need for affiliation was measured through the projective Thematic Apperception Test. The managers were shown a series of pictures and asked to write a story about each. These stories were then subjected to a rigorous analysis of content. No significant differences occurred between men and women in need for affiliation. In fact, though the women in Company 6 showed marginally higher amounts of need for affiliation than men of Company 6, the men of Company 19 showed higher levels of the need than the women of Company 19. For Company 6, achievement needs appeared much higher than affiliation needs for both men and women. However, in Company 19, affiliation needs were higher than achievement needs for men as well as women.

This pattern indicates that women managers do not have a greater need to affiliate than do male managers. Likewise, for the entire sample of women managers, the need to affiliate does not appear to be significantly greater than the need to achieve.

Need for Power.   Power needs were defined as the need to establish, maintain, or restore prestige or impact. The need for power has been shown by many researchers to be closely linked to managerial success.[37,52] McClelland and Burnham (p. 101) state, "The general conclusion of these studies is that the top manager of a company must possess a high need for power, that is, a concern for influencing people. . . . Moreover, the top manager's need for power ought to be greater than his need for being liked by people."[52]

It has been assumed that women have lower power needs than

men and that women would not be interested in positions of increased responsibility and influence. The research of Kanter contradicted that assumption.[34] She found that decreased interest in responsibility and influence were functions of status and power differences in organizational employment rather than a function of gender. Kanter concluded that in situations where women workers are accepted as equals and given realistic advancement opportunities, they no longer take the role of low-status persons but interact actively with their co-workers and display ambition and task orientation in accordance with their abilities.

Other authors have maintained that while level of power needs may be similar for men and women, such needs find expression in different ways. Jean Baker Miller noted women often have a fear of power.[54] She found the direct use of power by women frequently brought severe negative reactions from men. This resulted in women feeling the use of power was wrong and "destructive."

We predicted for our own sample that women managers would have power needs similar to those of male managers. As with needs for achievement and affiliation, we assessed power needs through the use of a variant of the Thematic Apperception Test. Results showed no significant differences between men and women managers at either company with respect to power motivation. As seen in Figure 4–1, power needs were somewhat lower for women than men at Company 6 but were higher for women than men at Company 19. For the entire sample, the mean score for power needs was higher than the scores for affiliation or achievement needs..

Dominance. Dominance has been defined as control over others, and as such, appears related to need for power. Campbell et al. described the trait of dominance as a compositive of aggressiveness, confidence, persistence, and independence, and claimed it was strongly related to leadership ability and managerial effectiveness.[10] Many studies have shown that women in the population had lower scores on measures of dominance than men.[12,46] Based on the wealth of studies supporting sex differences in dominance, we predicted that women managers would score lower than men on the Dominance Scale of the California Psychological Inventory. Results seen in Figure 4–1 found no significant differences between men and women on the measure of dominance. There was a tendency, however, for women in both companies to score slightly lower in this measure than did the men.

Self-Esteem. Self-esteem was defined as the degree of positive or negative regard one has for oneself. It has been shown to affect managerial success in a variety of ways. Hall[24] and Korman[36] found persons with high self-esteem were more likely to be "self-aware," making occupational choices that were in line with their own needs. In addition, high self-esteem persons were more likely to have high levels of ability.[36] Finally, high self-esteem persons were more able to assess accurately the probability of success given a particular level of effort. Thus, they were found to respond more predictably and realistically to their environment.[41]

Few differences in level of self-esteem have been found between men and women in the general population. Some evidence, however, has shown women choosing nontraditional careers have lower self-esteem than women in sex-appropriate, traditional roles. Tangri, for example, compared college women aspiring to male occupations with more traditional women and found that career-oriented women described themselves as "not too successful" or "always feeling one is acting; not being myself."[43] Bardwick stated that success for men increases their feelings of competence.[4] In contrast, success for women may decrease their self-esteem, which is also based on maintaining their feminine identity.

Based on these findings, we predicted men managers would show higher levels of self-esteem than women managers. Results revealed significant differences in the predicted direction between men and women in Company 6. No differences, however, emerged between the men and women of Company 19.

Motivation to Manage.   Miner spoke of motivation to manage being a composite of characteristics necessary for managerial effectiveness.[55] A measure devised by Miner to measure such motivation, the Miner Sentence Completion Scale, has been found to be a predictor of success in management jobs and desire for management careers.[55,57,58,59,60,61] That instrument included measures of desire to meet superiors' expectations, competitive needs, assertiveness, dominance, visibility needs, and comfort with routine aspects of administration.

Some evidence has shown that women scored lower than men on motivation to manage in the late 1960s and early 1970s.[58] More recent data, however, have shown no sex differences in overall motivation to manage or in measures of individual components of motivation to manage.[59]

Although our prediction was that no sex differences would be found in the overall motivation to manage score, we had predicted differences on the scales of "Imposing Wishes" and on the two scales measuring competitive drive: "Competitive Games" and "Competitive Situations." The rationale for the first prediction rested on an assumed relationship between imposing one's wishes and the trait of dominance on which we also had predicted sex differences. The basis for the second prediction of lower scores on competition was founded on the assumption that in our society, competition has been valued and rewarded in males' behavior but not in females' behavior. We reasoned that women would have ambivalence about competition that would be manifested in lower scores on the competition scales.

Results showed no significant differences between men and women in Company 19 on subscale scores or overall score. For Company 6, however, men had a much higher overall score on the measure of motivation to manage than did the women, although most of the overall score difference was accounted for by strong differences between men and women on the subscale of "Competitive Games." This subscale, designed to measure competitive drive and interest in sports and games, appeared to be the least work-related scale. On all other scales, including the more general scale of "Competitive Situations," the scores of men and women in Company 6 were not significantly different.

Attribution of Success

One of the determinants of managerial motivation has been found to be the extent to which managers believe in external versus internal control of the events influencing them.[13,40] Persons who are high in internal control feel they are able to influence their own destiny and are more likely to attribute their success to their own skills, efforts, or ability. Persons who are high in external control feel they have little influence over what happens to them, with the result that they are more likely to attribute success to external events such as luck or being in the right place at the right time.

Researchers have found that persons who believed strongly that effort would result in valued outcomes were more likely to put forth the effort needed to attain those goals. Similarly, persons who believed effort "won't pay off" were less likely to put forth the same degree of effort.[40]

Maccoby and Jacklin in a review of the research literature in the area of internal/external control found a strong tendency for women to be externalizers—that is, feeling that events affecting them are the result of luck or chance rather than the result of their own actions.[46] Men, on the other hand, were more likely to be internalizers—feeling that events are the result of their actions. Later studies revealed another interesting variant of this idea. Men were more likely to attribute *success* to their own actions but attribute failure to external events. Women were just the opposite: more likely to attribute *failure* to their own actions and success to external events.[18,38,53]

Given the importance of locus of control in contributing to a person's motivation, we chose to examine it by looking at success attribution. When asked what factors were responsible for their success, we expected male managers to mention skills, ability, or perseverance, whereas we expected female managers to emphasize luck, help from others, or being in the right place at the right time. Results showed a wide variety of answers. There was no indication, however, that more women than men attributed their success to external factors. In fact, the majority of both men and women felt their success was due to their hard work and good performance of responsibilities.

Goals and Aspirations

Level of Aspiration. It has long been recognized that level of aspiration affects subsequent performance.[3,42,51] Berlew and Hall identified the powerful impact of high goals for later work achievement.[6] Hall extended the notion to the working career as a whole by citing the importance of (1) challenging goals, (2) autonomy in selecting goals and how they are to be achieved, and (3) feedback as requisites to a feeling of psychological success in one's work career.[24,25] Such feelings of psychological success would be expected to have an important impact on the commitment, drive, and continued long-term effort required for success in a demanding professional career such as business management.[22]

Additional empirical research has found that women and men differ on level of aspiration. Jelinek and Harlan found significant differences between men and women MBA's with the men stating higher salary and career aspirations than the women.[26] Other researchers, as well, have found women having lower aspiration levels than men.[29,30,43] Our prediction in this study was that women would aspire to lower positions than men. Results supported this prediction.

In Company 6, 39 percent of the men spoke of aspiring to a top-management position (vice president or president) in contrast to 30.4 percent of the women. Only 8.7 percent of the men were content to remain in lower management compared to 30.4 percent of the women. In Company 19, the figures were even more striking. Forty-five percent of the men aspired to top-management positions as did only 18.2 percent of the women. In addition, 20 percent of the men spoke of remaining in lower-level management compared to 31.8 percent of the women.

Multiple reasons likely accounted for the lowered aspiration level of women managers. First of all, women may have been influenced by the subtle cues of others' expectations, both inside and outside the company. If others in the organization had little expectation that a woman manager would advance to top levels, this expectation may have been passed on to the manager and resulted in lowered aspirations.

A second factor that may have contributed to lower aspirations of women is the personal cost in terms of the amount of time and energy required to hold a top-level position. Some women felt the costs in time, outside interests, and family exceeded the benefits they would receive from the higher-management position. It is unclear whether women felt the costs of advancement were higher than did the men, that the benefits of advancement were lower, or whether a combination of both beliefs was operating. We will gain more clarity about this issue as our analysis proceeds.

Finally, women may have perceived less opportunity available and as a result lowered their own aspirations. This hypothesis was put forth by Kanter as an explanation of women's generally lower aspirations.[34] Preliminary analysis on a subsample of data indicated no differences in men and women's perceived opportunity in Company 6. However, in Company 19, men reported greater opportunity available to them than did women. Further analysis of the entire sample will be conducted to determine if differences in perceived opportunity account for much of the difference in aspiration level. Also, since it is possible that very high levels of aspirations are unrealistic for the majority of men as well as women managers, additional analysis will focus on whether the aspirations stated were "realistic" when compared to supervisory and top-management estimates of potential.

Personal Goal Setting.   Setting career goals has been thought to have a strong relationship with managerial success.[34,44] Hall stated that "a person's goals . . . intentions . . . and expectations have a strong influence on the direction and success of her activities" (p. 179).[24]

Some empirical research suggests that the process of setting career goals differs for men and women. Hennig and Jardim wrote of the lack of planning in women's careers.[31] They discussed how women arrive at particular jobs almost by luck rather than by setting goals and planning one's career. Harlan found male MBA's were better able to articulate career goals than were female MBA's.[27] Missirian found that goals and career orientation among a sample of twenty-one Boston businesswomen identified as "leaders" in 1963 differed from those typical of ambitious males and speculated that these differences might be one factor in the women's lesser career achievements between 1963 and 1973.[62]

We thought it likely that career goals and planning would be more characteristic of men than women in our sample. To measure the extent of career planning and goals, we asked each participant about both short- and long-term career goals. Surprisingly, we found few people of either sex who had done any long-range career planning. Instead, both men and women reported drifting into positions through a haphazard series of coincidences. The majority of managers did not speak of their next position as being a step toward meeting a long-term future goal. In fact, some managers described the process of planning and aiming for a future position as inhibiting their own career development. Some more successful managers preferred to examine the future in terms of the kinds of experiences they wanted over the next three to five years. This kind of planning they felt led to greater flexibility in being able to seize opportunities that would be beneficial to them.

The "drift" phenomenon that characterized the careers of most of our sample was revealed in a second way. When asked why they had chosen this particular occupation, approximately half of the male and female managers from Company 19 and half of the female managers from Company 6 indicated they "happened into their occupation with no deliberate thought." Only the male managers in Company 6 overwhelmingly reported they did not drift into the occupation.

Table 4–1 summarizes the comparisons between men and women managers on measures of psychological and personal background.

Table 4–1 Summary of Comparisons Between Men and Women Managers on Measures of Psychological and Personal Background

Variable	Results
Age	In both companies women were slightly older than men, but these differences were not statistically significant.
Education	In Company 6 there was a slight trend for men to have higher educational credentials than women. In Company 19 men had attained much higher educational levels than women.
Marital Status	There was a slight trend in both companies for a higher proportion of men than women to be married.
Parenting Status	Men in both companies had a somewhat higher likelihood of being parents than did women. In addition, there was an exceptionally low incidence of women managers having very young children (under the age of 6).
Need for Achievement	In Company 6 men scored higher than women on need for achievement in environments where conformance is valued. On two other measures of achievement, no differences were found. For Company 19 managers, no significant differences occurred on any of the three measures.
Need for Affiliation	No significant differences were found between men and women managers in either company.
Need for Power	No significant differences were found between men and women managers in either company.
Dominance	There was a tendency for women in both companies to score lower than men on the measure of dominance. However, these differences were not statistically significant.
Self-Esteem	Women in Company 6 showed lower self-esteem than men. However, there were no differences between men and women on this dimension in Company 19.
Motivation to Manage	In Company 6 women scored lower than men on overall motivation to manage and on the scale measuring interest in competitive games. No differences emerged for men and women in Company 19.

Table 4-1 (continued)

Variable	Results
Attribution of Success	There were no differences between men and women on this dimension. Most managers, regardless of sex, attributed success to hard work and good performance.
Level of Aspiration	Women in both companies reported aspiring to positions that were lower in the organizational hierarchy than those aspired to by men.
Personal Goal Setting	No differences were seen between men and women of either company in future goal planning. There was little career goal setting undertaken by men or women.

Comparison of Men and Women Managers on Measures of Organizational Experiences

We have begun analysis of the data in light of the expected differences in organizational experiences between men and women. We have labeled as "organizational experiences" those formal and informal interactions between the individual and the organizational structure, design, and process. Organizational experiences, in contrast to individual characteristics, can be directly influenced and changed by the organization through attention to organizational structure, design, and process. In other words, organizational experiences represent those areas in which organizations most readily can impact a person's success in management. In this section we will report on organizational power, formal and informal training, supervisory feedback, and appraisal.

Power

Kanter defined power as "the ability to get things done, to mobilize resources, to get and use whatever it is that a person needs for the goals he or she is attempting to meet" (p. 166).[34] Many researchers have viewed power as crucial to success and advancement in management.[17,34,35,52,83] Kotter stated that "as organizations have grown more complex, it has become more difficult, if not impossible, for managers to achieve their ends either independently or through persuasion and formal authority alone. They increasingly

need power to influence others on whom they are dependent"
(p. 125).[37]

The process of how one gets and exercises power has been sur-
rounded by controversy, with some researchers such as McClelland
reporting it emanates from the person's motive structure;[50] others,
such as Kanter, believe it stems from the organization.[35] We have
taken the approach that power is a multifaceted dimension that is
determined by personal motives in interaction with organizational
systems and structures. Since power motivation has been examined
earlier in this report, we will focus attention in this section on the
organizational components of power.

Based on her research, Kanter outlined three organizational
sources of power, all of which she found to be less available to
women than to men in organizations:

1. Supplies—having access to materials, money, and resources
   needed to meet the unit's goals and reward unit members.
2. Information—having access to and using organizational information.
3. Support—having the opportunity to make autonomous decisions knowing that the important organizational members
   will back your decisions.

Our prediction was that women would have less power available to
them in each of these areas than would men. We found mixed
results.

Power of Supplies. Using Kanter's sources of organizational
power, we measured power of supplies by gauging the extent to
which managers were responsible for corporate assets, able to
gather additional resources needed to meet goals, and able to get
rewards such as promotions or salary increases for those reporting to
them. In both companies, men had more control over company
assets and monies than did women. Sixty-one percent of the women
but only 32 percent of the men managers in Company 6 reported
direct control of less than $10,000 in company assets. In contrast,
over 40 percent of the men but only 22 percent of the women in
Company 6 controlled in excess of $1 million in company assets. In
Company 19 as well, the differences point to women's positions of
lesser fiscal responsibility. One third of the women managers and 8
percent of the men managers in Company 19 reported control of
less than $10,000 in company assets. Sixty-seven percent of the men
had responsibility for $1 million or more, as did 50 percent of the
women managers.

A second way we measured power of supplies was to ask the sample how often they had tried to place talented subordinates in desirable jobs, get approval for expenditures beyond their budgets, and get above-average salary increases for subordinates. In addition, we asked how often they were successful in these attempts. Results showed no differences between men and women in number of attempts or success rate of these activities.

Power of Information.   Access to information can be a strong indicator of power. Such access can come from a variety of sources: a mentor or company sponsor, a supervisor, a colleague, or a peer. We measured informational power by asking about frequency and sources of information and the purpose to which such information was put. The data revealed a tendency for men in both companies to attempt to get early information about decisions and policy shifts more often than women. In addition, men were more successful in these attempts. These differences were quite slight, and statistically nonsignificant in Company 6 but were highly significant in Company 19.

In addition, men and women from both companies spoke of being part of the informal network. While few differences existed between men and women in Company 6 in how these contacts were used, men in Company 19 had a broader informal system than did the women, more often including top executives as well as outside contacts and sources.

One way in which information has been thought to travel from one person to another has been in social interaction such as lunch, time conversations, sports activities, or after-work socializing. We asked the managers how often they saw people from work in a social setting and with whom they had lunch. We found the majority of men and women from both companies replied they socialized with other company employees on occasion but less frequently than once a month. We did discover some differences in lunching patterns. More men than women responded they had lunched with top executives, with their current supervisors, and with persons outside the company. Women reported more often than men of having lunch with personnel department employees.

Power of Support.   In order to determine if there were differences in support, we examined perceived input into fourteen types of work-related decisions. These decisions fell into five broader categories of decisions:

1. Decisions regarding work place and scheduling of work activities.

2. Decisions regarding staffing of unit's work.
3. Decisions concerning the distribution of rewards and sanctions to unit employees.
4. Decisions involving the handling of unexpected problems and occurrences.
5. Decisions concerning the establishment of organizational policy.

Only one of the fourteen items reflected differences between men and women in either company: the degree of autonomy in settling worker disagreements. To that item, Company 6 men reported a greater level of autonomy than did the women. There were no significant differences between men and women in Company 19. Despite the lack of significant differences, however, there was a consistent, though slight, trend for men to report higher levels of input into almost all decisions.

A final way in which we attempted to gauge power of support was to examine those individuals from whom organizational favors had been sought. We reasoned that support in the form of favors from higher-level organizational members would be a greater sign of power than from lower-level members and predicted the seeking of such higher-level support would be more characteristic of men than women. Results showed no differences in the number of influence attempts by men and women in Company 6. In Company 19, however, there was a trend for men to have attempted more influence attempts than women.

In analyzing from whom favors were sought, we found that Company 6 women had a somewhat greater tendency to have approached their current supervisors or previous supervisors for favors. Men in Company 6 were slightly more apt to have approached colleagues outside their own units, or personnel employees. In Company 19 men were found to have approached higher-level organizational members for favors more often than women. In that organization men were more likely to have sought favors from the company top executives, previous supervisors, colleagues outside the area, and personnel.

Training and Development

Formal Training. Programs designed specifically to enhance the skills and abilities of managers have been widely used by most organizations. Such programs have provided a means by which the company can increase the value of its managerial resources, thus contributing to the overall effective functioning of the company. The effects of training programs may go beyond simple skills acquisition and development, however. They have often served as a mechanism for increasing contact with other managers and enhancing informal communication. These effects have been seen as especially crucial to career advancement.[20,34]

We predicted that training programs would be seen by both men and women as important to job performance and career mobility. We further predicted no differences between men and women in access to formal company-sponsored training programs. Results showed formal training was offered in both companies in the form of workshops and seminars conducted by personnel as well as outside consultants. For some positions attendance in particular formal training programs was required, whereas for most positions such participation was voluntary. We found no indication that men were asked to attend or did attend such programs more often than women.

Informal Training. In most organizations informal training has been viewed as equally important as formal training. Informal training may come in the form of hints and suggestions from colleagues, advice from predecessors, or additional help from a company "sponsor" or "mentor." Many studies have suggested these informal means of training and development have excluded women, thus reducing their skill level, visibility, and opportunity.[31,34]

We predicted that men and women would emphasize the importance of informal training but that men would have greater access to informal training than women. Men and women managers in both organizations reported that once on a new job they had to learn new skills. This learning occurred primarily through informal training. Both sexes described the existence of an informal network that provided the necessary "how to" information. However, women reported they had to make a conscious effort to become a part of this network. Once they did, they were accepted and received the help they needed. Men indicated they were typically brought into the informal network without any effort on their part.

We also asked if people had "mentors" or "guardian angels," and if this kind of relationship was necessary to get ahead. Our data revealed in both companies that very few men and women have had one mentor who gave special help and attention over an extended period. What the managers described instead was a series of short-term helping relationships that facilitated their advancement.

These relationships most often involved a current or former supervisor who helped with a specific problem or mentioned their names for a particularly crucial job. When asked whether it was necessary to have a mentor or a guardian angel for advancement, both men and women managers felt it was not necessary to have such a person but that it was extremely helpful to have the multiple helping relationships described above.

Feedback and Appraisal. The appraisal process is a third form of organizational training and is critical to management development. A study conducted by Spriegel reported survey results showing that performance appraisals were extensively used in organizations as a means of training and development.[71] Such appraisal may occur as a formal review process or may represent informal feedback given on a daily basis. As with other forms of training and development, the importance of feedback for managerial success and development has been emphasized repeatedly.[10,24]

We had predicted sex differences in feedback quantity and quality based on the assumption that sex stereotypes might decrease the interest level a male supervisor would feel for a female manager's development, or might evoke fears of females becoming emotional if they were given negative feedback. Both men and women reported that feedback about job performance was received through a formal yearly performance appraisal as well as through informal day-to-day interactions with the supervisor. Few sex differences were seen with regard to the formal performance review, though there was some indication that the supervisors of men required the setting of formal job objectives more often than did supervisors of women. This could place women at a disadvantage in having performance measured, recognized, and rewarded.

In the evidence surrounding quality and quantity of informal feedback, strong differences emerged between men and women of Company 6. Women reported no differences in the amount and quality of feedback they received from their supervisors and the feedback they thought their male colleagues received. However, male participants often spoke of women receiving less critical feedback from supervisors. According to the men in the sample, supervisors were more likely to let errors of women go unmentioned. The effect on male managers was a feeling that their female peers were "getting away with something." This perception was later confirmed through conversations with the supervisors, who stated it was quite difficult to criticize a woman manager's performance. They stated that such feedback was especially uncomfortable because they feared women would become emotional; hence, there was a different quality to the feedback given women.

Additional data from Company 6 supported this finding as well. When asked whether or not they were criticized by their supervisors, women were somewhat more likely than men to say they were not criticized. Also, women were more likely than men to report their supervisors did not stress improving performance. When asked how effective their supervisors' comments were, only 18 percent of the men replied the feedback was not very effective in contrast to 35 percent of the women. In critiquing the effectiveness of the performance appraisal as a means of feedback on job performance, less than 10 percent of the men stated the appraisal feedback was ineffective, whereas 24 percent of the women felt this way. In Company 19 supervisory data collected supported the discomfort felt in giving women feedback on their performance, but this was not seen as a problem by the women or men managers in the Company 19 sample.

Table 4–2 summarizes the comparisons between men and women managers on measures of organizational experiences.

Extent and Nature of Sex Bias

The prevalence of sex bias in the form of sex stereotypes (beliefs concerning differences in personality traits and appropriate roles for men and women) has been well established in several studies.[5,7,69] In one study by Schwartz, top executives in three hundred "Fortune 500" companies and three hundred small businesses were surveyed.[69] Results from that study showed that the majority of respondents felt that women had less motivation, were not as good an investment, were not as committed to their careers, and did not take as much of an interest in their careers as men. Other research has shown that the characteristics deemed appropriate to managers had little overlap with characteristics considered appropriate to women, but substantial overlap with male characteristics.[67,68]

The fact that sex bias exists is not really the main problem. It is the behavioral results of this bias leading to inequitable treatment and harassment that is our greater concern. Studies have shown sex stereotyping results in the following: inequitable hiring, promotion, and supervision decisions;[14,65] lower salaries for women;[74] less

Table 4–2   **Summary of Comparisons Between Men and Women Managers on Measures of Organizational Experiences**

Variable	*Results*
Power of Supplies	In both companies men reported more control over assets than women. No differences between men and women were reported in the number of attempts to get above-average raises or desirable promotions for subordinates. Also, no differences were seen in the success rate of these attempts.
Power of Information	Men in both companies reported successfully attempting to get early information about decisions and policy shifts more often than women. In both companies men and women were a part of the informal network, but in Company 19 men reported using a broader informal system, including top executives and outside contacts.
Power of Support	In fourteen types of work-related decisions reflecting power of support, significantly more men than women reported greater autonomy in settling worker disagreements. In Company 19 a slight trend indicated men had more input into and tried to influence almost all decisions than women. In Company 6 differences were found between men and women in the breadth of network approached when seeking favors.
Formal Training	In both companies no differences were reported between men and women being asked or having attended formal training programs.
Informal Training	Men and women in both companies reported using the informal network to get informal training. Women, however, reported they had to make a conscious effort to become a part of the network, whereas men reported they gained membership without any effort. Men and women in both companies reported they had a series of short-term helping relationships, not one mentor, who facilitated their advancement.

Table 4-2 (continued)

Variable	Results
Feedback and Appraisal	No differences were reported between men and women in both companies in formal feedback received during the yearly performance appraisal. However, men had formal objectives for the coming year more often than women. In Company 6 male peers and supervisors reported that women received less critical feedback on job performance. Supervisors in both companies reported a level of discomfort when giving women feedback on performance. In Company 19 neither men nor women saw this as a problem.

powerful positions and more dead-end jobs for women;[34] fewer mentors or company sponsors for women employees;[31,34,79] segregation into "women's jobs";[2,34] and various forms of sexual harassment.[16]

We predicted that women in our sample would have faced some sex bias in their careers. We were especially interested in determining the forms that sex bias was taking in organizations today. Our prediction was that bias would be present in much more subtle forms such as dead-end jobs, fewer mentors and sponsors, and differences in power rather than in more blatant forms such as statements revealing stereotypic attitudes, sexual harassment, and salary inequities.

Stereotypic Attitudes

We found evidence of stereotypic attitudes in statements from both men and women in Companies 6 and 19. These attitudes were revealed in numerous comments reflecting an attitude that women were not as professional or as committed to a career as men. For example, both men and women reported women "gossiped," "complained," and had "cat fights" more than men. Also, women were seen as working only to supplement the family income—not because they were committed to a career. Additional statements suggested women were "bitchy" or overly aggressive. Some men reported it was an insult to their intelligence to be supervised by a woman. Both men and women preferred male supervisors to female, but many male managers preferred women supervisees. The reasons stated were "motivating women is easier than motivating men because you can appeal to a woman's better judgment" or "women are always trying to please."

Hiring, Promotion, and Occupational Segregation

We found no evidence that women were given preference in hiring and promotion decisions, although a minority of managers thought women were being moved too quickly or were being given preference over men in these decisions. The more general conclusion was that few managers admitted considering any criteria for hiring and promotion other than past performance or ability to do the job. The majority of managers stated that the final decision between a male and a female candidate would rest on ability, with sex having little or no impact.

There was a perception held by men and women in Company 19 that some jobs, both line and staff, were clearly "women's jobs" and some were clearly "men's jobs." What differentiated women's jobs from men's jobs appeared to be the stereotyped attitudes pertaining to men's and women's skills. Men were seen as having greater interests and abilities in typically masculine pursuits, such as those involving physical strength and stamina and those requiring a great deal of technical expertise. Women were seen as having greater interest and aptitude in artistic and homemaking endeavors and areas not requiring physical strength or technical knowledge.

There was some indication of such occupational segregation in Company 19. However, it was difficult to determine from these data whether this occurrence resulted from conscious or unconscious hiring and promotion practices or whether these differences resulted from individual employee choice regarding career movement. As we examine additional data collected, we will gain greater understanding of the scope and causes of this phenomenon in Company 19.

Supervision

The data indicated different patterns of supervision in both companies. Both men and women commented that women were placed in positions of having to prove themselves more often than men. Women saw themselves having to "fight it out" more often than men whenever a new position was entered. Men and women reported stricter supervisory control of women. They cited examples of supervisors insisting projects be completed by women but not by men well before they were due, and of women having little freedom to proceed on their own, needing to constantly check work with their supervisors. Also, in Company 19 women managers at retail stores reported being asked to fill typically female functions when additional staffing was needed before male colleagues or other males at lower levels were asked. The functions involved activities such as customer service or ringing up sales.

Another aspect of supervision that we had predicted would impact women's career mobility and might also be susceptible to sex bias was supervisory expectations. Locke looked specifically at the role of the supervisor as a source of motivation for an employee, especially in the area of job performance and satisfaction.[45] He found that the dynamic relationship between the supervisor's values, attitudes, and behavior and the employee's attitudes, values, and behavior were important factors in determining the ultimate level of employee satisfaction and performance. Allport also examined expectations.[1] He found that different expectations are often held for men and women and that these differing expectations can lead to discrimination.

We found data from managers and their supervisors that suggested lower professional commitment was expected from women than from men. In the coming months we will examine the supervisors' attitudes and expectations more closely to determine any relationships between stereotypic attitudes and supervisory ratings of promotability.

As reported earlier in this document, sex bias also emerged in the quality and quantity of feedback women received. Men in Company 6 reported that women received less critical feedback from supervisors and peers than did men. The reason given for this different behavior was the supervisors' fear that women would react emotionally when criticized. Some women, as well, commented on their female colleagues' ability to "turn on the tears" as a way to "handle men."

Sexual Harassment

Definitions of sexual harassment have described behaviors ranging from inappropriate comments and sexual innuendos to sexual propositions and coerced sexual relationships in exchange for job security, hiring or promotion. In past surveys conducted by *Redbook* magazine (November 1976, p. 149), Working Women United Institute, and the U.S. Navy, over 80 percent of the women respondents to those surveys reported knowledge of instances involving sexual harassment on the job. Despite these findings, we predicted we would find no evidence of sexual harassment in either of the companies examined. Our rationale was that overt sex bias was no longer acceptable behavior and that whatever sex bias was present would emerge in more subtle forms.

We found no evidence of women being coerced into sexual relationships in order to retain their positions or be advanced to better jobs. However, we did find women in Company 19 reporting that they experienced inappropriate comments and sexual remarks that interfered with their ability to do their jobs. Some of the reported comments ranged from male colleagues' testing the woman's sexual availability, "leering" at her during meetings, and suggesting she wear revealing clothes when top management was scheduled to make a visit. No women in Company 6 reported encountering overt sex bias in this form.

Table 4–3 summarizes the findings on the extent and nature of sex bias.

Effects of the Proportion of Women in Management on Organizational Life

Kanter proposed that the proportion of women in professional positions had important consequences for how women were responded to and perceived.[34] According to her formulation, if women comprised less than 15 percent of a total category, such as manager, the women could be labeled "tokens" since they would be seen as symbols of their group rather than as individuals. She further found that organizational dynamics shifted as the proportion of women increased. For women she labeled "tokens," she found increased performance pressures, greater isolation and exclusion from male groups, and greater distortion of their behavior by others in order to fit them into preexisting sex stereotypes.

Table 4–3   Summary of Findings on the Extent and Nature of Sex Bias

Variable	Results
Stereotypic Attitudes	In both companies there was evidence of stereotypic attitudes about women from men and women.
Hiring, Promotion, and Occupational Segregation	No evidence was found in either company that women were given preference in hiring or promotion decisions. There was some evidence of occupational segregation in Company 19, but the cause is unclear.
Supervision	Women in both companies were seen as having to prove themselves more than men. In Company 19, at the store level, women managers reported being asked to fill typically female functions when additional staffing was needed. In both companies there was evidence that supervisors expected lower professional commitment from women than men.
Sexual Harassment	There was no evidence in either company of women being coerced into sexual relationships to retain their position or be advanced to better jobs. In Company 19 women reported experiencing inappropriate comments and sexual remarks that interfered with their ability to do their jobs.

Based on Kanter's formulation, we predicted that women in Company 6 would experience greater pressure to prove their competence and greater difficulty gaining access to informal networks and would be more subject to stereotypes and misperceptions than women in Company 19. Some analyses have been conducted on the dimensions of performance pressure and stereotyping. Information on differences in access to informal networks will be analyzed and discussed in a later report.

Performance Pressure

Preliminary analysis found that women in both companies felt they had to work harder to prove themselves than did men. They described this phenomenon as "having their credibility tested" and gave examples of being challenged to prove themselves each time they were assigned a new task, supervisor, or subordinate. There was some indication that women in Company 19 experienced greater challenges to their authority and autonomy from supervisors and subordinates than did women in Company 6. Additional analysis on these data will be necessary to determine how performance pressures impact career advancement for women in the two companies.

Sex Stereotyping

Surprisingly, data revealed that women in Company 19 were subjected to much greater stereotyping than women in Company 6. This was precisely the opposite of what we predicted. Company 19 women felt they were not considered for some managerial positions, thus severely restricting the range of experiences and opportunities open to them. The positions from which women felt restricted occurred throughout the managerial hierarchy but were particularly evident at the upper-management level. Women in Company 6 reported opportunity to move throughout the entire organization. No cases were found of Company 6 women feeling they were excluded from nontraditional positions because of their sex.

The second way sex stereotyping was perceived by the women in Company 19 was in blatant sexual remarks and innuendos to which the women managers were subjected. These remarks, which were usually initiated by male supervisors or colleagues, resulted in the women feeling embarrassed, angry, and fearful of reprisal for telling anyone else of their experiences. Above all, the women felt the sexual remarks and suggestions were indications they were not being taken seriously as managers. Women in Company 6 did not report being subjected to such remarks. (See Table 4–4.)

Table 4–4   Summary of the Effects of the Proportion of Women in Management on Organizational Life

Variable	Results
Performance Pressure	In both companies women reported they felt they had to work harder than men to prove themselves. In Company 19, there was evidence that women experienced greater challenge to their authority and autonomy from supervisors and subordinates than did women in Company 6.
Sex Stereotyping	Data revealed women in Company 19 were subjected to much greater stereotyping than women in Company 6.

Discussion of Findings

Although much additional analysis remains to be completed, three main findings have emerged thus far:

1. Strong similarities exist in both the individual characteristics and organizational experiences of men and women managers.
2. Sex bias appears in subtle forms, which may be transformations of overt bias or may operate in conjunction with overt bias.
3. There is no simple, linear relationship between the extent of overt sex bias or stereotyping and the proportion of women in management.

Each of these findings and attendant implications is discussed below.

The Strong Similarities Between Men and Women Managers

The first major finding was the striking degree of similarity between men and women managers both in terms of individual characteristics as well as organizational experiences. Men and women were found to have very similar psychological profiles of high power and achievement needs, high self-esteem, and high motivation to manage. In addition, both men and women experienced difficulty in understanding and planning their careers, in obtaining balanced, useful feedback, and in obtaining opportunities for new skill development.

These results surprised us in view of the vast amount of literature on sex differences, both in terms of the organizational experiences and psychological characteristics of men and women. In retrospect, however, it appears that women's experiences have been compared to a "successful male myth" rather than to men's actual experiences. This myth, founded on sex stereotypes, assumes that men are highly successful, have well-planned careers, receive excellent training and development, have good working relationships with other company employees, have all their skills utilized in their work setting, and encounter no problems on the road to top management—the position to which all men aspire. When women are compared to this myth, any discrepancies between their experiences and the myth are labeled the result of sex discrimination or different socialization patterns that must be overcome. In fact, men and women encounter more similarities than differences in barriers to career advancement. The primary difference faced is the existence of sex bias, which will be discussed later in this report.

With regard to psychological differences, there are few reasons to suspect that women choosing the particular vocation of business management should differ substantially from men also choosing that vocation. Rand's study of college freshmen differentiated career-oriented women from family-oriented women.[64] She discovered that career-oriented women do indeed display more masculine characteristics than feminine characteristics. Other studies support this idea and suggest that career-oriented women have different motivational patterns than family-oriented women.[33,76,79,84]

The women in our study are part of a select group of women whose motivations are likely to be substantially different from women in more traditional roles. These women have chosen a demanding career and, in fact, represent only 5 percent of the female labor force. In addition, the women managers have worked side by side with men and have shared similar managerial responsibilities and functions.

Subtle Sex Bias as a Barrier to Women's Advancement

Subtle sex bias was most evident in Company 6 in the forms of feedback, supervision, and power differences between men and women. Women in Company 6 received less critical feedback from their supervisors. They also indicated supervisory comments were less effective in assessing job performance and that supervisors were less likely to stress the need for improving job performance. Such inequities are "subtle" in that they occur through unintentional and often unconscious individual behavior and organizational practices, yet still contribute to a person or class of people being discriminated against. Because they often operate below awareness levels, subtle forms of bias are especially difficult to measure and are resistant to change.

Relationship Between Sex Stereotyping and Proportion of Women Managers

One of the most startling results of this study to date has been the high incidence of overt sex bias and stereotyping in Company 19, but almost total absence of overt bias in Company 6. Exactly the opposite result had been predicted—that is, that much greater overt bias would emerge in Company 6 rather than Company 19. We think it is likely that the proportion of women in management is the critical variable that accounts for the differences observed in sex bias. Until now it has been assumed that as the proportion of women increased, sex bias would decrease in a linear fashion. However, we think there may be a curvilinear relationship between the two variables.

What we now hypothesize is high resistance by male managers to the first women managers in the company, followed by a rapid decrease in resistance as the percentage of women managers rises to approximately 10 to 15 percent. Rather than maintaining this low level of resistance, however, we predict a rapid upsurge in overt sex bias and a strengthening of stereotypic attitudes. The reasons behind this hypothesis rest on level of threat perceived by the men in the organization. In small numbers women are not seen as a real threat to the male majority for positions or resources. In fact, the presence of women could easily be rationalized as compliance to EEOC pressures in the company. As the proportion of women increases, however, their presence is more likely to be seen as a true threat, with women competing for and receiving jobs that normally would have gone to men. Women would be more visible as a group whose presence could no longer be ignored or explained away. Under such conditions, stereotypes and sexist behavior would be reactivated by male managers as a means of coping with the frustration and fear.

There is some theoretical base for this hypothesis. Labovitz and Hagedorn suggested that as groups which had previously been seen as subordinate increase in numbers, they will be seen as more powerful and able to actively compete for scarce resources formerly controlled by others.[39] The outcome will be increased antagonism toward the previously subordinate group. Essential to the activation of this antagonism, according to Labovitz and Hagedorn, is the group size, which must be large enough to be seen as powerful.

Although we have hypothesized the curvilinear relationship between overt sex bias and the proportion of women as an explanation of our data, alternate explanations cannot be ruled out at this time. Alternate hypotheses that merit attention and will be explored in the coming months are (1) the speed with which women moved into management and (2) company growth. It may be that differing proportions of women in management in the two companies reflect women's advancing at a faster rate in Company 19. The increased pace of assimilating women into the work culture may be counter-productive and lead to increased sex bias as a manifestation of resistance to change. In order to test this possibility, we are currently gathering and analyzing historical data from both companies that will allow us to determine the validity of this explanation.

Another alternate explanation for observed differences in sex bias in the two companies could be the differing growth rates of Companies 6 and 19. Despite the current economic conditions, Company 19 is expanding and opening new retail stores throughout the region. Company 6 is declining somewhat, as seen by recent store closings and reduced sales volume. We had predicted that as Company 19 grew, additional job openings would occur, which would reduce the perceived level of competition for higher positions. In addition, we had predicted that as Company 6 faced a decline in sales, job opportunities would decrease and competition for new jobs would remain high. It is possible that there is a critical ratio of numbers of jobs to number of employees competing for these jobs that must be attained in order for employees to perceive there is opportunity for advancement. In that case, Company 6 may have fallen below this critical ratio with too few jobs available for the number of employees would would normally compete for them. This would result in the actual competition being higher for Company 19 and accompanied by greater sex bias than Company 6.

In the coming months we will examine opportunity perceptions in more depth to determine the extent of opportunity perceived in Company 6 and Company 19. In addition, we will analyze growth rate by geographic region to determine if employees in high-growth regions differ substantially from stable or declining regions in opportunity perceived, competitive activities of managers, and level of sex bias.

Implications of Findings

The findings discussed above strongly suggest organizations need to invest in programs and efforts aimed at total human resource development. We would predict that total eradication of sex bias is not possible. Organizations, however, can reduce the impact of sex bias through a strong program of human resource management and development. At the minimum, such programs should address issues of supervisory training and managerial development, selection and promotion criteria, and affirmative action.

Supervisory Training and Managerial Development

Organizations should develop more comprehensive supervisory training programs for all supervisors. These programs would stress the importance of accurate feedback for employee development. If women are experiencing biased feedback by supervisors, it is quite possible other employees who are seen as different in ways other than gender also receive biased feedback. In addition, managers should be held as accountable for the training and development of the people reporting to them as they are for meeting other job objectives. Finally, those managers who provide good training for supervisees must then be rewarded.

In designing and conducting training programs for managers, efforts should be made to include both men and women and should focus on similar needs. These programs should include how to develop and train employees, plan career strategy, and heighten basic managerial skills. Special programs designed to help women managers would not be appropriate, as they would highlight perceived differences between men and women managers. Such programs could be seen in two ways, both of which are likely to add to the emergence of sex bias. First, women could be seen as deficient in some ways, thus needing more training than men. Secondly, women could be seen as receiving "favored" treatment that men do not get. Both of these assumptions would increase the alienation and tension between men and women managers in the organization.

Selection and Promotion Criteria

Job promotions and increased opportunity for growth and challenge are highly valued by both male and female managers. We suspect overt sex bias emerges, in part, as a result of competition for advancement opportunity. In the absence of sufficient information about available jobs and selection criteria, both men and women may overestimate the "competitive edge" the other sex has. Thus men assume women have a greater likelihood of attaining highly desirable positions because of affirmative action pressures, and women assume men are more apt to attain such positions because of the operation of an "Old Boys' Network," and bias against women.

Two steps are important to decrease the tension likely to result from promotion decisions. First, information about job opportunities must be made available to all interested, qualified persons, regardless of sex. One of the most efficient means of conveying this information is through a job-posting system. Second, valid criteria for selection should be identified and used in making the selection.

The first step in determining valid criteria should be the identification of competencies needed for successful job performance. This competency assessment would then form the base for job descriptions, selection procedures, and evaluation criteria. Selection criteria must change as needed competencies for job performance change. Thus follow-up at future points in time would be essential to determine needed competencies. This procedure not only makes the selection process easier and more likely to produce a better job-person fit, but also is especially helpful for men and women desiring to assess realistically their own performance and development needs. Care must be taken, however, to identify and use criteria that are not subtly biased in favor of one sex. The use of educational credentials, for example, is widely used by most organizations as a selection criterion for higher-level jobs despite its typically low validity in predicting future job performance and a high likelihood of operating against the selection of women and minorities.

Affirmative Action

Finally, in the area of affirmative action, company policies should be clear. Very few managers interviewed understood what the affirmative action policy of the company was and how it affected them. Many managers "assumed" women were given advantages in other parts of the corporation, although they personally reported not giving advantages on the basis of gender. In fact, good affirmative action policy and good human resource management go hand in hand. By clearly identifying competencies needed for job performance, selecting valid criteria, and using those criteria in hiring and promotion decisions, much of the bias inherent in less formal selection procedures will disappear with the effect that women will receive greater opportunity than before. Likewise, implementing strategies that ensure training and development opportunity for all employees is good management practice and will encourage better utilization of women as well as men.

Endnotes

1. G. W. Allport, *The Nature of Prejudice* (Reading, Mass.: Addison-Wesley, 1979).

2. A. Alvarez, K. G. Lutterman, and Associates, *Discrimination in Organizations* (San Francisco: Jossey-Bass, 1979).

3. J. M. Atkinson and G. H. Litwin "Achievement Motive and Test Anxiety Conceived as Motive to Approach Success and Motive to Avoid Failure," *Journal of Abnormal and Social Psychology* 60 (1960), pp. 52–63.

4. J. M. Bardwick. *Psychology of Women* (New York: Harper & Row, 1971).

5. B. M. Bass, J. Krusell and R. A. Alexander, "Male Managers' Attitudes toward Working Women," *American Behavioral Scientist* 15, 2 (1971), pp. 221–36.

6. D. E. Berlew, and D. T. Hall, "The Socialization of Managers: Effects of Expectations on Performance." *Administrative Science Quarterly* 11 (1966), pp. 207–24.

7. G. Bowman, N. B. Worthy, and S. A. Greyer, "Problems in Review: Are Women Executives People?" *Harvard Business Review* 43 (1965), pp. 14–45.

8. D. W. Bray, and D. L. Grant, The Assessment Center in the Measurement of Potential for Business Management, *Psychological Monographs* 80,(17, Whole No. 625, (1966).

9. L. K. Brown, Women and Business Management, *Signs* 5, 2 (1979), pp. 266–88.

10. J. P. Campbell, M. D. Dunnette, E. E. Lawler, III, K. E. Weick, Jr., *Managerial Behavior, Performance, and Effectiveness* (New York: McGraw-Hill, 1970).

11. P. C. Cummin, "TAT Correlates of Executive Power," in R. M. Steers and L. W. Porter, eds., *Motivation and Work Behavior* (New York: McGraw-Hill, 1975).

12. K. Deaux, "Women in Management: Causal Explanations of Performance" (Paper presented at the meeting of the American Psychological Association, Montreal, September 1974).

13. R. de Charms, *Personal Causation* (New York: Academic Press, 1968).

14. R. L. Dipboye, H. L. Fromkin, and K. Wiback, "Relative Importance of Applicant Sex, Attractiveness, and Scholastic Standing in Evaluation of Job Applicant Resumes," *Journal of Applied Psychology* 60 (1975), pp. 39–45.

15. P. Doeringer, and M. Piore, *Internal Labor Markets and Manpower Analysis* (Lexington, Mass.: D. C. Heath, 1971).

16. L. Farley, *Sexual Shakedown* (New York: Warner Books, 1978).

17. J. R. P. French, Jr., and B. H. Raven, "The Bases of Social Power," in D. Cartwright, Ed., *Studies in Social Power* (Ann Arbor: University of Michigan Institute for Social Research, 1959).

18. I. H. Frieze, "Studies of Information Processing and the Attributional Process in Achievement-Related Contexts" (Ph.D. diss., University of California at Los Angeles, 1973).

19. I. H. Frieze, J. E. Parsons, P. B. Johnson, D. H. Ruble, and G. L. Zellman, *Women and Sex Roles* (New York: W. W. Norton, 1978).

20. M. Granovetter, *Getting a Job* (Cambridge, Mass.: Harvard University Press, 1974).

21. R. M. Guion and R. F. Gottier, "Validity of Personality Measures in Personnel Selection," *Personnel Psychology* 18 (1965), pp. 135–164.

22. D. T. Hall, "A Theoretical Model of Career Subidentity Development in Organizational Settings," *Organizational Behavior and Human Performance* 6 (1971), pp. 50–76.

23. D. T. Hall, "A Model of Coping with Role Conflict: The Role Behavior of College Educated Women," *Administrative Science Quarterly* 17 (1972) pp. 471–86.

24. D. T. Hall, *Careers in Organizations* (Pacific Palisades, Calif.: Goodyear, 1976).

25. D. T. Hall and M. Morgan, "Career Development and Planning," in W. C. Hamner and F. L. Schmidt, eds., *Contemporary Problems in Personnel*, rev. ed. (Chicago: St. Clair Press, 1977).

26. A. Harlan, "A Comparison of Careers for Male and Female MBAs" (Paper presented at August 1976 meeting of the National Academy of Management).

27. A. Harlan, G. O. Klemp, and M. L. Schaalman, "Competence Assessment in Personnel Selection: Current Practices and Trends" (National Institute of Education report, ERIC CH: CE 027160, 1980).

28. L. Harmon, "Variables Related to Women's Persistence in Educational Plans," *Journal of Vocational Behavior* 2 (1972), pp. 143–53.

29. P. Hawley, "Perceptions of Male Models of Femininity Related to Career Choice," *Journal of Counseling Psychology* 19 (1972) pp. 308–13.

30. M. Henning and A. Jardim, *The Managerial Woman* (New York: Anchor Press, 1977).

31. M. Horner, "The Motive to Avoid Success and Changing Aspirations of College Women," in J. M. Bardwick, Ed., *Readings on the Psychology of Women* (New York: Harper & Row, 1972).

32. D. P. Hoyt and C. E. Kennedy, "Interest and Personality Correlates of Career Motivated and Homemaking Motivated College Women," *Journal of Counseling Psychology* 5 (1958), pp. 44–48.

33. M. Jelinek and A. Harlan, "MBA Goals and Aspirations: Potential Predictors of Later Success Differences Between Males and Females" (Paper presented at the meeting of the National Academy of Management, Detroit, August 1980).

34. R. M. Kanter, *Men and Women of the Corporation* (New York: Basic Books, 1977).

35. R. M. Kanter, "Power Failure in Management Circuits," *Harvard Business Review* 57 (1979), pp. 65–75.

36. A. Korman, "Self-Esteem as a Moderator of the Relationship Between Self-Perceived Abilities and Vocational Choice," *Journal of Applied Psychology* 51 (1967), pp. 65–67.

37. J. P. Kotter, "Power, Dependence, and Effective Management," *Harvard Business Review* 55 (1977), pp. 125–36.

38. A. Kukla, "Attributional Determinants of Achievement-Related Behavior," *Journal of Personality and Social Psychology* 21 (1972), pp. 166–74.

39. S. Labovitz, and R. Hagedorn, "A Structural-Behavioral Theory of Intergroup Antagonism," in F. J. Davis, ed., *Understanding Minority-Dominant Relations* (Arlington Heights, Ill.: AHM Publishing, 1979).

40. E. E. Lawler, III, *Pay and Organizational Effectiveness: A Psychological View* (New York: McGraw-Hill, 1971).

41. E. E. Lawler, III, *Motivation in Work Organizations* (Monterey, Calif.: Brooks/Cole, 1973).
42. K. Lewin, "The Psychology of Success and Failure," *Occupations* 14 (1936), pp. 926–30.
43. J. Lipman-Blumen, "How Ideology Shapes Women's Lives," *Scientific American* 226 (1972), pp. 34–42.
44. E. A. Locke, "Toward a Theory of Task Motivation and Incentives," *Organizational Behavior and Human Performance* 3 (1968), pp. 157–89.
45. E. A. Locke, "The Supervisor as Motivator: His Influence on Employee Performance and Satisfaction," in R. M. Steers and L. W. Porter, eds., *Motivation and Work Behavior* (New York: McGraw-Hill, 1975).
46. E. E. Maccoby, and C. N. Jacklin, *The Psychology of Sex Differences* (Stanford: Stanford University Press, 1974).
47. D. C. McClelland, *Personality* (New York: Dryden Press, 1951).
48. D. C. McClelland, *The Achieving Society* (Princeton, N.J.: Van Nostrand, 1961).
49. D. C. McClelland, "Business Drive and National Achievement," *Harvard Business Review* 40 (1962), pp. 99–112.
50. D. C. McClelland, *Power, the Inner Experience* (New York: Irvington, 1975).
51. D. C. McClelland, J. W. Atkinson, R. A. Clark, and E. L. Lowell, *The Achievement Motive* (New York: Irvington, 1953).
52. D. C. McClelland, and D. H. Burnham, "Power is the Great Motivator," *Harvard Business Review* 54 (1976), pp. 100–110.
53. I. D. McMahan, "Sex Differences in Causal Attributions Following Success and Failure" (Paper presented at the meeting of the Eastern Psychological Association, April 1971).
54. J. B. Miller, *Toward a New Psychology of Women* (Boston: Beacon Press, 1976).
55. J. B. Miner, *Studies in Management Education* (New York: Springer, 1965).
56. J. B. Miner, "The Early Identification of Managerial Talent," *Personnel and Guidance Journal* 46 (1968), pp. 586–91.
57. J. B. Miner, "Motivation to Manage among Women: Studies of Business Managers and Educational Administrators," *Journal of Vocational Behavior* 5 (1974), pp. 197–208.
58. J. B. Miner, "Motivation to Manage Among Women: Studies of College Students," *Journal of Vocational Behavior* 5 (1974), pp. 241–50.
59. J. B. Miner, *Motivation to Manage: A Ten-Year Update on the "Studies in Management Education" Research* (Atlanta: Organizational Measurement Systems Press, 1977).
60. J. B. Miner, "The Miner Sentence Completion Scale: A Reappraisal," *Academy of Management Journal* 21 (1978), pp. 283–94.
61. J. B. Miner, and J. F. Brower, "The Management of Ineffective Performance," in M. D. Dunnette, Ed., *Handbook of Industrial and Organizational Psychology* (Chicago: Rand McNally, 1976).
62. A. Missirian, "The Female Manager as a Shelf-Sitter," *Human Resource Management* 17 (1978).
63. N. C. Morse, and R. S. Weiss, "The Function and Meaning of Work and the Job," *American Sociological Review* 20 (1955), pp. 191–98.
64. L. M. Rand, "Masculinity or Femininity? Differentiating Career Oriented

and Homemaking Oriented College Freshman Women," *Journal of Counseling Psychology* 15 (1968), pp. 444–50.

65. B. Rosen, and T. H. Jerdee, "Sex Stereotyping in the Executive Suite," *Harvard Business Review* 52 (1974), pp. 45–58.

66. J. E. Rosenbaum, "Career Paths and Advancement Opportunities," in R. A. Alvarez, K. G. Lutterman and Associates, eds., *Discrimination in Organizations* (San Francisco: Jossey-Bass Publishers, 1979).

67. V. E. Schein, "The Relationship Between Sex Role Stereotypes and Requisite Management Characteristics," *Journal of Applied Psychology* 57 (1973), pp. 95–100.

68. V. E. Schein, "Relationship Between Sex Role Stereotypes and Requisite Management Characteristics Among Female Managers," *Journal of Applied Psychology* 60 (1975), pp. 340–44.

69. E. G. Schwartz, *The Sex Barrier in Business* (Atlanta: Georgia State University Press, 1971).

70. Robert Seidenberg, *Corporate Wives–Corporate Casualties?* (New York: AMACOM, 1973).

71. W. R. Spriegel, "Company Practices in Appraisal of Managerial Performance," *Personnel* 39 (1962), pp. 77–83.

72. B. A. Stein, *Getting There: Patterns in Managerial Success* (Working paper, Center for Research on Women, Wellesley College, Wellesley, Mass., 1976.

73. S. S. Tangri, "Determinants of Occupational Role Innovation among College Women," *Journal of Social Issues* 28 (1972), pp. 177–99.

74. J. R. Terborg, and D. R. Ilgen, "A Theoretical Approach to Sex Discrimination in Traditionally Masculine Occupations," *Organizational Behavior and Human Performance* 13 (1975), pp. 352–76.

75. J. Veroff, J. W. Atkinson, S. C. Feld, and G. Gurin, "The Use of Thematic Apperception to Assess Motivation in a Nationwide Interview Study," *Psychology Monograph 74, 12*, Whole No. 499 (1960).

76. L. Vetter, and E. C. Lewis, "Some Correlates of Homemaking vs. Career Performance among College Home Economics Students," *Personnel and Guidance Journal* 42 (1964), pp. 593–98.

77. V. H. Vroom, *Motivation in Management* (New York: American Foundation for Management Research, 1965).

78. B. Weisbrod, and P. Karpoff, "Monetary Returns to College Education, Student Ability, and College Quality," *Review of Economics and Statistics* 5 (1968), pp. 491–97.

79. M. S. White, "Psychological and Social Barriers to Women in Science," *Science* 170 (1970), pp. 413–16.

80. W. H. Whyte, Jr., "The Wives of Management," *Fortune* 42 (October 1951).

81. W. H. Whyte, Jr., "The Corporation and the Wife," *Fortune* 42 (November 1951).

82. D. Wise, "Academic Achievement and Job Performance," *American Economic Review* 65 (1975), pp. 350–66.

83. A. Zaleznik, "Power and Politics in Organizational Life," *Harvard Business Review* 48 (1970), pp. 47–60.

84. C. Zissis, "A Study of the Life Planning of 550 Freshman Women at Purdue University," *Journal of the National Association of Women Deans and Counselors* 27 (1964), pp. 153–59.

Chapter 5

MOVING FORWARD, STANDING STILL: WOMEN IN WHITE COLLAR JOBS

by Julianne M. Malveaux

At some point between 1960 and 1980, perceptions of women in the labor force changed. Part of the attitudinal change was attributable to rising labor force participation of women—for mothers, for single women, and for women of all age groups. In 1960 one in three women worked, while in 1980 female labor force participation rose past the 50 percent mark. Only the labor force participation of black female teens dropped. A major contributory factor to the changing perceptions of women in the labor force has been the increasing visibility of these women. Magazines such as *Savvy* and *Working Woman* have focused solely on "executive women." Profiles of these women have been featured in popular magazines. Television, the vast disseminator of cultural values, has featured the working woman and her lifestyle in an attempt to sell everything from perfume to bacon.[1]

Change? Maybe. The occupational distribution of women indicates that the proportion of women who hold managerial jobs has increased. Additionally, there has been limited movement for black women out of private household jobs into clerical jobs. Detailed occupational data also show the entry of women, albeit in minute numbers, into occupational positions that had been formerly almost all male.[2]

Change? Maybe not. Despite perceptual changes and the in-

101

crease in the number and proportion of working women, the types of jobs that women hold and the income disparities that women experience remain about the same. In fact, although almost two thirds of working women hold white collar jobs, nearly half of those jobs are clerical. More than a quarter of all black women and a sixth of all white women are employed in service jobs, compared to about half as many men in each case. In nonclerical occupations the phenomenon of occupational crowding remains strong: in sales jobs almost four in five women hold retail jobs, while only one in three males in a sales job works in retail sales. In professional, technical, and kindred occupations, more than 60 percent of the women work in the female-stratified occupations of noncollege teacher and nonphysician health professionals (for example, nurses and dietitians). Within occupational categories, there is further occupational segregation. For example, preliminary investigations indicate that managerial women are more likely to hold staff jobs that have more limited upward mobility than are managerial males;[3] similarly, more managerial women work in the public sector than do their male counterparts.

This chapter discusses the phenomenon of occupational segregation and the changes that have taken place in the occupational distribution of women, especially white collar women (professional, managerial, sales, clerical) since 1970. A discussion of the uneven distribution of women in certain industries supplements this analysis and shows that changes in occupational attainment represent only one aspect of the movement toward income equality for women. The combination of occupational and industrial segregation for women has resulted in the traditional inequality in wages among sexes. Data on earnings by industry and occupation highlight this point. A final contributory factor in the slow movement of improved labor force status of women is the issue of comparable worth. Even where work is comparable and where qualifications are nearly identical, women may earn less because they hold jobs that have been historically "female."

Given the persistence of occupational segregation, what is projected for women workers in the future? Growth is projected in industries that have had heavy concentrations of women in the past (such as the health services). To the extent that these industries account for a disproportionate number of *new* jobs that women hold, unequal occupational patterns will remain.

The Dynamics of Occupational Segregation

Theories of Occupational Segregation

The consequences of occupational segregation are apparent in both the lower earnings and the higher unemployment that women workers experience. In the most straightforward explanation of the phenomenon, women on the one hand are denied access to some occupations and are "crowded" into a limited number of occupations where pay, then, is lower and unemployment higher.[4] On the other hand, some researchers assert that women "choose" crowded occupations—since they plan to leave the labor force intermittently, then decide to work in jobs where skills deteriorate least with absences from the labor force.[5]

Researchers have attempted to differentiate occupational segregation by cause. In other words, a demand-based theory of occupational segregation would deal with the direct discrimination that the "crowding" hypothesis speaks to. An example of such would be to have "male" and "female" job titles for similar jobs. In the publishing industry for example, Michael Korda notes that male entry jobs were titled "writer," while female entry jobs were titled "researcher." Although educational qualifications were similar, the "writer" jobs were higher paying than were the "researcher" jobs.[6] A supply-based theory of occupational segregation is more consistent with a human capital theory of the labor market and would find women "choosing" stratified jobs.

Although discrimination laws may prevent the rigid occupational segregation described in the crowding hypotheses, they can do little to attack more subtle causes of crowding. For example, as long as there is a perception of "male" and "female" jobs as well as sex-based preferences, however unstated, on the part of employers, the occupational preferences of employees will be shaped. Nonetheless, Beller noted that occupational segregation began to diminish during the 1970s.[7]

Magnitude of Occupational Segregation

Another study of occupational changes between 1970 and 1977 bears out Beller's assertion by showing some movement by women out of female-stratified jobs and into traditionally male jobs.[8] The proportion of women who worked as elementary and secondary school teachers dropped, and the proportion of engineers and physicians grew somewhat (but remained small—one tenth of 1 percent of all women hold engineering jobs, compared to 2 percent of all men; two tenths of 1 percent of all women were physicians in 1977, compared with more than 1 percent of all men). During the 1970–1977 period, the proportion of women managers among black and white women increased about 50 percent. In sales occupations, although the proportion of women employed remained about the same, fewer women were employed in "crowded" retail jobs; more worked in nonretail sales. The proportion of women in clerical jobs remained about the same for white women and increased by 25 percent for black women. The increased representation of black women in clerical jobs can be viewed as complementary to their decreasing representation in private household jobs.

If occupational status is viewed by age, indications of change are more pronounced. Despite the fact that occupational choice often has "lock-in" effects, women who were 25 to 34 years old in 1968 experienced considerable occupational upgradings by 1977 (when they were 35 to 44). The trends discussed for all women were similar but more pronounced for this age group—3 percent fewer women worked in clerical jobs, and the proportion of managers in this cohort more than doubled between 1968 and 1977.[9] Among white women there was an increase in the proportion of women in sales; the increase was largely in nonretail sales jobs. Among black women, there was a smaller increase in the proportion of sales workers; here, the increase was in traditional female retail sales jobs. These changes can be put into perspective by viewing the rate of change in the occupational composition of other segments of the age cohort in question between 1968 and 1977. For example, in 1968 nearly 9 percent of all white males between 25 and 34 years old were managers. By 1977, more than 13 percent in that cohort (now 35 to 44 years old) were managers—an increase of about 50 percent. On the other hand, as mentioned, the proportion of white female managers more than doubled—from 3.5 percent in 1968 to 7.4 percent in 1977. Further, the proportion of black female managers nearly tripled—only 1.3 percent were managers in 1968, while 3.5 percent were managers in 1977.

Sales occupations provide a similar example. Although the proportion of white males in the cohort in question remained fairly constant in sales occupations between 1968 and 1977, representation in retail sales dropped for these white males during this time period. The proportion of white women in sales occupations rose from 4.8 to 6.5 percent in the 1968 to 1977 period; most of the increase was in nonretail sales. On the other hand, the slight increase (from 2.0 to 2.3 percent) in the proportion of sales workers among black women was entirely accounted for by an increase in the proportion of retail sales workers.

If changes in the distribution of white males in the same age cohort (25 to 34) in 1968 are used as a benchmark to indicate "normal" amount of occupational change that might take place during a ten-year period, then it is reasonable to assume that the additional improvement in the occupational distribution of women is indicative of some affirmative action policy on the part of firms. The overall composition of the labor force began to shift away from manufacturing and laborer jobs and toward white collar jobs in the 1970s.[10] These changes affected the employment profile of black workers more than the profile of women workers.

Equally interesting when viewing these young women is the fact that occupational improvement of white women is more clearly associated with movement out of female-stratified jobs than the mobility of black women. For example, black women maintained or increased their proportional representation as noncollege teachers and retail sales workers, while the proportion of white women in these jobs decreased. Further, because of larger initial representation, the proportion of white women in managerial jobs was more than twice that of black women. Finally, in nonwhite collar jobs, more than a third of the 35- to 44-year-old black women in 1977 remained in service work and private household jobs, compared to a sixth of the white women.

Looking at the two-digit occupations only tells part of the story of occupational segregation, however. The detailed occupations for white collar workers in 1979 and the percentage of workers in each of these occupations that are female are revealing. If we categorize occupations as Jusenius did[11]—as being typically female if more than 46.7 percent of the employees are female (46.7 percent is 5 percent plus the female portion of the 1979 labor force, 41.7 percent)—we observe variation within major occupations in the sexual composition of detailed occupations. For example, in the sales occupation, although the proportion of women is higher than that of

the proportion of women in the total labor force, women are concentrated as retail sales clerks, demonstrators, peddlers, and real
estate agents and brokers. The highest paid of the detailed occupations in the category, stock and bond sales agents, has one of the
lowest proportions of women in the category. Similarly, among managers, there are only three typically female occupations—building
managers, office managers, and health administrators. Although
women dominate the clerical occupation, some occupations are
"typically male" in that job category—shipping clerks, dispatchers,
postal clerks, and messengers among them.

In the professional and technical occupations, significant variation
is observed. Although the proportion of women in these jobs is
fairly close to the proportion of women in the labor force, "typically
female" occupations include noncollege teachers, social workers,
counselors, nurses, dietitians, therapists, and librarians. Women
represent, however, fewer than 10 percent of all engineers,
architects, and dentists and fewer than 20 percent of all lawyers,
chemists, and physicians. Within these occupations, the patterns of
concentration by sex show patterns interesting enough to warrant
further investigation. For example, although less than 3 percent of
all engineers are women, 7 percent of all industrial engineers are
women. Similarly, in the social sciences, the proportion of female
psychologists is double the proportion of female economists (see
Table 5–1).

The three-digit occupation captures the changes in occupational
stratification as well. Zellner reported that in 1960, 71 percent of all
women worked in occupations that were more than half female,
with most of these women working in occupations that were more
than 80 percent female.[12] By 1978, 61 percent of all women worked
in occupations that were more than half female, a reduction of about
15 percent. Further, only two thirds as many women (28 percent)
worked in the most stratified occupations—those 80 to 100 percent
female—in 1978 than in 1960.[13]

A follow-up on the earlier point that the upward mobility of black
women workers is less pronounced than that of white women can
also be made from the three-digit data. For example, while 9 percent of all secretarial workers were black in 1975, fewer than 2
percent of the legal and medical secretaries were black.[14] Similar
differences in the job mix of black and white women exist in other
occupations.

Table 5-1   Women as a Percentage of Total Employment in White Collar Jobs, 1979

Occupations	Percentage Female
Professional and technical	43.3
Accountants	32.9
Architects	6.0
Computer specialists	26.0
Computer programmers	29.0
Computer systems analysts	24.3
Engineers	2.9
Aeronautical and astronautical engineers	1.6
Civil engineers	2.5
Electrical and electronic engineers	2.2
Industrial engineers	7.3
Mechanical engineers	1.3
Foresters and conservationists	8.8
Lawyers and judges	12.4
Lawyers	12.8
Librarians, archivists, and curators	78.1
Librarians	80.9
Life and physical scientists	18.9
Biological scientists	36.4
Chemists	15.2
Operations and systems researchers and analysts	21.2
Personnel and labor relations workers	45.5
Physicians, dentists, and related practitioners	11.9
Dentists	4.6
Pharmacists	24.4
Physicians, medical, and osteopathic	10.7
Nurses, dieticians, and therapists	93.2
Registered nurses	96.8
Therapists	72.9
Health techologists and technicians	69.5
Clinical laboratory technologists and technicians	71.9
Radiologic technologists and technicians	73.1
Religious workers	13.3
Clergy	4.6
Social scientists	34.5
Economists	24.4
Psychologists	50.5
Social and recreation workers	61.4
Social workers	64.3
Recreation workers	52.6
Teachers, college and university	31.6
Teachers, except college and university	70.8

Table 5-1 (continued)

Occupations	Percentage Female
Adult education teachers	51.3
Elementary school teachers	84.3
Prekindergarten and kindergarten teachers	97.4
Secondary school teachers	50.7
Teachers except college and university, n.e.c.	75.9
Engineering and science technicians	15.9
Chemical technicians	21.4
Drafters	14.8
Electrical and electronic engineering technicians	9.6
Surveyors	3.5
Technicians, except health, engineering, and science	17.3
Airplane pilots	—
Radio operators	46.6
Vocational and educational counselors	53.3
Writers, artists, and entertainers	37.8
Athletes and kindred workers	38.1
Designers	28.5
Editors and reporters	42.3
Musicians and composers	35.9
Painters and sculptors	46.6
Photographers	21.5
Public relations specialists and publicity writers	43.8
Research workers, not specified	37.1
All other professional and technical workers	39.1
Managers and administrators, except farm	24.6
Bank officials and financial managers	31.6
Buyers and purchasing agents	30.4
Buyers, wholesale and retail trade	40.0
Credit and collections managers	40.0
Health administrators	48.1
Inspectors, except construction and public administration	12.5
Managers and superintendents, building	50.0
Office managers, n.e.c.	63.0
Officials and administrators, public administration, n.e.c.	26.6
Officials of lodges, societies, and unions	29.2
Restaurant, cafeteria, and bar managers	35.4
Sales managers and department heads, retail trade	39.8
Sales managers except retail trade	8.6
School administrators, college	32.8
School administrators, elementary and secondary	37.5
All other managers and administrators	17.7

Table 5-1   (continued)

Occupations	Percentage Female
Sales workers	45.1
Advertising agents and sales workers	41.0
Demonstrators	93.2
Hucksters and peddlers	79.8
Insurance agents, brokers, and underwriters	23.8
Newspaper carriers and vendors	28.6
Real estate agents and brokers	49.4
Stock and bond sales agents	19.7
Sales workers and sales clerks, n.e.c.	45.8
Sales representatives, manufacturing industries	17.1
Sales representatives, wholesale trade	10.4
Sales clerks, retail trade	70.7
Sales workers, except clerks, retail trade	20.0
Sales workers, services and construction	39.1
Clerical workers	80.3
Bank tellers	92.9
Billing clerks	90.1
Bookkeepers	91.1
Cashiers	87.9
Clerical supervisors, n.e.c.	71.3
Collectors, bill and account	59.5
Counter clerks, except food	77.9
Dispatchers and starters, vehicle	35.5
Enumerators and interviewers	76.7
Estimators and investigators, n.e.c.	55.8
Expediters and production controllers	38.1
File clerks	86.6
Insurance adjusters, examiners, and investigators	55.5
Library attendants and assistants	79.4
Mail carriers, post office	10.3
Mail handlers, except post office	50.3
Messengers and office helpers	31.5
Office machine operators	74.9
Bookkeeping and billing machine operators	89.5
Computer and peripheral equipment operators	61.6
Key punch operators	95.3
Payroll and timekeeping clerks	81.4
Postal clerks	34.4
Receptionists	97.2
Secretaries	99.1
Secretaries, legal	99.3
Secretaries, medical	100.0
Secretaries, n.e.c.	99.1

Table 5-1   (continued)

Occupations	Percentage Female
Shipping and receiving clerks	21.3
Statistical clerks	78.8
Stenographers	93.4
Stock clerks and storekeepers	31.9
Teachers aides, except school monitors	93.4
Telephone operators	91.7
Ticket, station and express agents	44.4
Typists	96.7
All other clerical workers	76.4
Total, white-collar workers	52.8
All occupations, 16 years and over	41.7

SOURCE: U.S. Bureau of Labor Statistics, *Employment and Earnings*, January 1980.
n.e.c. = Not elsewhere classified.

Occupational Segregation and Differential Unemployment

Another consequence of occupational segregation is the differential unemployment that women experience. Although female unemployment dipped below that of males for one month in 1980, generally female unemployment exceeds male unemployment. And although some explanations of high female unemployment suggest that women are more casually attached to the labor force than men and that they experience higher employment because they can afford higher search, even in those occupations where full-time employment and a strong attachment to the labor force are the rule rather than the exception (for example, in managerial and some professional occupations), women experience more unemployment in these occupations than do men. Further while twice as much female unemployment as male unemployment can be attributed to initial entry or reentry to the labor force, female job leaving accounts for about the same amount of unemployment (16 percent) as does male job leaving (14 percent). Nearly 40 percent of female unemployment is explained by job losing, as is slightly more than 60 percent of male unemployment.[15]

Explanations of unemployment differentials that focus on supply side characteristics of workers (such as age, education, training) cannot explain why women are clustered in lower-paying and higher-unemployment occupations than males who have similar human capital characteristics. However, a view of the demand side of the unemployment equation may indicate differences in the factors that determine unemployment in female stratified occupations.

A reduced form equation of a model of the supply and demand sides of the labor market was estimated by this researcher (see appendix for model detail).[16] The equation estimated had several "components," including education and skills, nonwork options, personal characteristics, and institutional factors. The institutional variables, which attempted to measure the strength of the demand side, were industry profits, unionization for the industry, and class of worker.

One case where there is little skill difference between two occupations with different demographic compositions is durable and nondurable goods operatives. About a third of all durable goods operatives were women in 1975, while 60 percent of all nondurable goods operatives were women. The Jusenius characterization of occupations as "female" would clearly categorize the nondurable operatives occupation as a female one. Significantly, the percentage of unionization is positively correlated with work for durable goods workers but is insignificant for nondurable goods workers.[17] This is consistent with Madden's model of discrimination as male power to unionize—a power that female workers lack.[18]

This finding indicates a direction for further research. Since the work done focused on two-digit occupations, there were few other parallels as straightforward as the durable/nondurable goods one. When three-digit occupations are considered, there are clear parallels, but the number of observations is often too small for robust analysis.

Some of these patterns might be merely interesting; but when the sex label has an effect on earnings and employment (especially where the skill required is similar), then our understanding of income inequality between men and women is enhanced by understanding occupational segregation. In fact, for women in low- and medium-skill groups, Jusenius found that when training, education, and job tenure are controlled for, the sex label of an occupation exerts downward pressure on wages.[19] Similarly, Ammot found that rising female shares of employment lowered male wages until an occupation is about a third female, illustrating the male interest present in maintaining occupational segregation.[20]

A persistent wage and unemployment differential exists between men and women, which has long-run implications, not only for those who earn lower wages but also in many cases for their families (an increasingly important concern as the number of female-headed families rises). Thus, whether occupational segregation is a supply-based or a demand-based phenomenon, its persistence remains extremely important in explaining the inferior position of women in the labor force. Further progress in removing occupational barriers for women is critical in narrowing wage gaps between men and women.

Women and Industrial Concentrations

Although occupation is important in explaining what kind of work is done and the level of skill that a worker must have, type of industry is important in discussing the work environment, and to some extent, the profit picture (and thus the wage package) available to workers. Therefore, although a measurement can be taken that a clerical worker earns less than a professional worker, there may be wage variations by industry in either occupation. Similarly, unemployment varies by industry.

Variation Among Industries

How do industries vary and why is this important to women and work? Highly capitalized, highly unionized, and highly concentrated industries tend to offer better wage packages than do other industries. Jobs in marginal industries, with more competition, less machinery, and low profits generate low wage or secondary labor market jobs. Thus, patterns of industrial concentration by sex are important in measuring the position of women in the labor force.

Earlier research by this writer notes differences in the industrial representation of the labor force by occupation and demographic group.[21] Except in occupations that are "typically female" (especially the clerical occupations), males have a broader industrial distribution than do females. A broader industrial distribution generally minimizes any negative effects that the entire work force may suffer because of variation in one particular industry. White males have the broadest distribution, with black females concentrated in the narrowest of industrial ranges. Just as an occupational distribution has concentrations of "typically female" jobs, there are typically female industrial pockets in the industrial distribution. Women are overrepresented in service industries, and in finance, insurance, and real estate, but are underrepresented in manufacturing, transportation, public administration, mining, and construction industries. A view of detailed industry information reinforces the notion of industrial segregation (see Table 5–2. While almost 60 percent of the workers in the finance, insurance, and real estate industry are women, fewer than 40 percent of those employed in security, commodity brokerage and investment companies are women. Similarly, while women are overrepresented in service industries, they are most heavily concentrated in the personal and professional (including health) services and in entertainment services. When average hourly earnings by industry are examined, it is clear that women are concentrated in those industries that pay least well.[22]

In an effort to measure how the female share of industrial employment has changed as a larger number of women entered the labor market, Rider-Pinches developed a shift-share analysis to measure both the proportion of women in a given industry and the changes in the proportion of women in an industry over time. Her analysis looks at the upward shift in female employment and how this increase is distributed among the several industries—thus the terminology "shift-share." The purpose of this method of analysis is to measure changes in the industrial segregation that women experience as their overall employment increases. Rider-Pinches finds that the health industry consistently (between 1963 and 1975) accounted for the largest share of the net upward shift in employment; it also accounted for most of the growth in female employment. The concentration of women in the health industry indicates an increase in sex segregation by industry since the health industry is "typically female" and since the percentage of female employees in this industry increased over time.[23] In a finding consistent with industrial distributions mentioned earlier, Rider-Pinches notes that female employment grew more rapidly than did total employment in the period that she analyzed, but this growth was concentrated in a smaller number of industries.

Table 5–2   Women as a Percentage of Total Employment in Detailed Industries, 1979

Industry	Percentage Female
Agriculture, forestry, and fisheries	19.8
Agriculture production	18.8
Agriculture services except horticultural	41.4
Horticultural services	8.5
Forestry	26.6
Fisheries	9.5
Mining	11.8
Metal mining	6.2
Coal mining	4.5
Crude petroleum and natural gas extraction	18.5
Nonmetallic mining and quarrying, except fuel	7.9
Construction	7.4
General building contractors	7.1
General contractors, except building	6.8
Special trade contractors	7.4
Not specified construction	9.6
Manufacturing	30.9
Durable goods	25.1
Lumber and wood products, except furniture	12.1
Logging	3.7
Sawmills, planing mills, and mill work	12.3
Miscellaneous wood products	21.9
Furniture and fixtures	34.0
Stone, clay, and glass products	19.4
Glass and glass products	29.4
Cement, concrete, gypsum, and plaster products	9.1
Miscellaneous nonmetallic mineral and stone products	17.6
Primary metal industries	11.7
Blast furnaces, steelworks, rolling, and finishing mill	9.0
Other primary iron and steel industries	10.0
Primary aluminum industries	12.2
Other primary nonferrous industries	20.3
Fabricated metal products	19.9
Cutlery, hand tools, and other hardware	33.9
Fabricated structural metal products	14.0
Screw machine products	21.0
Metal stamping	24.7
Miscellaneous fabricated metal products	19.9

Table 5-2 (continued)

Industry	Percentage Female
Machinery, except electrical	19.8
Engines and turbines	14.4
Farm machinery and equipment	14.3
Construction and material handling machines	13.9
Metalworking machinery	16.5
Office and accounting machines	31.3
Electronic computing equipment	33.0
Machinery, except electrical, n.e.c.	18.4
Electrical machinery, equipment, and supplies	43.0
Household appliances	40.5
Radio, TV, and communication equipment	41.7
Electrical machinery, equipment, and supplies, n.e.c.	43.8
Transportation equipment	16.6
Motor vehicles and motor vehicle equipment	17.4
Aircraft and parts	18.5
Ship and boat building and repairing	10.6
Mobile dwellings and campers	14.1
Professional and photographic equipment and watches	45.0
Scientific and controlling instruments	43.0
Optical and health services supplies	54.7
Photographic equipment and supplies	27.9
Ordnance	27.7
Miscellaneous manufacturing industries	48.3
Nondurable goods industries	39.9
Food and kindred products	29.2
Meat products	31.1
Dairy products	19.5
Canning and preserving fruits, vegetables, and seafood	44.1
Grain-mill products	23.4
Bakery products	26.8
Confectionery and related products	51.3
Beverage industries	14.3
Miscellaneous food preparation and kindred products	30.5
Tobacco manufacturers	28.1
Textile mill products	46.6
Knitting mills	65.2
Yarn, thread, and fabric mills	42.9
Miscellaneous textile mill products	36.4
Apparel and other fabricated textile products	79.1
Apparel and accessories	81.4
Miscellaneous fabricated textile products	62.7
Paper and allied products	22.2

Table 5-2   (continued)

Industry	Percentage Female
Pulp, paper, and paperboard mills	11.4
Miscellaneous paper and pulp products	35.2
Paperboard containers and boxes	25.4
Printing, publishing, and allied industries	38.8
Newspaper publishing and printing	36.7
Printing, publishing, and allied industries except newspapers	39.8
Chemicals and allied products	25.4
Industrial chemicals	17.2
Plastics, synthetics and resins, except fibers	20.5
Synthetic fibers	25.6
Drugs and medicines	40.3
Soaps and cosmetics	43.6
Paints, varnishes, and related products	22.1
Agricultural chemicals	26.3
Miscellaneous chemicals	18.2
Petroleum and coal products	16.1
Petroleum refining	16.9
Rubber and miscellaneous plastic products	34.2
Rubber products	25.7
Miscellaneous plastic products	40.9
Leather and leather products	63.3
Footwear, except rubber	67.0
Leather products, except footwear	63.6
Transportation, communications, and other public utilities	24.4
Transportation	19.2
Railroads and railway express service	6.3
Street railways and bus lines	37.1
Taxicab service	13.2
Trucking service	10.2
Warehousing and storage	23.6
Water transportation	11.6
Air transportation	30.3
Services incidental to transportation	55.3
Communications	47.3
Radio, broadcasting, and television	35.0
Telephone (wire and radio)	50.0
Telegraph and miscellaneous communication services	35.7
Utilities and sanitary services	15.2
Electric light and power	14.5
Electric gas utilities	20.1
Gas and steam supply systems	20.8
Water supply	16.6
Sanitary services	7.0

Table 5-2 (continued)

Industry	Percentage Female
Wholesale and retail trade	46.0
Wholesale trade	25.5
Motor vehicles and equipment	22.0
Drugs, chemicals, and allied products	29.3
Dry goods and apparel	40.6
Food and related products	24.3
Farm products—raw materials	25.6
Electrical goods	29.2
Hardware, plumbing, and heating supplies	22.7
Machinery, equipment and supplies	24.6
Metals and minerals, n.e.c.	22.5
Petroleum products	25.7
Scrap and waste materials	8.5
Alcoholic beverages	18.5
Paper and its products	27.5
Lumber and construction materials	18.0
Wholesalers, n.e.c.	34.0
Retail trade	50.8
Lumber and building material retailing	22.3
Hardware and farm equipment stores	29.3
Department and mail-order establishments	69.3
Limited price variety stores	75.1
Vending machine operators	35.1
Direct-selling establishments	77.4
Miscellaneous general merchandise stores	67.7
Grocery stores	44.7
Dairy product stores	58.7
Retail bakeries	63.7
Food stores, n.e.c.	50.9
Motor vehicle dealers	14.7
Tire, battery, and accessory dealers	16.5
Gasoline service stations	13.7
Miscellaneous vehicle dealers	21.1
Apparel and accessory stores, except shoe stores	76.6
Shoe stores	50.0
Furniture and home furnishing stores	35.6
Household appliances, TV, and radio stores	26.2
Eating and drinking places	60.7
Drug stores	62.9
Liquor stores	30.3
Farm and garden supply stores	30.0
Jewelry stores	60.1
Fuel and ice dealers	20.7
Retail florists	66.9
Miscellaneous retail stores	57.7

Table 5–2   (continued)

Industry	Percentage Female
Finance, insurance, and real estate	57.6
Banking	71.0
Credit agencies	67.6
Security, commodity, brokerage, and investment companies	39.5
Insurance	56.0
Real estate, including real estate-insurance-law offices	46.3
Service industries	61.2
Business and repair services	32.2
Advertising	43.7
Services to dwelling and other buildings	35.4
Commercial research, development and testing labs	27.8
Employment and temporary help agencies	70.5
Business management and consulting services	52.0
Computer programming services	38.4
Detective and protective services	18.2
Business services, n.e.c.	53.7
Automobile services, except repair	22.5
Automobile repair and related services	9.3
Electrical repair shops	12.9
Miscellaneous repair services	14.2
Personal services	73.7
Private households	88.1
Hotels and motels	58.9
Lodging places, except hotels and motels	77.9
Laundering, cleaning and other garment services	59.6
Beauty shops	88.7
Barber shops	15.2
Dressmaking shops	93.0
Miscellaneous personal services	48.9
Entertainment and recreation services	38.4
Theaters and motion pictures	35.1
Bowling alleys, billiard, and pool parlors	36.9
Miscellaneous entertainment and recreation services	40.5
Professional and related services	65.6
Offices of physicians	66.5
Offices of dentists	67.8
Hospitals	76.5
Convalescent institutions	88.3
Office of health practitioners, n.e.c.	58.3
Health services	70.8

Table 5-2   (continued)

Industry	Percentage Female
Legal services	49.6
Elementary and secondary schools	70.9
Colleges and universities	48.9
Libraries	82.6
Educational services, n.e.c.	67.5
Museums, art galleries, and zoos	56.6
Religious organizations	40.4
Welfare services	72.2
Residential welfare facilities	66.9
Nonprofit membership organizations	55.8
Engineering and architectural services	19.2
Accounting, auditing, and bookkeeping services	46.1
Miscellaneous professional and related services	42.8
Public administration	34.2
Postal services	23.0
Federal public administration	37.2
State public administration	40.7
Local public administration	32.6
All occupations, 16 years and over	41.7

SOURCE: U.S. Bureau of Labor Statistics, *Employment and Earnings*, January 1980.
n.e.c. = Not elsewhere classified.

Occupational Segregation Within Industries

Rider-Pinches has also developed an index to measure occupational segregation within industries.[24] She finds that with an index of 100 (where zero indicates no occupational differences by sex in an industry and 100 indicates total occupational segregation in an industry), the lowest amount of occupational segregation is present in eating and drinking places (but here, occupational segregation has *increased* over time, with an index value of 21 in 1967 and 29 in 1975). Other industries with low amounts of occupational segregation (indices with values under 40) include some nondurable goods manufacturing industries (which also have a high concentration of female workers), education (where there was a reduction in the amount of occupational segregation since 1967, from 46 in 1967 to 35 in 1975), and personal services. Industries with large amounts of occupational segregation include the mining and construction industries, some of

Table 5-3   **White Collar Occupational Distribution by Industry and Sex, 1979**
                 (percent)

Industry		Professional	Managerial	Sales	Clerical
Agriculture	M	2.0	1.0	0.2	0.2
	F	2.9	0.9	0.5	12.1
Mining	M	14.5	8.1	0.7	3.8
	F	16.7	5.9	—	67.6
Construction	M	2.9	12.1	0.4	1.7
	F	3.9	6.7	1.3	72.8
Manufacturing	M	12.9	9.0	2.6	5.3
	F	5.8	2.8	1.5	27.0
Durable	M	14.1	8.1	1.6	5.1
	F	5.6	2.8	0.7	30.7
Nondurable	M	10.6	10.6	4.5	5.5
	F	6.1	2.8	2.4	23.3
Transportation	M	9.5	10.4	0.7	9.7
	F	6.7	8.1	1.3	62.7
Trade	M	2.5	26.0	18.8	5.0
	F	1.5	11.0	23.3	32.2
Wholesale	M	4.0	24.1	28.6	5.9
	F	3.5	9.1	9.5	63.1
Retail	M	1.9	26.6	15.3	4.7
	F	1.2	11.2	25.0	28.6
FIRE (Finance,	M	7.6	29.9	33.5	13.7
Insurance, and	F	3.9	11.3	13.7	68.2
Real Estate)					
Service	M	42.9	12.1	0.9	4.8
	F	32.4	4.1	0.4	27.1
Public	M	21.5	14.1	0.1	20.1
Administration	F	15.9	10.1	0.2	64.9

Note: Rows do not sum to 100 since blue-collar occupations are excluded.

Source: U.S. Bureau of Labor Statistics, *Employment and Earnings*, January 1980.

the transportation industries, and some of the FIRE (finance, insurance, and real estate) industries.

In general, Rider-Pinches notes that those industries with the smallest female concentrations also are the industries with most occupational segregation. Usually, but not always, women have broader occupational distributions in the industries that they dominate. Table 5-3 illustrates this point. The largest share of female professional workers is found in the service industries, where there is also a high overall concentration of women. But there are few female managers, even in this industry—most female managers are found in retail trade, in the FIRE industries, and in public administration. In some of the industries where women are underrepresented, such as mining and construction, the bulk of the female representation is in the clerical occupation. Although the percentage of women in public administration does not exceed the percentage of women in the total labor force, women do relatively well in this occupation, both as professional workers and as managers. This raises interesting questions about the enforcement of discrimination laws being more vigorous in the public as opposed to the private sector.

The Effect of Occupational and Industrial Segregation on Wages

The impact of occupational and industrial segregation on earnings is shown in Table 5–4. Because the earnings presented are for all workers, an adjustment for full-time workers only would adjust female-male earnings ratios upward, since more women than men work part-time. However, from Table 5–4 we see that female clerical workers fare best (in terms of absolute earnings) in the transportation, communication, and public utility industries, and in public administration. Women in the professional and related service industries fare relatively poorly—there clerical workers fare better than women in any occupation-industry group. Overall, white collar women workers seemed to do better, relatively, in public administration, transportation, and durable goods industries. White collar women fared least well, relatively, in the personal service industries, in the FIRE industries, and in wholesale trade. The industries in which women fare worst are those industries where the concentration of women workers is highest, again illustrating the negative effects of occupational and industrial segregation on women.

The inclusion of aspects of the industrial distribution, then, is important in measuring income inequality by sex. The attainment of professional occupational status may have only a minor effect on relative wages for women, particularly when they find jobs in industries that are female-dominated and which have resultingly low relative wages for women. This is important since much of the employment growth that has occurred in the past two decades has been in occupations and industries that are female-stratified. Cleri-

Table 5–4 Earnings by Industry and Occupation, 1976 (in dollars)

Industry	Male	Female	Female/Male Ratio
Total, all occupations	12,665	6,011	.47
Agriculture	7,641	2,999	.39
Mining	14,982	(B)	—
Construction	11,446	5,955	.52
professional and managerial	17,962	(B)	—
clerical and sales	14,801	6,067	.41
craft and operative	10,767	(B)	—
other	6,651	(B)	—
Manufacturing	13,432	6,714	.50
professional and managerial	19,914	10,069	.51
clerical and sales	12,780	7,663	.60
craft and operative	11,859	5,906	.50
other	9,110	5,921	.65
Durable	13,570	7,452	.55
professional and managerial	19,919	11,025	.59
clerical and sales	13,046	8,103	.62
crafts and operative	12,044	6,672	.55
other	9,340	6,221	.67
Nondurable	13,184	6,077	.46
professional and managerial	19,905	9,247	.46
clerical and sales	12,450	7,150	.57
craft and operative	11,512	5,339	.46
other	8,674	5,555	.64
Transportation, Communication and Public Utility	14,114	8,397	.59
professional and managerial	19,215	9,976	.52
clerical and sales	12,982	8,955	.69
craft and operative	13,525	4,749	.35
other	9,438	—	—
Wholesale Trade	14,335	7,056	.49
professional and managerial	19,562	—	—
clerical and sales	14,859	6,714	.45
craft	10,758	5,514	.51
other	7,716	—	—
Retail Trade	9,200	4,165	.45
professional and managerial	14,220	6,901	.49
clerical and sales	8,064	4,147	.51
craft and operative	8,609	4,990	.58
other	4,631	3,015	.65

Table 5–4 (continued)

Industry	Male	Female	Female/Male Ratio
Finance, Insurance, Real Estate	15,824	6,681	.42
professional and managerial	19,162	9,183	.48
clerical and sales	15,970	6,336	.40
craft and operative	9,534	—	—
other	6,911	—	—
Business and Repair Services	10,321	5,652	.55
professional and managerial	16,544	8,062	.49
clerical and sales	12,225	5,474	.45
craft and operative	8,443	—	—
other	5,545	3,786	.68
Personal Services	7,509	2,748	.37
professional and managerial	12,021	4,481	.37
clerical and sales	(B)	4,378	—
craft and operative	7,072	3,415	.48
other	5,392	2,416	.45
Entertainment and Recreational Service	9,132	5,172	.57
Professional and Related Service	15,493	6,754	.44
professional and managerial	18,824	8,882	.47
clerical and sales	7,141	5,646	.79
craft and operative	10,333	4,006	.39
other	6,483	4,230	.65
Public Administration	14,691	8,727	.59
professional and managerial	17,438	10,502	.60
clerical and sales	13,524	8,362	.62
craft and operative	13,363	—	—
other	13,110	6,027	.46

SOURCE: U.S. Department of Commerce, *Social and Economic Characteristics of the Population, 1977 and 1970.*

cal and service jobs continue to have high growth rates projected, as do industries such as health and food. Although projected growth in these areas has been positive in terms of female employment, it has done little to broaden the opportunities that women face in the labor force. Furthermore, although growth in traditionally female occupations and industries has intermittently narrowed the unemployment gap between men and women, it has done nothing to narrow earnings differentials.

When discussing wage differentials, it is useful to measure the size of the difference attributable to differences in the occupational and industrial distribution of males and females. An adjustment that takes differences in the distributions into consideration was done as follows:

$$E'_w = \sum_{i=1}^{49} D_{mi} * E_{wi} \qquad i = \text{occupational-industrial cell,} \qquad (5\text{--}1)$$

where E'_w are the adjusted earnings of women, the product of D_m, or the male occupational-industrial distribution, and E'_w, mean female earnings.

The industrial breaks used are for the fourteen major industries. The occupational breaks are broader, as shown in Table 5–4. These occupational groupings combine at least two of the twelve major occupations. The effect of combining the groups is to obscure some of the differences in earnings levels between major occupations groups. On the other hand, because 1977 CPS data are used (and sample size is a consideration) in this approximation, the groupings make cell sizes more robust.

Where the major industrial classifications are used in conjunction with the occupational groupings discussed (as opposed to detailed groupings), it is clear that the adjustment made here is a first approximation of differences due to employment distributions. A further flaw in the data is that they are not adjusted for full- or part-time work effort. Since proportionately more women than men work part-time, our estimate is a lower bound of the differences measured due to distributions. Data that disaggregated full- and part-time workers are not available by both occupation and industry.

Another flaw in the data has to do with the dynamics of occupational segregation itself. More than 15 percent of all males are distributed in occupational-industrial cells where the number of women is too small to yield a statistically reliable mean earnings figure. (The corresponding number of women in these cells is nine tenths of 1 percent of the females.) Thus, in general, the E_w figure reflects mean earnings; but for those cells where population size is small, mean earnings for the *industry* are used. About a quarter of the forty-nine cells used (the agricultural, mining, and entertainment service industries do not disaggregate by occupation) are so affected.

When the adjustment shown in Equation 5–1 is undertaken, mean female earnings rise from \$6,011 to \$6,915, an increase of 16 percent. Thus, female earnings would be 16 percent higher if women were distributed across broad occupation-industry cells in the same way as men. This adjustment does not capture those within-cell differences that exist—most notable may be differences in detailed occupational distribution, as discussed in the early part of this chapter.

It is possible to hold the female distribution fixed, and approximate female incomes when *male* earnings are earned:

$$E''_w = \sum_{i=1}^{49} D_{wi} * E_{mi} \qquad \text{where } i = \text{occupational-industrial cell,} \qquad (5\text{--}2)$$

where E''_w are the adjusted earnings of females, the product D_w, the female occupational-industrial distribution, and E_m, the male earnings. If the female occupational-industrial structure is held fixed but male earnings are substituted, E''_w is $10,833, 15 percent lower than the $12,665 actual mean earnings of males.

Although, as mentioned, these adjustments are a first approximation, they indicate that the occupational and industrial differences between males and females are responsible for a *minimum* of 15 percent of the earnings distribution differential. In an alternative measure, changes in the earnings gap as opposed to the earnings poles may be considered. In such case the adjustments measured above account for between 13.5 and 27.5 percent of the wage-earnings gap. In either case these adjustments are a first approximation, and they measure differences in the distribution among cells and not the within-cell differences. Some of the remaining earnings differential can be explained by the inexactness of this approximation, especially where cell size is concerned, as well as by the different full- and part-time status of males and females, differences in job tenure, and other differences that, while superficially sex-neutral, are significant because they impact female earnings more strongly than they empact male earnings.

The Impact of Occupational and Industrial Segregation—1980 and Beyond

In examining data on occupational and industrial segregation, it appears that women have experienced limited progress in the labor force. Although female labor force participation has increased markedly, most of the increase has been in jobs that women traditionally hold. Where we observe improvements in women's occupational status—for example, in the managerial occupation—much of the increase may be in industries that are also typically female. Furthermore, although the number of women who hold "female" jobs has decreased, the decline has been limited. Additionally, because of the way occupational data are classified, changes in the occupational distribution can only be sketched. For example, managerial jobs may include managers in a range of industries, management trainees, chief executive officers, and employees in staff as well as line jobs. The patterns that we have observed regarding occupational segregation may well extend to these subdivisions.

Much of the research on the advancement of women in jobs has focused on entry jobs. But will these women be promoted? Or will they participate in a "revolving door," where one or two women work at a firm for a finite period of time and then are replaced by new women? Although it is clear that certain, highly visible women have made inroads in select male bastions, how will their career advancement compare to that of their male colleagues? Further, what does their isolated experience have to do with the employment experience of most women—those who earn fifty-nine cents for every dollar that males earn?

The seventies were a decade of legislation and litigation for the rights of women in the workplace. Since the 1972 amendments to the Civil Rights Act of 1964, Title VII covers employment practices and discrimination in private firms with more than fifteen employees, as well as state and local governments and educational institutions. Additionally, due to the monitoring of regulatory agencies, consent decrees have been developed to ameliorate effects of past discrimination on women. But some issues are yet to be resolved. Because of the sex-based way that job titles have developed, the issue of comparable worth is important—that is, do women who have similar skills and similar jobs earn less than males because of different job classifications? Similarly, the issue of sexual harassment has surfaced as an issue important to women in the workplace. While the district courts originally held that a claim of sexual harassment does not state a cause of action under Title VII, circuit courts have ruled differently on the statute.[25] The grounds for litigation for sexual harassment are not clearcut, and the issues are complicated because they transcend the context of the labor market to deal with issues of how men and women relate in society. However, they most certainly will be redefined as more complaints are filed in this area.

Perhaps more important than shaping the kind of work women will do in the 1980s is the changing demographic profile of the population. Women remain single longer, and they more often head families. They are more frequently divorced and thus are more concerned about their work histories and financial security in terms of pensions and Social Security benefits. Thus the dynamics of occupational and industrial segregation, and the fact that wages for women remain relatively low, may be seen as more critical when the effects of lower women's wages are seen as other than temporary.

The conclusion of this review of occupational and industrial segregation of women is necessarily pessimistic. To the extent that growth continues in occupations where women are already heavily represented, there will be little improvement in the income earnings differential observed between males and females. Further investigations of the issue of comparable worth may produce alterations in the way that wage schedules and occupational classifications are organized in general and for white collar women in particular. Despite the fact that the legislative and litigative environment that women encounter when they work has been altered, the gripping effects of occupational and industrial segregation remain a significant factor in explaining unequal female earnings.

Endnotes

1. Gail Bronson, "Sexual Pitches in Ads Become More Explicit and More Pervasive," *Wall Street Journal*, November 18, 1980, p. 1.
2. U.S. Department of Commerce, *Survey of Income and Education* (Microdata), 1976.
3. Julianne Malveaux and Phyllis Wallace, "Attacking the Myth of the Twofer," *Ms. Magazine*, forthcoming.
4. Barbara Bergmann, "Occupational Segregation, Wages and Profits When Employers Discriminate by Race or Sex," *Eastern Economic Journal* 1 (April/July 1974), pp. 103–10.
5. Simon Polachek, "Occupational Segregation: Theory, Evidence and a Prognosis," in Cynthia B. Lloyd, Emily S. Andrews, and Curtis L. Gilroy, eds., *Women in the Labor Market* (New York: Columbia University Press, 1979).
6. Michael Korda, *Male Chauvinism* (New York: Random House, 1973).
7. Andrea Beller, "Occupational Segregation by Sex: Determinants and Changes" (Presented at Eastern Economic Association Meetings, May 1980).
8. Julianne Malveaux, "Unemployment Differentials by Race and Occupation," (Ph.D. diss., MIT, 1980), pp. 34–37.
9. Ibid.
10. Constance Dicesare, "Changes in the Occupational Structure of U.S. Jobs," *Monthly Labor Review* 98, 3 (March 1975).
11. Carol Jusenius, "The Influence of Work Experience and Typicality of Occupa-

tional Assignment on Women's Earnings" in *Dual Careers* (Manpower Research Monograph No. 21, 81, 4, U.S. Department of Labor, Washington, D.C., 1976).

12. Harriet Zellner, "Determinants of Occupational Segregation" in Cynthia Lloyd, ed., *Sex, Discrimination and the Division of Labor* (New York: Columbia University Press, 1975).
13. U.S. Bureau of Labor Statistics, *Employment and Earnings* 27, 1 (January 1978).
14. Julianne Malveaux, "Unemployment Differentials by Race and Occupation," p. 28.
15. U.S. Department of Labor, *Employment and Training Report of the President*, (Washington, D.C., September, 1980).
16. Malveaux, "Unemployment Differentials by Race and Occupation," pp. 129–39. Detailed results from this model may be obtained from the author.
17. Ibid., pp. 167–78.
18. Janice Madden, "Discrimination and Male Market Power," in Cynthia Lloyd, ed., *Sex, Discrimination and the Division of Labor.*
19. Carol Jusenius, "The Influence of Work Experience."
20. Theresa Ammot, "Mechanisms of Occupational Segregation: Some New Empirical Evidence" (Paper presented at the Eastern Economic Association Meetings, Montreal, May 1980).
21. Malveaux, "Unemployment Differentials by Race and Occupation," pp. 121–22.
22. U.S. Bureau of Labor Statistics, *Employment and Earnings* 27, 1 (January 1980).
23. Christine Rider-Pinches, "Employment Segregation by Sex" (Paper presented at the Eastern Economic Association Meetings, Montreal, May 1980).
24. Ibid.
25. Allan Goldberg, "Sexual Harassment and Title VII," in D. A. Neugarten and Jay M. Shafritz, eds., *Sexuality in Organizations* (Oak Park: Moore Publishing, 1980).

Additional References

1. Francine Blau and Laurence M. Kahn. "Race and Sex Differences in the Probability and Consequences of Voluntary Turnover" (University of Illinois, mimeograph, September 1978).
2. Council of Economic Advisers, *Economic Indicators* (Washington, D.C.: U.S. Government Printing Office, October, 1980).
3. Duane E. Leigh, *An Analysis of the Determinants of Occupational Upgrading* (New York: Academic Press, 1978).
4. Michael Reich, David Gordon, and Richard C. Edwards, "A Theory of Labor Market Segmentation," *American Economic Review* 63, 2 (May 1973), pp. 359–65.

5. U.S. Bureau of Labor Statistics, unpublished occupational data, Tables 23–27, 1968–1977.
6. U.S. Department of Commerce, *Social and Economic Characteristics of the Metropolitan and Nonmetropolitan Population,* 1977 and 1970 (Washington, D.C.: U.S. Government Printing Office, 1978).
7. U.S. Department of Labor, *Employment and Training Report of the President* (Washington, D.C.: Government Printing Office, 1979).
8. Howard Wachtel and Charles Betsey, "Employment at Low Wages." *The Review of Economics and Statistics* 54, 2 (May 1972).
9. Phyllis A. Wallace, *Black Women in the Labor Force* (Cambridge, Mass.: MIT Press, 1980).

Appendix

EMPLOYMENT EXPERIENCE MODEL

A model of the supply side of the labor market is

$$E_s = S(W,K,O,PC,Q), \qquad (A-1)$$

where

E_s = employment supplied,
K = education and skills,
O = nonwork options,
PC = personal characteristics,
W = wage, and
Q = stability characteristics (such as number of jobs held and turnover).

Similarly, a model of the demand side of the labor market is

$$E_d = D(W,Q,I.), \qquad (A-2)$$

where

E_d = employment demanded,
W = wage,
Q = stability characteristics, and
I = institutional factors.

Thus,

$$E_s = S(W,Q,Z) + \epsilon_1 \text{ and} \qquad (A-3)$$

$$E_d = D(W,Q,X) + \epsilon_2, \qquad (A-4)$$

where

Z $\quad$ = supply factors K,O,PC,
X $\quad$ = demand factors I,
ϵ_1, ϵ_2 = respective error terms.

A reduced form of equations (A–3) and (A–4) that measure unemployment is

$$U_i = S(W,Q,Z) - D(W,Q,X) = H(W,Q,X,A). \qquad \text{(A–5)}$$

The causation between W and Q on the right-hand side and the dependent variable U is two-way. Thus it is conceivable that U might appear as an independent variable in an equation explaining either W or Q. The reduced form of the equation, then, does not include these endogenous variables:

$$U_i = H(X,Z) + \epsilon_i. \qquad \text{(A–6)}$$

This equation can be modified to show the detail of the components of X and Z:

$$U_i = H(K,O,PC,I) + \epsilon_1. \qquad \text{(A–7)}$$

A Proxy for Unemployment

In attempting to explain differences in employment experience, weeks worked seemed to be a good choice of a dependent variable. While the discussion earlier has been developed in terms of unemployment rates, it is not possible to use unemployment rate as a variable in a cross-sectional analysis of individuals since it is the composite of the employment experience for a segment of the population. However, the unemployment rate, U, is expressed in terms of weeks worked as follows:

$$\frac{\sum_{i=i}^{N} E_i}{\sum_{i=1}^{N} W_{LFi}}$$

where

E = weeks worked for individual i
W_{LFi} = weeks in the labor force for individual i.   (A–8)

The flaws of using weeks worked when comparing men and women rest in the fact that (as noted) the source of labor supply (job loss, quitting, entry, and reentry, etc.) differ by sex.

The employment experience model is summarized as follows:

Variable and Component Definitions

$$E_s = S(W,Q,K,O,PC)$$
$$E_d = D(W,Q,I)$$
$$E_i = H(K,O,PC,I)$$

K—Skill Component

SVP   Specific Vocational Preparation is a job trait associated with the three-digit occupation in which a person works. These data were compiled from the Employment Probability Analysis Project.* Range from 0 to 8.

HS   Dummy Variable. 0 if less than 12 years of education completed; 1 if more than 16 years of education.

COLL   Dummy. 0 if less than 16 years of education completed; 1 if more than 16 years of education.

EDUC   Years of schooling completed. Range from 0 to 20.

0—Options Component

PUB   Dummy Variable for Public Assistance receipt. 0 if neither AFDC nor Food Stamps nor other Public Assistance was received, 1 if any of those items noted were received.

UN   Dummy Variable for receipt of unemployment-associated benefits. 0 if neither Unemployment Insurance nor Workmen's Compensation is received. 1 if either is received.

---

* Lynn B. Ware, *Industry Characteristics Data for 1970 Census Industry Titles* (Chestnut Hill, Mass.: Social Welfare Research Institute, 1976).

PUN   Composite variable of PUB and UN. 1 if either PUB or UN is 1, zero otherwise.

EARNERS or EARN   Dummy variable that is zero if a family has only one earner and 1 if there are multiple earners.

CHILD6   Number of children six years old or younger. Range 0 to 5.

CHSEX   Child variable with a sex interaction term. Range 0 to 5. (CHILD6*SEX)

I—Institution Effects Component

PROFITS   Profits for the industry in which the individual works. These data were obtained from the Employment Probability Analysis Project.*

UNION   Percentage of unionization for all workers for the industry in which the individual works. These data were obtained from Freeman and Medoff.†

CLW   Class of Worker. Dummy Variable. 0 for private workers and 1 for public (federal, state or local) workers.

PC—Personal Characteristic Component

AGE   Age. Continuous Variable with person-age in years.

SEX   Dummy Variable. 0 for males, 1 for females.

RACE   Dummy Variable. 0 for whites, 1 for blacks.

CMAR or MAR   Dummy Variable. 0 if never married, divorced or separated. 1 if married (with spouse present or in the armed forces).

---

* Lynn B. Ware, *Industry Characteristics Data for 1970 Census Industry Titles* (Chestnut Hill, Mass.: Social Welfare Research Institute, 1976).

† Richard Freeman and James Medoff, "New Estimates of Private Sector Unionism in the U.S.," *Industrial and Labor Relations Review* 32, 2 (January 1970).

Chapter 6

WOMEN AND NONTRADITIONAL BLUE COLLAR JOBS IN THE 1980s: AN OVERVIEW

by Brigid O'Farrell

The 1970s were a time of "firsts"—the first woman mechanic, plumber, telephone installer, and coal miner—the first women to enter nontraditional blue collar jobs. The 1980s will be a time of ongoing change as women continue to enter the world of paid work in increasing numbers with growing economic needs and heightened awareness of alternatives to traditional female work. Employers can make the 1980s a time of substantial, productive change. In this chapter we look specifically at what managers can and should do to increase the opportunities available to women while improving the overall training and quality of their blue collar work force.[1]

Women are and always have been blue collar workers. Similar to the employment picture in general, however, blue collar women and men work in different occupations, industries, plants, and jobs. Women are operatives, while men are craft workers. Women work in the textile industry while men work in the steel industry. Women

This paper was written under a research grant (RO1MH30767) from the Center for Work and Mental Health, National Institute of Mental Health, Department of Health and Human Services. I would like to thank my colleagues on this project, Sharon Harlan and Priscilla Douglas, for their continuing contributions to this paper and more generally to the study of women in nontraditional blue collar work.

135

assemble small electronic components in one plant while men build jet engines in another plant. Within these plants men set up and repair machines while women operate them. After fifteen years of equal employment opportunity legislation there has been some change, but progress continues to be slow. Skilled blue collar jobs remain predominantly male.

Many employers attribute the limited integration of blue collar jobs to social or psychological factors over which they have little control; for example, women's perceived preference for light, clean work or the sexist behavior of male coworkers. A small but growing body of research, however, offers additional explanations. The systematic study of women and blue collar work, especially nontraditional work, is still quite new, but the studies reviewed in this chapter suggest that there are both personal barriers and organizational constraints on women's mobility, which managers can directly influence. These studies find that women are interested in nontraditional blue collar work, and those who stay in the jobs report relatively high satisfaction with both increased pay and challenging work. But these women remain a small group, at least in part, because of barriers to recruitment and hiring and problems on the job.

Overcoming barriers such as arbitrary age limits that conflict with women's family life cycles, the lack of information on apprenticeship and skilled trades, the hostile behavior of male coworkers and foremen, or restrictive job posting and bidding procedures provide an important challenge for managers. As more and more women enter the labor force looking for better jobs, the development of new programs and procedures for outreach, recruitment, training, support and job mobility will be important if employers are to meet not only the letter but also the spirit of the law—that is, to provide equal employment opportunity regardless of sex, with women and men working in cooperative and productive environments.

Blue Collar Work: Definitions and Change

Blue collar workers represent a major section of our work force. In November 1980, the U.S. Department of Labor reported that there were over 30 million of these workers, representing 32 percent of the labor force.[2] Statistics for blue collar workers come from the census category covering craft and kindred workers, operatives, and nonfarm laborers. The blue collar category is not as clear as it once was in that it often overlaps with references to "pink, white, and grey collars" and the related category of service work, but it continues to reflect a large group of workers who use predominantly manual skills—for example, carpenters, plumbers, welders, stitchers, checkers, and assembly line workers.

Although the proportion of blue collar jobs is declining (white collar jobs are growing at a faster rate), the actual number of blue collar jobs continues to increase. In fact, Amitai Etzioni, sociologist and former White House adviser, recently predicted a period of "reindustrialization" and thus a return to familiar blue collar work: casting steel, transporting beams, mining coal. He reminds us:[3]

> *There will be good money in blue collar work. Already many blue collar jobs pay better than white collar ones. Especially lucrative is blue collar work related to the field of energy.*

Despite steel plant closings and a slump in the automobile industry, employment projections for the 1980s show a need for workers in jobs such as auto mechanic, plumber, pipefitter, welder, and machine operator.[4] It seems likely that blue collar work will remain a significant part of the labor force for the foreseeable future. It is important therefore to look at opportunities for women in the blue collar sector. We begin by defining nontraditional blue collar jobs in the context of occupational segregation and the change that has occurred in the last two decades.

Nontraditional Jobs Defined

In their analysis of Census data by occupation and sex, Reubens and Reubens define nontraditional jobs as those "in which women form a considerably smaller proportion of the work force than their current share of the total employed population."[5] In 1980 women represented 42 percent of all employed workers 16 years and over (see Table 6–1).

Using the above definition we find that all but three of forty-one detailed craft occupations listed by the Department of Labor are nontraditional. Bakers, decorators and window dressers, and tailors are 42.9 percent, 71.1 percent and 46.2 percent female, respectively. Only one traditional craft, printing, is more than 20 percent female (22.7 percent), and all the others are 15 percent or less female. Among operatives, which are approximately 40 percent female, over half of the thirty-eight specific occupations are nontraditional and nine out of ten nonfarm laborer occupations are nontra-

Table 6-1   Employed Persons by Occupation, Race, and Sex

| | | Percent of Total | |
Occupation	Total Employed (in thousands)	Women	Black and Other
Total Workers, 16 Years and Over	97,270	42.4	11.2
White Collar Workers	50,809	53.3	8.4
Professional, technical	15,613	44.3	8.9
Managers, administrators	10,919	26.1	5.2
Sales workers	6,172	45.3	5.1
Clerical workers	18,105	80.1	11.1
Blue Collar Workers	30,800	18.5	12.7
Craft, kindred	12,529	6.0	8.3
Operatives, except transport	10,346	40.1	15.3
Operatives, transport	3,468	8.0	15.3
Laborers	4,456	11.6	16.9
Service Workers	12,958	62.0	19.4
Farm Workers	2,704	18.0	7.4

SOURCE: Bureau of Labor Statistics, U.S. Department of Labor, *Employment and Earnings.* 28, 1 (January 1981), Table 23, pp. 180–81.

ditional. Animal caretaker, which is 51 percent female, is the one nonfarm laborer exception. Table 6–2 lists sixteen of the most nontraditional craft occupations.

These nontraditional blue collar jobs can be better understood in the context of four distinct types of segregation:[6] occupational, industry, firm, and job. Occupational segregation refers to the concentration of women and men in different occupational categories, shown in Table 6-1. In the most general form, women are concentrated in white collar and service occupations. Only 18.5 percent of blue collar workers are female. Differences then persist within categories; 40 percent of operatives are women compared to only 6 percent of the craft workers.

Within the occupational category women and men are found in different industries. Women operatives run machines in the shoemaking, dry cleaning, textile, apparel industries, and assemble small components in the electronics industry. Men, on the other hand, run grinding machines and lathes in the steel industry and

Table 6-2   Selected Nontraditional Blue Collar Jobs*

Occupation	Total Employed	Percent of Total	
		Women	Black and Other
Craft, Kindred	12,529,000	6.0	8.3
Carpenters	1,185,000	1.5	5.7
Brickmasons, stonemasons	168,000	0.1	16.1
Electricians	648,000	1.2	5.7
Road machinery operators	456,000	0.9	9.6
Painters, construction, maintenance	469,000	6.0	11.3
Plumbers and pipefitters	478,000	0.6	9.2
Roofers and slaters	139,000	0.7	10.8
Machinists	567,000	3.4	8.3
Millwrights	108,000	0.9	4.6
Sheetmetal workers, tinsmiths	161,000	3.1	6.2
Tool and die makers	176,000	2.8	2.3
Mechanics, automobiles	1,197,000	0.7	9.1
Mechanics, other	2,123,000	2.6	7.5
Crane, derrick, hoist operators	148,000	0.7	17.6
Electric powerline workers	117,000	0.9	8.5
Stationary engineers	182,000	1.1	9.3

SOURCE: Bureau of Labor Statistics, U.S. Department of Labor, *Employment and Earnings*, 28, 1 (January 1981), Table 23, pp. 180–81.

* Includes only craft occupations where the total employed is 100,000 or more and women are 6 percent or less of total employed.

assemble and weld in automobile manufacturing. At the firm level, women have typically been employed in types of firms described as small, marginal, nonunion enterprises with low capital investment, low profit margins, irregular personnel practices, high turnover, and low pay.

Furthermore, within industries and firms women and men do different jobs. For example, in apparel firms men are skilled cutters and pressers while women run sewing machines. In electronics women run machines while men set up and repair them; women assemble small circuit boards while men assemble jet engines. Jobs in the type of firms that employ men are characterized by better pay, fringe benefits, security and training, which in turn reflect greater unionization than white or blue collar jobs traditionally held by women. In both construction and manufacturing these jobs are at the top of a job hierarchy in the internal labor market.[7]

Table 6–3   Mean Earnings for Selected Occupations by Race and Sex (Year-Round Full-Time Workers, 18 Years Old and Over)

	Men		Women	
Occupation	*White*	*Black*	*White*	*Black*
Sales workers	$19,314	(B)	$8,741	(B)
Clerical, kindred	15,542	$12,801	9,479	$9,823
Craft, kindred	16,374	14,128	10,263	(B)
Operatives	14,425	12,278	8,564	8,376
Laborers	12,731	10,390	8,654	(B)
Service workers	12,402	10,170	6,979	7,182

SOURCE: Census Bureau, U.S. Department of Commerce, *Money Income of Families, 1978*, Current Population Report, Series P-60, No. 125 (June 1980), Table 57, p. 257.

B = Base less than 75,000.

As shown in Table 6–3, men, both minority and nonminority, earn more than women in either white or blue collar predominantly nonmanagement jobs. Higher wages and other benefits associated with nontraditional blue collar jobs are related to union membership. In 1977 23.8 percent of all wage and salary workers belonged to labor unions. Nearly 43 percent of blue collar workers are union members, however, compared to 18 percent of white collar workers and 19 percent of service workers. Within occupational categories, machinists are more organized (56 percent) than sewers (10 percent), and the automobile workers are more organized (71 percent) than electrical components workers (32 percent).[8] Union members are more likely to have fringe benefits such as retirement plans, health insurance, overtime pay provisions, and cost-of-living increases. Job advancement and security are enhanced through job posting and bidding procedures, bumping, lay-off and recall provisions, and strict seniority requirements. Formal training and skill development is best exemplified in apprenticeship programs combining classroom and on-the-job training. Access to apprenticeship positions that lead to journeyman status and actual referral to construction jobs are determined by joint apprenticeship committees and referral halls, both of which are run largely by unions.[9]

In 1978, 15.4 percent of the total female labor force belonged to a labor union, representing 24.4 percent of all union members. Like men, women in blue collar jobs are more likely to be union members than white collar or service workers, and union women earn more than nonunion women. In general, however, union organization reflects the segregation of the marketplace. The majority of women are concentrated in a few unions in industries that historically employ women.[10]

There are further occupational and wage differences for minority workers, and particularly for black women. In 1980 36 percent of workers who were members of minority groups were in blue collar jobs. Like women, minority groups have long been part of the blue collar world, but in the most undesirable, lowest-paying jobs. Exclusion of black and other minority workers from skilled craft work was highlighted in the 1960s by attempts to integrate construction sites, which has led to Hometown plans that include goals and timetables, and some progress has been made for minority men.[11]

Over three quarters of a million minority women hold blue collar jobs. Like white women, they are concentrated in the operative category and are further segregated by industry, firm, and job. Unlike white women, however, minority women are increasing in the operative job category while white women are declining.

Research shows that black and Puerto Rican women are tracked into less desirable blue collar jobs, while white women have greater mobility into white collar jobs than similarly situated minority women. It appears that minority women are moving from service jobs, particularly domestic service, to manual blue collar jobs, while white women are going from manual blue collar jobs into white collar clerical jobs.[12] These trends leave open the question of whether or not women, minority or white, have the opportunity to move to the higher-paying, skilled blue collar jobs.

Changes in Rates of Blue Collar Employment

In 1960 only 3 percent of those employed in skilled trades were women. Federal legislation and court decisions in the 1960s and 1970s have led to some changes.[13] From 1960 to 1970 women increased from 3 percent to 5 percent of workers employed in skilled trades, which was eight times the rate of increase for men in that period.[14] More current examples of women carpenters, welders, and telephone pole climbers are reported in such diverse papers as the *Boston Globe*, the *Wall Street Journal*, and *Steel Labor*. In 1976 the United Steelworkers of America devoted two pages of *Steel Labor* to women steelworkers, "Blue Collar All the Way."[15] *The Engineering and Mining Journal* reported that a survey showed a 100 percent increase in the number of women in mining in U.S. and Canadian mining companies in the last ten years.[16]

A striking example of women filling jobs when they are actually available is found in Alaska. The Alyeska Pipeline Service Company reported an increase in the employment of women in nontraditional blue collar construction jobs from 21 to 1,702 between June 1974 and December 1975.[17] The Department of Labor established goals and timetables for women in the construction trades, and in 1975 the secretary announced there were "3,118 women apprentices in training, representing an increase of 66 percent over 1973."[18] The most widely available data on women in nontraditional blue collar jobs comes from AT&T. In 1973 it was publicly documented that women in the Bell System had historically been excluded from craft jobs. Under a court-ordered affirmative action plan, AT&T increased the number of women in their nontraditional blue collar jobs from 11,413 in 1973 to 23,819 in 1979. The number of women in outside craft jobs, telephone installers and repairers, rose from 972 to 6,313 during that period.[19]

According to the Department of Labor, however, only 2.6 percent of all apprentices were women and only 1.9 percent of apprentices in the construction trades were women. The largest gains were in only four categories: bakers, window dressers, typesetters and painters.[20] By 1980 only 6 percent of all craft workers were women. No more than 2 percent of carpenters, electricians, mechanics or tool and die makers were women (Table 6–1 and 6–2). In Reubens and Reubens, analysis of nontraditional occupations showed some growth for women in the skilled categories of molders, upholsterers, drillers, sawyers, furniture finishers, bartenders, recreation attendants, and inspectors. These are occupations where the female share rose by 5 percentage points or more and male growth was small. Crafts with a strong growth of males, however, did not show much increase in female employment. They conclude that "A closer look must be taken at congratulatory reports on the erosion of sex stereotyping in the crafts."[21] Employers, women's groups, researchers and government officials conclude that change is occurring, but it is slow. We turn now to more detailed explanations of change and the change process.

Getting In: Interest and Barriers

Employers report less success recruiting women for nontraditional blue collar jobs than recruiting women for management jobs. During the last decade they have continually attributed this lack of success to women's preference for other types of work. In 1974 Norma Briggs reported a survey of seventy-eight establishments that trained Wisconsin state-registered apprentices. There were no women apprentices, but three quarters of the respondents felt some trades, such as sewing and interior decorating, were particularly suited to women and two thirds said they would hesitate to consider a woman for other trades. Over half explained that their reluctance was due to the 'unsuitable' working conditions of the trade: the work involved long hours, was 'dirty' or 'heavy.' "[22]

In 1976 psychologists Meyer and Lee interviewed men and women workers and managers in ten public utilities. Managers reported that getting women into blue collar jobs was a problem and that clerical women in particular were reluctant to enter the male factory world.[23] A 1979 Conference Board study by Shaeffer and Lynton involving a survey and interviews with personnel staffs in over two hundred large corporations confirmed the earlier employer attitudes. Managers concluded that, "There is no ready supply of female applicants for nontraditional blue collar jobs . . . in-house or external."[24]

There is a growing body of research, however, that contradicts these claims. Recent studies find that women are interested in nontraditional blue collar work; the problem continues to be the reluctance of employers to hire women and the persistence of organizational barriers that discourage women moving to jobs that are technically open to them within a firm. The findings, discussed below, suggest that women are available for nontraditional blue collar jobs despite personal obstacles and that several of the organizational barriers can be reduced by employers.

Women's Interest

Past interest in nontraditional blue collar jobs was displayed by women during war years when Rosie the Riveter was hailed as a wartime heroine. One example from Chafe's analysis of the American woman from 1920 to 1970 is illustrative. In 1940, 36 women were involved in the construction of ships. By December 1942 over 160,000 women were employed welding hatches, riveting gun emplacements and binding keels. "As stevedores, blacksmiths, foundry helpers and drill-press operators, they demonstrated they could fill almost any job no matter how difficult or arduous."[25]

Despite surveys showing that women wanted to keep their jobs, after the war they left the higher-paying more skilled jobs almost as quickly as they had entered them. Some war-related factories closed altogether, and returning veterans were given preference for almost all jobs. Just as employers, the media, and government had strongly encouraged women to join the war effort, after the war they encouraged women to return to their homes and families. Women returned, not to home, however, but to waitress, clerk, and assembly jobs.[26]

More recently it has been shown that companies are able to find women for nontraditional jobs when they are under pressure to hire women. The successful impact of goals and timetables is now being well documented for minorities and more recently for women.[27] In an evaluation of ten government-sponsored programs to train women for apprenticeship programs, Kane and Miller state that where goals and timetables have been implemented, they have produced remarkable results:[28]

In the year following the issuance of the revised regulations (29CFR 30 and 41CFR 6.4), there was a rise in the percentage of women apprentices in every state except Missouri. There was a total rise of all women apprentices from 1.7 percent in 1976 to 3.1 percent in 1978 to 3.7 percent in 1979.

Ullman and Deaux report similar effects for the consent decree and resulting affirmative action program in their ongoing study of two midwestern steel companies.[29]

Kane and Miller further report that programs to train women for apprenticeship have more applicants than they are able to serve. One program reported 250 women applicants in one day after an announcement of project funding appeared in the local newspaper. In a survey of over 200 women in traditionally female jobs in a large corporation, O'Farrell and Harlan found that almost all of the women thought women should have the opportunity to do nontraditional blue collar work; most said they had considered nontraditional blue collar work, and 30 percent had taken some action toward a move to such work.[30] Although these studies do not suggest that overwhelming numbers of women are beating down the doors for these jobs, they do support the need for a closer look at barriers beyond women's personal preference that might limit their access to new job opportunities.

Barriers to New Hires and Transfers

Most of the programs and research on women in nontraditional blue collar jobs have focused on apprenticeship in the construction trades. Understandably, apprenticeship is the traditional route to the most skilled and most visible craft jobs—for example, plumbers, electricians, and carpenters working on building sites in the community.[31] However, much of the litigation and court-ordered consent decrees and, in fact, most of EEOC's systemic approach have focused on major corporations such as AT&T, General Electric, Ford, and the steel industry. Ullman and Deaux point out that there are more craft workers in manufacturing than in any other industrial group. In 1978, 19.3 percent or 4,144,000 workers in manufacturing were in craft positions.[32] As a result of more recent research on industrial craft workers, discussion of access is divided into two categories: barriers to hiring women from outside the firm and barriers restricting women from transferring within the firm.

Hiring

Hiring barriers that limit access to the skilled trades affect people who are unemployed, working in another company, in school, or presently not participating in the labor market—in other words, people who are not currently part of the organization that is hiring for the trades. Companies often refer to employing these people as "hiring off the street." This is the major source of hiring for apprenticeship programs run by joint apprenticeship councils and is one form of hiring for companies seeking people for apprenticeship, entry level, and skilled jobs. Off-the-street hiring is usually geared to vocational training programs, manpower training programs, and high school recruitment.

Age Limits. One of the most serious barriers for women wanting to enter apprenticeship training or entry-level jobs in a plant that provides opportunities for on-the-job training advancement, is age limits. This barrier combines attitude, life cycle, and arbitrary organizational constraints. In short, external recruitment and hiring focuses on people under 25. While this is a common informal employment practice, apprenticeship programs often have formal upper-age limits of 25 to 27, which have yet to be found discriminatory by the courts. Yet these age limits combine with traditional attitudes and women's life cycles to form a formidable barrier.[33]

Unlike teenage boys, teenage girls are not trained, counseled, or expected to enter nontraditional jobs. The majority of young women cling to the stereotype that they will soon marry, leave the work force, and raise a family, despite the continuing trends to the contrary.[34] Thus, employers report a lack of success in recruitment—a lack of interest on the part of women.

The attitudes of many young women, however, do not mean that women do not want these jobs. Rather, women become interested in these jobs later in their life cycle. In six sample programs the median age of women in apprenticeship training was 25 to 26.5 years, while 40 to 50 percent of women in several research studies were in their late twenties to early forties.[35] Women with children returning to work for economic reasons, newly divorced or widowed women, or single women who have never left the work force begin to view work roles differently. In their late twenties and early thirties or forties, they have twenty or thirty years left in the paid labor force and they want to make the most of it. The Department of Labor has acknowledged but has done little to remove the age limit barrier:[36]

> Studies have shown that most women enter apprenticeship after they have already had some experience in the work force, usually in low skill, low paid jobs. By the time that many women in their twenties or early thirties discover that skilled trades offer both opportunity and satisfaction, they are too old to apply.

Although employers rarely have the formal upper-age limits for hiring, the stability and low turnover sought through on-the-job training and promotion from within strongly encourages hiring young men who will acquire specific skills and benefits that keep them with the same employers for a long time. This emphasis on youth, also reflected in low entry-level salaries and the need for after-work nonpaid training time, form a slightly different barrier for women employed in traditional jobs in companies that also have nontraditional work (discussed in the section on transfer barriers).

Traditional Recruitment. High schools, vocational schools, and manpower training programs have made little progress in placing young girls in nontraditional training roles. Sex bias among counselors and traditional attitudes of administrators, students, and families all contribute to the continued segregated training in these programs. These problems are complex, but it appears unlikely that employers or joint apprenticeship councils who rely on these traditional recruitment sources will have much success recruiting women in the immediate future.[37]

Lack of Information. Coupled with the discriminatory procedures and outcomes of the traditional recruitment sources is a general confusion and lack of information on nontraditional opportunities. Information on trades and training is generally not available to women or high school counselors. This lack of information is particularly damaging since the process for application is often confusing.[38]

Military Service and Veteran's Preference. Military experience offers two advantages to men in access to nontraditional jobs. Familiarity and training in blue collar trades (entry level, semiskilled and skilled) is often acquired while men are in the military service. Far fewer women, of course, benefit from this training. Furthermore, those who serve in the military are often given preference in hiring over women and other nonveterans.[39] Efforts to have veteran's preference rules changed or extended to widows and children of veterans have been unsuccessful.

Lack of Confidence. Lack of confidence in the ability to learn new jobs is a concern raised by many women. Can they do the work?[40] If they have not been exposed to this nontraditional work, then it is likely that they don't know what might be required. In one plant where women have fought very hard to enter a nontraditional job, their own jobs were similar to the men's and they knew they could do the work.[41] Women who have succeeded in nontraditional jobs often report that they had experience or exposure unusual for a woman somewhere in their background. They not only knew that they could do the work, but also that they liked the work.[42] While lack of information and confidence are personal barriers, they are also ones that employers can do something about through recruitment and training programs.

Transfer

Transfer barriers refer to organizational constraints within large industrial plants where women are already employed in two different types of traditionally female jobs: blue collar factory and white collar clerical. Information about barriers for these women is based in large part on my own research, referred to here as the Harbor Case. In 1978 intensive interviews were conducted in one large industrial firm with nineteen women in nontraditional blue collar jobs, seventeen men in these same jobs, and fourteen women in traditional factory and clerical jobs. These interviews were supplemented by twenty-seven interviews with local and international union officials and review of collective bargaining agreements, court cases and related historical information.[43] This work suggests different barriers for traditional blue collar and clerical workers.

Traditional Blue Collar Workers.   Heavy, dirty, manual work does not appear to be a major barrier for many women. As we pointed out earlier, women have been doing manual factory work for a long time. Women in traditionally female factory jobs would seem to be a particularly good source of recruits for traditionally male jobs because they are already performing hard, dirty, factory jobs. One of the worst jobs in the Harbor Case was done by women:[44]

> *The Black Job that was a dirty job. Your hands were in water and kerosene. I use gloves. A lot of girls' hands used to peel; took the skin right off. We had uniforms because the tar would get all over you. And that smell gets in your clothes and never comes out.*

The job was not the first choice of men or women. Like many entry-level male jobs, people did it because of economic need and very limited alternatives. In Wisconsin, Briggs found that women had long been doing dirty, difficult work. Thirty-four of the seventy-eight plants in her survey found women in "unsuitable" working conditions, noisy, dirty, messy, with irregular hours.[45] Manual work is hard, insecure, and a life that many fathers don't want for their sons, much less their daughters. Yet daughters are part of this world and the men's jobs, while difficult, are in many ways better than those traditionally available to women.

Although the work itself may not be a barrier restrictive job-bidding systems that result in loss of pay and seniority are valid immediate barriers for many women. Job posting and upgrading procedures characterized by rigid pay structures and seniority systems, while nondiscriminatory on their face, can have a negative impact on women because of previous discriminatory practices. For example, in the Harbor Case the majority of blue collar women were segregated not only into predominantly female jobs but also into predominantly female plants. Although there was one local union and one company, the women and men worked in physically separate plants manufacturing different products. The company moved people back and forth between plants when they felt it was necessary, but the general policy in effect in 1978 was that people in one plant could not bid on jobs in the other plant. To get a nontraditional job a woman would have to quit her job and take a chance on starting in an entry-level job in the predominantly male plant.

Loss of pay and seniority often result from restrictive bidding procedures or department or plant seniority systems. Starting in an entry-level training position may require a currently employed person to take an immediate loss of pay and seniority. To enter the nontraditional job-training programs in the Harbor Case, women in the predominantly female plant had to give up seniority and take a cut in pay for anywhere from five months to three years. Loss of seniority was an issue also raised by Shaeffer and Lynton, who concluded that "Women with established seniority rights have rarely been willing to give up those rights."[46] Internal movement can have a very high cost despite possible long-term gains.

Clerical Workers. Shaeffer and Lynton found companies reporting the strongest resistance from clerical workers. Companies in this study reported very little success in moving women from clerical to plant jobs, even when the women would not lose seniority and the plant jobs paid more. The Harbor Case raised several factors that may influence clerical workers' decisions not to move to nontraditional jobs.

The first of these factors is the area of benefits. Although improved wages are the focus of much research and discussion about women and nontraditional jobs, benefits beyond wages, like retirement plans, health insurance, and sick leave, must also be taken into account. Clerical jobs, as well as other traditionally female jobs, may have some nonwage benefits that are better than the nontraditional jobs. In the Harbor Case, for example, nontraditional blue collar jobs paid more than clerical jobs, but the clerical jobs had a better leave policy. Women transferring to craft jobs would trade twenty days of sick/personal leave for two days of sick leave. The blue collar workers received only five days sick leave after twenty years of service. Sick leave was a benefit that women with young children were particularly reluctant to give up.

A second factor revolves around layoff and bumping rights. In blue collar jobs, procedures to determine layoffs can be equally as important as procedures for moving up. In the Harbor Case, layoffs were common, and people were bumped out of jobs by seniority within job and then department where the person had experience.

Men reported bumping around into many different jobs during
their first ten years with the company. Thus, they gathered experience and skill to help them move up, but also to help them in time
of layoff when they had to move down. Women in clerical jobs had
seniority but very limited experience. They risked a higher chance
of layoff in the male jobs, with seniority to bump down only in their
clerical jobs. For many clerical women the increased pay was not
sufficient to offset the threat of layoff, although they all wanted and
needed higher pay.

A third problem in trying to move to nontraditional jobs had to do
with past experience. Companies may now have jobs open and
encourage clerical workers to try them. Foremen may now be willing to have women on their crews. On the other hand, women may
very well remember negative experiences of a few months or years
ago. In the Harbor Case several women reported stories of women
being told they couldn't do the job; they "wouldn't want to be there
with all the animals" or "they were not the kind of jobs a girl would
want." Women were asked to lift weights or move equipment that
was not part of anyone's job. Companies are small communities and
news travels fast. Once such stories circulate, it may take strong
efforts and repeated successes for managers to overcome them.

The fourth organizational issue for internal transfer of clerical
workers, and to some extent factory workers, is the structure of the
white collar jobs. Reubens and Reubens refer to this as "vertical
mobility in office settings."[47] Although the focus is more on professional and technical levels, the Harbor Case again provides a very
specific example of mobility within the nonmanagement salaried
classification. The salaried category had a structure in which jobs at
the very top of the classification paid almost as much money as the
most skilled factory jobs and had been done only by men in the
past—for example, production and purchasing control clerks.
Although there were few openings, there was a potential opportunity for jobs that the women had every confidence they could do and
still maintain their benefits. These jobs were the first choice of
several clerical workers. Reubens and Reubens conclude:[48]

*Male intensive occupations in white collar fields offer the same or
superior working environments and conditions and higher earnings,
than the related female intensive occupations. This feature leads to
less conflict over choices than women face at the lower end of the
occupational scale and establishes clearer upward mobility patterns
from female intensive to male intensive occupations.*

On the Job: Satisfaction and Problems

Getting a job or getting into a training program is one thing. Staying on the job and performing adequately is yet another. Current research suggests that women who move to nontraditional blue collar jobs and stay in those jobs enjoy a higher level of job satisfaction than workers in sex-typical jobs, but they have also had to overcome problems. Unfortunately, none of the studies currently available are able to report in any depth on the women who left nontraditional jobs. We have no way of evaluating whether the women who hold these jobs are typical of all the women who have held these jobs. Studies to address this question are unlikely in the future because of the difficulties involved in locating the sample and collecting longitudinal data, which companies fear could provoke more discrimination lawsuits. Thus, the satisfaction and problems discussed here are real but are not all-inclusive.

Women's Job Satisfaction

Women in nontraditional blue collar jobs appear to be satisfied with their jobs and more satisfied than women in traditionally female jobs with pay and the content of the work. While money is an important motive for working in general, and taking blue collar jobs in particular, women cite interest, challenge, skill, and security as important aspects of their nontraditional jobs.

Seventy-five percent of the 73 women in public utility companies interviewed by Meyer and Lee liked their jobs very much or fairly well.[49] The majority of the 56 women in nontraditional workingclass jobs interviewed by Walshok at two different points in time, projected high levels of job satisfaction and described their jobs as complex, interesting and challenging.[50] In Schreiber's study of 100 women and men in one corporation (50 in nontraditional and 50 in traditional jobs) and O'Farrell and Harlan's survey of 338 women in one company (101 in nontraditional and 237 in traditional jobs) women and men in sex-atypical jobs were significantly more satisfied with their jobs than their counterparts in sex-typical jobs.[51]

In Muriel Lederer's book, which encourages women to try blue collar jobs, she states that "working women are looking for challenge, responsibility, promotion opportunity and financial security."[52] Women in nontraditional jobs suggest that they have found these things both in the absolute and comparatively when they look at traditionally female jobs. One woman machinist described her "sense of accomplishment after a hard day's work. . . . I can say to myself 'Hey! I did that.'" For other women "a skill means job security."[53]

The comparison with traditionally female jobs is also important. Women don't take, assess, or keep jobs in a vacuum. They compare current jobs with other jobs in the plant, with other traditionally female jobs, with jobs in other companies, trades, and cities. A woman apprentice described the difference between her former female assembly job and her current machine repair work:[54]

> I had been doing the same thing for so long that I didn't have to use my head anymore. I could do that job with my eyes closed it was so tedious. Now it is something different all the time. It's really interesting and you have to use your head.

Women also compare their jobs to the traditional homemaker role as well as paid work, and Walshok concludes, "Their nontraditional jobs give them more challenge, autonomy and pay than they can find elsewhere."[55] The high levels of satisfaction and diverse reasons, calling on both extrinsic and intrinsic factors of long concern to managers, should be quite encouraging for the women's future in these jobs.

Problems: Hostility, Training, Health and Safety

We also know, however, that even the most successful women face difficulties on the jobs. Three important and related problems facing women in nontraditional jobs include the hostility of male coworkers and foremen, exclusion from important on-the-job training, and health and safety of the work environment. But the findings discussed here suggest that managers can initiate programs and procedures to substantially reduce the problems.

Hostility.   Personnel managers in the Shaeffer and Lynton study report that "the blue collar world is where the sex stereotypes really reside."[56] It is well documented that the first women to enter these jobs face resentment from both coworkers and lower-level managers. The hostility ranges from practical jokes to threats of violence and in some instances actual violence. Meyer and Lee, Walshok, Schreiber, O'Farrell and Harlan all report harassment by coworkers and foremen. They found, however, that harassment was not reported by the majority of women, that it lessens over time, and is then often attributed to a small number of men. These researchers also report that some men are helpful to the women in learning and carrying out the jobs. In Lederer's handbook one woman describes the situation: "You have to prove yourself beyond what any man would have to do on the job. Once you pass the bath of fire, you are generally accepted."[57]

To reduce hostility we must move beyond the labels, however, to the reasons for hostility, which, like women's interest in nontraditional jobs, are affected by the organization as well as the men's personal attitudes and beliefs. In the Harbor Case men's attitudes were explored more fully. The men who expressed general disapproval of women in their jobs were a small group. They felt women belonged at home and were taking jobs away from men. Although this attitude is based in part on men's job-related definitions of their own masculinity, there are at least three other factors that may play a part in male hostility for many more men.

One factor is a general fear of change—anticipation of the unknown. Women and men interviewed in the Harbor Case said that hostility seemed to lessen over time as men worked with women. Men who actually had experience working on the job with women had more positive attitudes toward women in nontraditional jobs than did those who were still in all-male work groups. Meyer and Lee report similar findings but caution that women who were ill-equipped to do the work had a very negative impact, reinforcing all of the old stereotypes.[58]

Qualifications—being able to do the work—is another important concern to the men on the job. If a woman can't do the work it has direct implications for the other workers; they'll have to do more. In the clearest sense it will be seen as unfair. In the Harbor Case, women, both traditional and nontraditional, shared this concern. They all felt it was very important for women to be able to do their "legitimate" share of the work. A woman welder in the case study explained: "I resent it very much when they [women] go on a man's job and they don't do it right. . . . They ruin it for the next girl."[59]

A third reason for hostility is concern for job security. Economist Lester Thurow states that it is easier to lay a worker off in the United States than anywhere else in the world.[60] Plant layoffs were very common for workers in the Harbor Case even though the company was considered one of the best in the area. Anyone with more seniority was unwelcome in a department for it meant the people in that department might lose their jobs. Thus, the women most likely to be able to transfer because of their seniority also face the most resentment because of their seniority. One man described how some of the men felt:[61]

> *I guess the fellows are scared for their jobs. Because if she has more service than them then the next one in line might be worried. There are a few men who strenuously objected to women coming in because the women coming in had more service than they did.*

One man told of turning down a job because he had more service than the other men in the work group. He explained that he didn't like the bitterness that went with the promotion. "They can make your life miserable. So I refused the job."[62]

Another reason for hostility may also have to do with the way in which the women first get the jobs. It appears that those who have to fight very hard—that is, file grievances or go to the federal government—may meet more hostility than women who are offered the jobs and don't have to fight for them. All of these reasons for hostility suggest that women who follow the pioneers will face less hostility. Women are already there proving they can do the job, and the major fight has been won. This does not mean it is easy, however. If there are even a few men left who are resentful, whether they be coworkers or foremen, they can make life unpleasant.

Training.   Learning the job presents several problems that employers can now anticipate. Women still come to jobs with less background than men. Government training has certainly not compensated for women's lack of familiarity with tools from fathers, high school, or the military service. Furthermore, if most or part of the job is learned through on-the-job training from coworkers or foremen, a change will have to be made, at least for the first women. Resentful men will not adequately train women, who then find themselves in a "Catch 22." The men resent them because they can't do the work but the same men also refuse to train them so the women can't learn to do the work. In one company, even though there was extensive formal training, managers and workers estimated that 80 percent of the craft jobs were learned on the job. And while foremen were technically responsible for on-the-job training, it was usually done by coworkers.[63]

Health and Safety.   As more women are hired and hostility begins to lessen, women report more "subtle" problems: having to do the job better than everyone else, being the only woman on a night crew of all men (even if they are friendly), poor lighting and restroom facilities, physically difficult work, and perhaps most difficult, health and safety problems.

Those concerned with quality of work life issues focus in large part on blue collar jobs. Alienation and worker dissatisfaction are closely linked to "blue collar blues." This dissatisfaction is often equated with alcoholism, wildcat strikes, sabotage, and mental health problems for thousands of assembly line workers, to name just a few.[64] These jobs and these workers are the focus of much of the occupational health and safety legislation: brown lung for textile workers, black lung for miners, cancer for asbestos and steelworkers.

Women's awareness of health and safety problems is illustrated in the Harbor Case. The women interviewed seem more likely to see real dangers in some of the blue collar work that men have accepted. (If they complain, however, they may be accused of not being able to do the work.) In contrast to the men, these women were very satisfied with their wages and thought union leaders should give the highest priority to health and safety problems: eye strain, steel chips in eyes, asbestos fibers, noxious fumes. Health and safety issues had been raised most specifically for pregnant women. Men in the plant have lived with these conditions for years, but women may not be as willing to put up with them. Some of these very problems may be keeping other women from even trying these jobs.

Conclusions: New Programs and Procedures

The 1980s will be a time of continued movement for women into traditionally male blue collar jobs. A recent survey projects openings for women in auto mechanics, electrical work, machine operation, plumbing, pipefitting and welding. The Department of Labor foresees no change in the steadily increasing number of women available to enter these jobs into the 1990s.[65]

But the integration of nontraditional blue collar jobs is complex. A woman going into a coal mine, working with molten iron in the foundry of an automobile plant, or picking up the tools of the metal worker or electrician represents a significant change—not only for the woman but for the other men and women with whom she works and lives. This change touches individuals and families, coworkers, and bosses. Established values and norms are contradicted, often painfully so.

Although the blue collar aristocrats—the construction craft workers—earn good wages and like and respect their work, the majority of blue collar jobs that women are trying to enter are more ambiguous.[66] Women's interests and men's reactions must be seen in the context of blue collar work in general—that is, from the perspectives of women and men who currently work in all types of blue collar jobs and from the majority of clerical workers who are married to blue collar workers.[67] "Hard hats—authoritarian, racist and overpaid" is a stereotype not a reality.[68] Much of the work is difficult and insecure, and the majority of blue collar workers fall between the Department of Labor's intermediate budget of $16,236 and the lower budget of $10,041 for a family of four.[69] Yet many of these jobs represent a major improvement for women, and they find help and support among their male coworkers, friends, and families.

My point is that despite the complexities of early socialization and traditional attitudes and/or discrimination, women are interested in nontraditional blue collar jobs. Those who succeed are very satisfied with work that is hard but not harder than many traditionally female jobs. Nontraditional jobs usually pay more, and women report that they are more interesting and challenging. Certainly not all women will choose blue collar work if given the opportunity, but there is sufficient interest and incentive to counter employers' attributing lack of success at integrating jobs to the personal interests of most women. To facilitate the integration of these jobs in an efficient and productive manner, employers can undertake several types of interventions and programs that have developed from the research.

Outreach and Recruitment

Research has shown that traditional recruitment methods designed for young boys and men are not appropriate for attracting women to nontraditional blue collar jobs. Recruitment, both within a company and from a wider community, should provide women with information about job opportunities, what the jobs are like, how to apply, tests required, and advantages beyond pay such as interest, challenge, and skill. This information should include realistic assessments of the difficulties and problems without being self-defeating. Recruiters might effectively use women who have succeeded to encourage other women. Shaeffer suggests four more ways companies can help to provide information:[70]

1. Clear non-technical descriptions of jobs including physical demands, training, support and promotion opportunities
2. Sound slide presentations that show the work environment and explain hours, pay, seniority rules, etc.
3. Walk-through tours of the work area
4. Opportunities to try parts of a job and become familiar with the tools

Job Posting, Bidding, and Seniority

Companies need to carefully assess the impact of current procedures on employees' internal mobility—procedures for job posting and bidding, seniority systems, and benefit plans. Where there is a collective bargaining agreement, the union should be involved in designing plans and programs and bringing equal employment issues to the collective bargaining table. Additional steps to encourage internal transfers include job posting systems, extended probationary periods, and plant or companywide seniority systems. Perhaps most important is the introduction of interim transition programs for women with seniority and proven commitment to the organization so that they do not lose seniority, pay, or benefits to reach longer-term opportunities in skilled blue collar work.

Training

Organizations need to carefully assess how their training is actually accomplished, both formally and informally. They may need to set up some preemployment training and establish more formal on-the-job training. The program should involve hands-on experience as well as classroom training. Perhaps most important, it should be very directly job related. Trainees should be placed with foremen or coworkers carefully selected to be both competent and supportive teachers. The best craftsman may not be the best trainer. As with many other aspects of affirmative action, developing new training programs may very well improve training for all workers. Ultimately training programs that improve skills for both women and men will be most effective. There are few organizations that could not benefit from improved worker training.

While women may need basic training in shop-related areas, men need a different kind of training and support. Men in blue collar jobs face many insecurities and changes in their work and personal lives. They need more information on working women and changing roles to put their situations in a broader perspective. Two specific groups of men, foremen and shop stewards, need much more extensive training on their legal and social roles and responsibilities to help implement affirmative action and ensure equal opportunity. They need to be involved in planning changes from the beginning. They know the jobs and incumbent workers the best, but may well be the last to be informed of changes in hiring, training, and placement procedures. Frustrations may then be focused on the new employees.

Assignments

Initial assignments for the first women to enter nontraditional blue collar jobs are very important. Managers should place women with supportive supervisors, identifying groups that don't have major problems such as work conflicts, job reductions, or many grievances. Managers should also consider placing women in pairs so that one woman is not completely isolated in a job, shift, department, or building. Improved lighting on night shifts and changes in restroom facilities may also be necessary.

Support

Encouraging women to get together for counseling and support once they are on the job should be an ongoing part of an affirmative action program. Emotional strains may continue for some time, and a chance to "air feelings, share problems, and exchange ideas and alternatives for handling tough situations" may be very valuable, especially for the first women.[71]

Independent Recruitment and Training

Special programs to recruit and train women for skilled trades have been effective. Over two hundred independent groups are now training women for nontraditional work in such organizations as Women's Enterprises in Boston, Advocates for Women in San Francisco, and Wider Opportunities for Women in Washington,

D.C.[72] Most of these programs, however, are not directly linked to employers. There are no guarantees of placement or follow-up. According to Kane and Miller, women's placement may have more to do with the "staff capabilities, training, knowledge of apprenticeship, and their relationship with JAC's and employers" than with the individual capabilities of the women.[73]

These programs have valuable experience in recruiting, training, and providing support, which could be adapted to specific locations and employers. They need to be more closely linked to joint apprenticeship councils and employers. Employers should actively seek out these groups to work with them as one of the steel companies in Ullman and Deaux's study had done. These researchers concluded that:[74]

Nearly all of the gains to date in female craft employment in the steel mills have come as a result of nontraditional recruitment and training programs. Most of the increase of female workers in Company A is a result of the outreach and training activities of NPA, a non-profit agency working with Company A to increase female and minority craft employment.

Removing Age Limits

Where upper-age limits exist, they should be eliminated. Where more informal practices focus on hiring young workers, they should be changed to open the horizons to consider workers who are somewhat older and to bring different, often complementary experiences to the job. Recognizing responsibilities for childbearing as a normal interruption in a woman's work life rather than an end that limits her to dead-end, low-paying jobs could greatly enhance women's opportunities to both reenter the work force and change career direction.

In conclusion, women taking jobs in the predominantly male blue collar world must be placed in a broader perspective. Placing women in nontraditional jobs is one strategy for expanding women's opportunities and improving their currently inequitable position in the work force; it is not the only strategy. Programs suggested here must go on simultaneously with efforts to reach equal pay for equal work as well as equal pay for work of comparable value.

All of these problems challenge the management of human resources. Employers have a legal obligation to provide women with equal opportunities in employment. Women have economic, psychological, and social reasons, as well as legal rights, to work in jobs of their choice for good pay. Achieving equal employment opportunity also provides the incentive and the opportunity to reassess the standard ways of doing business and to come up with better recruitment, training, planning, and working conditions for all workers. The necessary changes are gradually occurring. They can be facilitated by responsible programs that benefit men, women, and ultimately the organizations in the 1980s.

Endnotes

1. The focus on management is not meant to exclude the responsibilities of other key actors in this change process. The current and potential roles of women themselves, schools, families, and unions are discussed at length in other publications. For example, the kinds of initiatives such as training and interviewing that women can initiate to get into the current system are detailed by Muriel Lederer in *Blue Collar Jobs for Women: A Complete Guide to Getting Skilled and Getting a High Paying Job in the Trades* (New York: E. P. Dutton, 1979). Pamela Roby reviews the problems and possible alternatives for the vocational education system in "Vocational Education," in Ann F. Cahn, *Women in the U.S. Labor Force* (New York: Praeger Publications, 1979), pp. 203–24. The current and potential role of labor unions in implementing affirmative action for women is described by Ronnie S. Ratner and Alice H. Cook in "Women, Unions and Equal Employment," National Commission on Employment Policy, Washington, D.C., 1980, and by Brigid O'Farrell in "Equal Employment Opportunity, Women and Unions: An Industrial Union Alternative," Final Report, The Upjohn Institute for Employment Research, Kalamazoo, Michigan, 1981.

2. U.S. Department of Labor, Bureau of Labor Statistics, *Employment and Earnings*, Volume 27, No. 12 (Washington, D.C.: U.S. Government Printing Office, December 1980), p. 35.

3. Amitai Etzioni, "A Blue Collar Decade? Semiskilled Workers May Be the New Economic Elite," *The Boston Globe*, Section A-1, August 17, 1980.

4. Fern Schumer, "Getting Women into Men's Jobs," *The Boston Globe*, September 1, 1980, p. 37. Unpublished data from the Bureau of Labor Statistics, U.S. Department of Labor in "National Recruitment Survey," *The New York Times*, Section 12 (October 12, 1980), p. 15.

5. Beatrice G. Reubens and Edwin P. Reubens, "Women Workers, Nontraditional Occupations and Full Employment," in Ann F. Cahn, ed., *Women In the U.S. Labor Force*, 1979, p. 106.

6. Several theories of sex segregation and wage differentials in employment have been developed in the last two decades. For reviews of the literature from several disciplines see Hilda Kahne and A. I. Kohon, "Economic Perspectives on the Roles of Women in the American Economy," *Journal of Economic Literature* (December 1975), pp. 1256–62; Martha Blaxall and Barbara

Reagan, eds., *Women and the Workplace* (Chicago: The University of Chicago Press, 1976); Phyllis A. Wallace and Annette M. LaMond, eds., *Women, Minorities and Employment Discrimination* (Lexington, Mass.: Lexington Books, 1977); Ann H. Stromberg and Shirley Harkness, eds., *Women Working* (Palo Alto, California: Mayfield Publishing Co., 1978); and Jo Freeman, *Women: A Feminist Perspective* (Palo Alto, California: Mayfield Publishing Co., 1977).

7. For a discussion of internal labor market theory and how it relates to women see Mary H. Stevenson, "Internal Labor Markets and the Employment of Women in Complex Organizations" (Working Paper, Wellesley College Center for Research on Women, 1977); and Sally Hillsman Baker, "Women in Blue Collar and Service Occupations" in Ann H. Stromberg and Shirley Harkness, eds., *Women Working*, 1978.

8. Bureau of Labor Statistics, U.S. Department of Labor, *Earnings and Other Characteristics of Organized Workers*, May 1977, Report 566, 1979.

9. The role of unions in apprenticeship and referral and its relationship to discrimination is discussed in William B. Gould, *Black Workers in White Unions: Job Discrimination in the United States* (Ithaca, N.Y.: Cornell University Press, 1977) and Benjamin W. Wolkinson, *Blacks, Unions and the EEOC* (Lexington, Mass.: Lexington Books, 1973).

10. Ronnie S. Ratner and Alice H. Cook, "Women, Unions and Equal Employment," 1980.

11. For a review of black and other minority workers in the construction trades see William B. Gould, *Black Workers in White Unions*, 1977; Robert W. Glover and Ray Marshall, "The Response of Unions in the Construction Industry to Antidiscrimination Efforts," in Leonard J. Hausman, et al., eds., *Equal Rights and Industrial Relations* (Madison Industrial Relations Research Association Services, 1977). The role of unions and employers in the construction industry is further discussed in Brigid O'Farrell, "Equal Employment Opportunity, Women and Unions: An Industrial Alternative," 1981.

12. Research on women in blue collar jobs in general and minority women in particular is very recent. The lack of previous research is well documented by Pamela Roby, *The Conditions of Women in Blue Collar Industrial and Service Jobs: A Review of Research and Proposals for Research Action and Policy* (New York: Russell Sage Foundation, 1974). Research on the vocational training of minority women is presented in Sally H. Baker, "Women in Blue Collar and Service Occupations," 1978, pp. 359–61. For a summary of the black women's working history see Priscilla H. Douglas, "Black Working Women: Factors Affecting Labor Market Experience" (Working Papers, Wellesley College Center for Research on Women, March 1980). Douglas is now carrying out a study of black women factory workers, which will be available late in 1981. She is specifically addressing this question of movement of black women to white collar clerical jobs reported by Beatrice G. Reubens and Edward P. Reubens, "Women Workers, Nontraditional Occupations and Full Employment," in Ann F. Cahn, ed., *Women in the U.S. Labor Force* 1979, pp. 118–19.

13. The overall impact of federal legislation and its limitations has been the subject of much debate. It is generally concluded that three major pieces of legislation and Executive Orders (Title VII of the 1964 Civil Rights Act as amended, the

Equal Pay Act of 1963, and Executive Order 11246) have been important but not sufficient to bring about equal employment opportunity. See Ronnie S. Ratner, ed., *Equal Employment Opportunity Policy for Women: Strategies for Implementation in the United States, Canada and Western Europe* (Philadelphia: Temple University Press, 1980); Ralph E. Smith, ed., *The Subtle Revolution* (Washington, D.C.: The Urban Institute, 1979); and Ann F. Cahn, *Women in the U.S. Labor Force*, 1979.

14. Janet N. Hedges and Stephen Bems, "Sex Stereotyping in the Skilled Trades," *Monthly Labor Review* 97 (May 1974), p. 16.

15. "Women in the Workplace," *Steel Labor* 41 (July 1976), pp. 10–11.

16. June Lasky, "Woman Power: A New force in the Mining Labor Pool," *Engineering and Mining Journal*, reported in *Womanpower*, May 1976.

17. "To Form a More Perfect Union," Report of the National Commission on the Observance of International Women's Year (Washington, D.C.: U.S. Government Printing Office, 1976), pp. 58–59.

18. *Womanpower Newsletter*, April 1976.

19. Herbert Northrup. *The Impact of the AT&T-EEO Consent Decree* (Philadelphia: University of Pennsylvania, Wharton School, 1979).

20. Joseph C. Ullman and Kay K. Deaux, "Recent Efforts to Increase Female Participation in Apprenticeship in the Basic Steel Industry in the Midwest" (Paper presented at the Conference on Apprenticeship Training: Emerging Research and Trends for the 1980s, ETA, U.S. Department of Labor, Washington, D.C., May 1, 1980), p. 1.

21. Beatrice G. Reubens and Edwin P. Reubens, "Women Workers, Nontraditional Occupations and Full Employment," 1979, pp. 113–14.

22. Norma Briggs, "Apprenticeship," in Ann F. Cahn, ed., *Women in the U.S. Labor Force*, 1979, p. 227.

23. Herbert Meyer and Mary D. Lee, *Women in Traditionally Male Jobs: The Experience of Ten Public Utility Companies*, R&D Monograph No. 65, U.S. Department of Labor, ETA (Washington, D.C.: U.S. Government Printing Office, 1978).

24. Ruth G. Shaeffer and Edith F. Lynton, *Corporate Experiences in Improving Women's Job Opportunities*, Conference Board Report No. 755 (New York: The Conference Board, 1979), pp. 67–71.

25. William H. Chafe, *The American Woman* (London: Oxford University Press, 1972), Chapter 6, pp. 35–150.

26. Ibid., Chapter 8, pp. 174–95.

27. See *Federal Register* 42, 158 (Tuesday, August 16, 1977), p. 41379, 41380, for a summary of the effects of goals and timetables in the maritime industry.

28. Roslyn D. Kane and Jill Miller, "Availability of Women for Apprenticeship, Preliminary Findings" (Paper presented at the Conference on Apprenticeship Training: Emerging Research and Trends for the 1980s, ETA, U.S. Department of Labor, Washington, D.C., May 1, 1980), p. 13.

29. Joseph C. Ullman and Kay K. Deaux, "Recent Efforts to Increase Female Participation in Apprenticeship in the Basic Steel Industry in the Midwest," 1980, p. 19.

30. Brigid O'Farrell and Sharon Harlan, "Clerks and Craftworkers: The Effect of Male Coworker Hostility on Women's Satisfaction with Nontraditional Jobs," *Social Problems*, forthcoming, 1981, p. 15.

31. Glover and Marshall outline three reasons why the black community initially targeted the construction trades for affirmative action: (1) the high pay and visibility of skilled trades; (2) the undenied exclusion of minorities and women from these unions; and (3) the resistance of these unions to any change (Glover and Marshall, 1977), p. 121.

32. Joseph Ullman and Kay Deaux, "Recent Efforts to Increase Women's Participation in Apprenticeship in the Basic Steel Industry," 1980, p. 3.

33. An excellent critique of age limits in apprenticeship and their negative effect on women is presented by the League of Women Voters Education Fund in a Petition to Amend 29C.F.R. Part 30 to Prohibit the Use of Maximum Age Limits as Entrance Requirements in Registered Apprenticeship Programs filed with the U.S. Department of Labor, June 4, 1980, and the U.S. Equal Employment Opportunity Commission, December 1980.

34. Nancy Barrett, "Women in the Job Market: Occupations, Earnings and Career Opportunities," in Ralph Smith, *The Subtle Revolution*, 1980.

35. See the League of Women Voters Education Fund Petition and a review of several research studies by O'Farrell, "Women and Blue Collar Work," Industrial Liaison Symposium, MIT, January 1978 (Working Paper, Wellesley College Center for Research on Women, 1978).

36. Women's Bureau, Office of the Secretary, U.S. Department of Labor, *Women's Guide to Apprenticeship*, 1978.

37. In addition to the findings of Briggs (1979), Meyer and Lee (1978), Ullman and Deaux (1980), and Kane and Miller (1980) and Roby (1974, 1980), Harlan reviews the problems for women in CETA programs in enrollment, assignment and outcomes in Sharon Harlan, "Sex Differences in Access to Federal Employment and Training Resources Under CETA: An Overview" (Working Paper, Wellesley College Center for Research on Women, June 1980).

38. Norma Briggs, "Women in Apprenticeship—Why Not?," Manpower Research Monograph No. 33 (Washington, D.C.: U.S. Department of Labor, 1974).

39. For a discussion of military experience and veteran's preference see Brigid O'Farrell, "Affirmative Action for Women in Craft Jobs: Change in the Small Industrial Work Group" (Working Paper, Wellesley College Center for Research on Women, 1977); and Norma Briggs, "Women in Apprenticeship– Why Not?," 1974.

40. Women's concern over their ability to do nontraditional work is reported in three studies: Meyer and Lee, "Women in Traditionally Male Jobs," 1978; Carol Schreiber, *Changing Places* (Cambridge, Mass.: The MIT Press, 1979); and Brigid O'Farrell, *Women in Nontraditional Blue Collar Jobs: A Case Study of Local I*, Final Report, Research and Development Grant No. 21-25-78-21, U.S. Department of Labor, ETA (Washington, D.C.: U.S. Government Printing Office, 1980).

41. Brigid O'Farrell, *Women in Nontraditional Blue Collar Jobs*, 1980, pp. 37–47.

42. Mary L. Walshok, "Factors Affecting Success for Women in Skilled Blue Collar Jobs" (Paper presented at the Annual Meeting of the Society for the Study of Social Problems, Boston, 1979).

43. Brigid O'Farrell, *Women in Nontraditional Blue Collar Jobs*, 1980.

44. Ibid., p. 76.

45. Norma Briggs, "Apprenticeship" in Ann F. Cahn, ed., *Women in the U.S. Labor Force*, 1979, p. 227.

46. Ruth Shaeffer and Edith Lynton, "Corporate Experiences in Improving Women's Job Opportunities," 1979, p. 71.
47. Beatrice Reubens and Edwin Reubens, "Women Workers, Nontraditional Occupations and Full Employment," in Ann F. Chan, ed., *Women in the U.S. Labor Force*, 1979, p. 120.
48. Ibid.
49. Herbert Meyer and Mary D. Lee, "Women in Traditionally Male Jobs," 1978, p. 31.
50. Mary Walshok, "Occupational Values and Family Roles: A Descriptive Study of Women Working in Blue Collar and Service Occupations," *The Urban and Social Change Review* 11, 1, 2 (1978), pp. 16–18.
51. Brigid O'Farrell and Sharon Harlan, "Craftworkers and Clerks," 1980, pp. 9–11.
52. Muriel Lederer, *Blue Collar Jobs for Women*, 1979, p. 4.
53. Brigid O'Farrell, *Women in Nontraditional Blue Collar Jobs*, 1980, p. 39.
54. Ibid.
55. Mary Walshok, "Occupational Value and Family Roles," 1978, p. 18.
56. Ruth Shaeffer and Edith Lynton, "Corporate Experiences in Improving Women's Job Opportunities," 1979, p. 67.
57. Muriel Lederer, *Blue Collar Jobs for Women*, 1979, p. 5.
58. Herbert Meyer and Mary D. Lee, "Women in Traditionally Male Jobs," 1978, pp. 10–11.
59. Brigid O'Farrell, *Women in Nontraditional Blue Collar Jobs*, 1980, p. 41.
60. Lester C. Thurow, *The Zero-Sum Society* (New York: Basic Books, Inc., 1980), p. 7.
61. Brigid O'Farrell, "Women in Nontraditional Blue Collar Jobs," 1980, p. 99.
62. Ibid., p. 100.
63. Brigid O'Farrell, "Affirmative Action for Women in Craft Jobs," 1977.
64. *Work in America*, Report of a Special Task Force to the Secretary of Health, Education and Welfare (Cambridge: The MIT Press, 1972), p. 29.
65. *Handbook of Labor Statistics–1978*, Bureau of Labor Statistics, U.S. Department of Labor (Washington, D.C.: U.S. Government Printing Office, 1979), p. 486.
66. E. E. LeMasters, *Blue Collar Aristocrats* (Madison: University of Wisconsin Press, 1971).
67. Andrew Levinson, *The Working Class Majority* (New York: Coward, McCann and Geoghegan, Inc., 1974), p. 29.
68. *Work in America*, 1972, pp. 34–35.
69. *Employment Perspectives–Working Women*, Bureau of Labor Statistics, U.S. Department of Labor, Report No. 551, No. 4, 1978.
70. Ruth Shaeffer and Edith Lynton, "Corporate Experiences in Improving Women's Job Opportunities," 1979, p. 69.
71. Herbert Meyer and Mary Lee, "Women in Traditionally Male Jobs," 1978, p. 120.
72. The Directory of Nontraditional Occupations (NTO) Programs for Women was sent to the author by Jo Shuchat, Project Director, Women's Outreach Project, Technical Education Research Centers, Cambridge, Mass., December 1980.

73. Roslyn Kane and Jill Miller, "Availability of Women for Apprenticeship," 1980, p. 13.
74. Joseph Ullman and Kay Deaux, "Recent Efforts to Increase Women's Participation in Apprenticeship in the Basic Steel Industry," 1980, p. 20.

Chapter 7

CORPORATE EXPERIENCES IN IMPROVING WOMEN'S JOB OPPORTUNITIES

by Ruth Gilbert Shaeffer and Edith F. Lynton

There has been measurable improvement in the job opportunities being provided to women, so it seems worthwhile to examine the nature of the change efforts that very large companies have undertaken—and also to consider their views of what has helped or hindered the success of these efforts thus far. The following findings are based (1) on the responses of 265 very large corporations to a Conference Board survey questionnaire in late 1976 and (2) on nearly 200 follow-up telephone interviews or on-site visits, spread both by industry and by geographic area, during 1976–1977. These findings do, therefore, represent the experience-based opinions of a much larger number of companies than provided us with matched 1970 and 1975 employment statistics. Even so, the views expressed are not necessarily typical of all very large U.S. corporations.

The Focus of the Efforts

Most of the companies report it has been necessary to try to increase the representation of women in at least some of the jobs in all of their EEO-1 job categories—except for the office and clerical

This chapter is reprinted with permission of The Conference Board from Report 755 by Ruth G. Shaeffer and Edith F. Lynton, *Corporate Experiences in Improving Women's Job Opportunities* (New York, The Conference Board, 1979).

category.[1] However, the greatest emphasis is clearly being given to improving the opportunities for women as officials and managers and as professionals (especially in male-intensive industries). A limited number of companies say that the greatest stress is being given to certain kinds of sales jobs. But very few of the companies employing blue collar workers say they have been placing their greatest emphasis on increasing the overall representation of women in such jobs, whether at the entry, semiskilled, or skilled-craft level.[2]

Among the reasons commonly offered for this heavy emphasis on the higher-level white collar jobs are: the greater availability of qualified, willing candidates both internally and externally; the restricted availability of blue collar job openings; the higher visibility of the managerial or professional jobs; the importance of providing female role models at higher organizational levels in order to encourage women at lower levels to try to move up, too; the fact that these are the entry jobs for recent female college graduates, who are likely to move on up in management; the greater control exerted by the headquarters personnel group with respect to these jobs; the need for the whole headquarters unit to take a leadership role so that it can then insist on other units following suit; pressure from compliance review officers; and (especially from some companies in male-intensive industries) the fact that these categories are likely to be the most difficult ones in which to make progress.

Even though the greatest emphasis has clearly been placed on only two particular occupational categories, it should not be assumed that most companies have set up special programs to hire, train, or otherwise help to prepare *women* to move into these jobs. The clearest and most important finding with respect to how major companies are going about increasing the representation of women at these organizational levels is that they are relying on working through the organization's basic staffing processes for filling individual job openings and not primarily on special programming.

The problem of increasing the higher-level job opportunities being provided to women (and to minorities as well) is generally being addressed as a problem that the whole organization must solve and not as one that can be delegated to the personnel department. Such staff specialists are obviously playing important supporting and assisting roles in the overall process—including devising many broad-scale improvements in corporate personnel procedures, policies, and practices that have the effect of opening up more opportunities for women when they are applied evenhandedly to all individuals, regardless of sex. But in most of the companies, at these levels it is the line managers who are expected to implement the organization's staffing processes and who are being held accountable for making sure that appropriate results for women are actually achieved. Moreover, it is generally not merely the lower or middle levels of line management that are being expected to take appropriate action. Top management is very much involved, especially in the more successful efforts. Interrelated goals and timetables are being established for improving the representation of women on jobs where they are underutilized at all higher organizational levels—taking realistic account of the expected staffing flows, of the genuine qualifications required to perform the various jobs, and of the maximum present and probable future availability of appropriately qualified women, assuming significant employer effort.

This is, of course, essentially what is called for under the Executive Order, but the scope of the planning being done is much larger than the regulations require. That is, the planning is being done on an interrelated basis for *the whole organization*, not merely for each separate establishment. Thus, far from considering a "goals and timetables" approach as a meaningless paperwork exercise needed to satisfy government reporting regulations, most of the companies now say goals and timetables are being used as corporatewide planning and control tools with respect to the appropriate utilization of human resources, especially at the managerial and professional levels.

The fulfillment of these plans is regarded as just as much a part of each line manager's job as any other aspect of managing a work unit. Indeed, some companies note that they have found meeting EEO goals and timetables to be one of the key indicators likely to distinguish good line managers from less successful ones. Thus, those who are constructively and successfully assisting the organization to meet its EEO challenge are reported to be among those most likely to benefit substantially from their managerial performance, both in terms of bonuses and salary increases and also in terms of further promotions—even though from now on a larger share of all such promotions will probably be going to qualified women and minorities.

Consistent evidence was found throughout the interviews and the responses to the questionnaire that the majority of the companies taking part in The Conference Board survey—especially the largest ones—are convinced that an overall management-by-objectives approach to human-resource utilization is the most appropriate response to the EEO challenge their organizations face under federal laws and regulations. This chapter first considers some of the overall perceptions and opinions companies have drawn from their experiences to date; then subsequent sections describe some of the constants as well as some of the changes in basic staffing processes and report in more detail on some of the successful and unsuccessful experiences companies have had in moving more women into managerial and professional roles.

Factors Contributing to the Overall Success of the Company's Efforts

Those responding to the questionnaire were presented with a "laundry list" of twenty-three factors (plus room to add more) and were asked to number from one to ten those they considered to have made the greatest contribution to the overall success of their company's efforts. The order of responses, when combined in appropriately weighted form, is as follows:

1. Awareness of federal laws and regulations;
2. Commitment on the part of the chief executive officer;
3. Establishment of goals and timetables for action;
4. Development of an equal employment opportunity policy;
5. Analyses of the company's utilization of women;
6. Awareness of large backpay awards in class-action suits;
7. Monitoring of EEO results against plans;
8. Dissemination of the EEO policy;
9. Identification of special problem areas in utilizing women; and
10. Changes in personnel practices or special programs to improve opportunities for women.

The order of the first three items on the list is very clear-cut. It is noteworthy that changes in personnel practices and special programming for women barely made the "top ten" list. And, although the general goals and timetables approach called for under the Executive Order received high marks, the risk of losing government contracts and rigorous compliance reviews as a government contractor both received scant mention, while the risk of a Title VII class-action suit was perceived as very real. (Under this law individuals, as well as the EEOC itself, can bring class-action lawsuits that may require backpay for large groups of employees.) On the other hand, relatively few companies reported that an actual complaint, investigation, or lawsuit alleging sex discrimination had had special importance in spurring their efforts to improve job opportunities for women. An even smaller number reported that the formation of a women's caucus or council within the company—or pressure from an outside women's group—had made a significant difference.

One of the personnel executives interviewed summed up the situation this way:

> *It may seem surprising in these days of Watergate, bribery scandals, and whatnot, but I really do believe that most large U.S. corporations try very hard to be law-abiding citizens. EEO was an area where it took us a while to understand what the law really meant, but those class-action lawsuits proved very effective teachers. And, when the light finally dawned, we really went to work on it. Besides, we now realize that it makes darn good sense.*
>
> *How do you go about achieving EEO results in a company? The same way you achieve any other results. You analyze the problem carefully, determine what you need to do, and then set up an overall management planning and control system to make very sure it happens—and on schedule.*

The Importance of a Results-Oriented Management Planning and Control System

Prior survey research on the changing nature of the corporate personnel function had already indicated that centralized planning and monitoring systems were being developed with respect to EEO matters.[3] Moreover, during the pilot study for this research, a number of companies reported that the single most successful action their organizations had taken to equalize job opportunities for women and minorities was to set up an overall, results-oriented management planning and control system in order to ensure that the achievement of this objective received appropriate attention at all levels of the organization on an ongoing basis.

To test the current prevalence and perceived effectiveness of such a corporate approach, the companies participating in the full-scale survey were asked their reactions to it, based on their own experiences. About two thirds of the companies said they rely on such an *overall* management system in the EEO area and the vast majority ascribe important positive value to it. Indeed fully one third of the corporations utilizing such an approach say it is the single most successful action regarding EEO matters their companies have ever taken. Companies with huge numbers of employees give especially high marks to this kind of overall EEO management system. There appears to be least experience with this approach in the transportation industry, among gas and electric utilities, and in retailing.

Profiles of Successful and Disappointing Experiences

Companies were asked to describe in considerable detail one of their more successful experiences in improving job opportunities for women. It could be a broad effort or a limited program; the only stipulation was that it must have been in actual operation long enough for them to be able to evaluate its success. Then, in an exactly parallel format, they were asked to describe a disappointing experience. This device permitted comparison of the profiles of the two sets of experiences, sometimes holding constant some characteristic such as the nature of the jobs being filled.

All told, 195 successful experiences and 106 disappointing experiences were reported, with more than three fourths of each group of experiences reported as beginning in 1973 or later. While it relates only to the examples the companies chose to report and not to the whole of their efforts on behalf of women, this information about timing does tend to confirm that significantly greater corporate action followed the AT&T consent decree.

The proportions of the success stories dealing with the various EEO-1 job categories are shown in Table 7–1.

This information not only confirmed the emphasis reportedly being given to higher-level white collar occupations, but is also in conformity with other available information about the general nature of corporate staffing efforts.[4]

By contrast, the disappointing experiences that were reported tend to be much more evenly spread across the various EEO-1 job categories, with much lower proportions of them dealing with the

Table 7-1 Proportion of Successful Job-Improvement Experiences, by Job Category

Job Categories	Percentage of Success Stories
Officials and managers	52%
Professionals (with a substantial number of the reports also dealing with the managerial category)	48
Technicians (with a substantial number of the reports also dealing with both the professional and managerial categories)	20
Sales workers	20
Office and clerical workers	7
Skilled craft workers	9
Semiskilled operatives	10
Unskilled laborers	9
White collar trainees (especially in banks and insurance companies)	9
Production trainees	1

officials-and-managers category (29 percent), professionals (25 percent), technicians (8 percent), and sales workers (11 percent); and much higher proportions dealing with blue collar jobs (skilled crafts—24 percent; semiskilled operatives—22 percent; unskilled laborers—17 percent).

Some of the success stories dealing with blue collar jobs involve unionized employees; a much larger proportion of the disappointing experiences do. But the total number of reports is so limited and there are so many other factors, such as the recession, influencing the situation that it seems inappropriate to generalize on this point.

Differences in Staffing Strategies

There is a major distinction between the general staffing strategies followed in the successful instances and the disappointing ones:

	Successful Experiences	Disappointing Experiences
Bringing in women as new employees	24%	44%
Upgrading, transfering or promoting present female employees	29	26
Both	44	20
Other or no answer	3	10

This difference holds true even when the kinds of jobs being filled are held constant. The fact that the emphasis is much more likely to be on *both* initial hiring and internal movement of women in the successful cases again seems to signal reliance on an ongoing, managed process rather than on special programming.

Differences in Staffing Activities

The questionnaire provided a list of twenty-four different kinds of activities that might be part of an effort to improve women's job opportunities, and space to add others. Companies could indicate which ones were part of each successful or disappointing experience. As a separate item, they could also indicate which activities were crucial to that experience. Many of the listed activities, such as recruiting, selection and job-related training and development, tend to be mentioned with about equal frequency in the success stories and in the disappointing stories. A few of the activities are not only much more likely to be mentioned in the success stories, but are also much more likely to be regarded as crucial to such experiences. No matter what kinds of jobs are involved, these three activities are more often associated with success than with failure:

1. Job analysis;
2. Career planning or pathing; and
3. Special preparation of supervisors and managers.

In the successful experiences dealing with white collar jobs, there is also somewhat greater use of job posting and self-nomination procedures, especially in the female-intensive industries, and greater likelihood that attention is being given to both monitoring and feeding back the results being achieved to the line managers. For blue collar jobs, job posting has not proven as successful, and serious difficulties are apparently being encountered with external recruiting, too.

Follow-up interviews indicate that the supervisory preparation noted in so many successful efforts is most likely to deal with the organization's overall EEO obligations and with the basic responsibility of line managers for achieving EEO results. It often includes some guidance with respect to interviewing and evaluating female candidates' qualifications and subsequent job performance fairly. Only in rare instances does it deal with matters of female psychology. Indeed, there are experience-based warnings that this kind of emphasis can easily backfire unless it is handled by specially qualified experts. Problems have also been encountered with "consciousness-raising" sessions for male managers, which did not take place within the authority structure of the organization and did not offer them a constructive way to release any anxiety generated—for example, by enlisting their active cooperation in helping the organization to meet its EEO challenge.

Differences in Who Has Been Involved

The questionnaire also provided an opportunity for companies to indicate what individuals or groups were involved in various aspects of the successful and disappointing experiences. Once again there is much overlap in what is being reported. But even when the kinds of jobs being filled are held constant, the following are more often found in the successful experiences:

1. Top management and the personnel executive (not merely personnel staff members) are more likely to be crucially involved in initially planning and organizing the effort.
2. Top management and the personnel executive are more likely to be crucially involved in providing ongoing advice or counsel.
3. Line managers are more likely to be involved in carrying out the activities. But for professional jobs, the personnel staff is also likely to have a major role in college recruiting.
4. The personnel executive (not merely personnel staff members) is more likely to be officially monitoring the results.
5. Top management is more likely to be receiving feedback of the results.
6. Top management, line managers, and the personnel executive are all more likely to have the assigned accountability for the success of the effort. (In successful blue-collar efforts, members of the local personnel staff rather than corporate personnel staff members are likely to be among those being held accountable).

In short, regardless of the kind of jobs being filled, the successful experiences reported are clearly more likely to be part of a corporatewide managed effort than are the disappointing experiences. However, because a much larger proportion of the successful experiences than of the disappointing experiences deal with improving the job opportunities for women in the officials-and-managers and professional job categories, this finding may also indicate that few of the surveyed companies have as yet extended their *overall* corporate human resource planning and control systems to cover all the EEO-1 job categories. Indeed, many of these organizations may not yet have the kind of computer-based information system covering all their U.S. employees that is needed to do this.

Turning Disappointing Experiences into More Successful Ones

A considerable number of companies say that several of their experiences with moving women into better jobs initially seemed quite disappointing but that, by adopting a problem-solving approach, they have often been able to turn such situations around and make them more successful. Usually this has required having an affirmative action officer or other personnel staff member discuss the situation separately with the individual manager and the individual employee. But sometimes it has also proved necessary to bring the two together to discuss how each views the problem and then jointly to seek solutions with staff assistance. Indeed, sometimes it has proved important and useful to bring groups of managers and groups of female employees together to find out what is really going on and what practical solutions can be devised. Companies note that this approach has the advantage of making the discussions more impersonal.

A few companies in female-intensive industries say they have established a forum for an ongoing dialogue between top management and women who work for the company by instituting a women's council, typically with rotating membership, that meets periodically to exchange views with key executives. And many companies in both male-intensive and female-intensive industries say they have arranged group meetings between managers and some or all of the women who report to them to deal with specific problem situations on an ad hoc basis.

For example, one insurance company reported that, because the sales results of women were not turning out to be equivalent to those of men, a series of meetings between district sales managers and some of the women sales representatives was arranged, with members of the corporate personnel staff facilitating a problem-solving approach.

Early in the meetings it was established that many of the women had previously worked in the company's regional or district sales offices doing clerical or supervisory work. Because they already knew most of the "lingo" used to describe the company's products, the sales managers had assumed they did not need full product-knowledge training—or even training in selling skills.

During the meetings it became increasingly obvious—even to the district sales managers—that they had not been regarding the women as part of the "regular" sales force. They were considered to be in some "special" category of sales employees that did not need, or merit, the same managerial consideration and assistance given to the men, who were thought of as making up the "regular" sales force. In fact, the district managers had not even bothered to be careful to select only *qualified* women.

By the end of the series of meetings, the district sales managers had agreed

1. To consider all women as well as all men chosen for this job to be "regular" sales representatives.
2. To improve their selection interviewing of all candidates. This meant they would be sure to cover all matters clearly relevant to job performance—such as availability to work evenings and weekends—but they would avoid asking women such sexist questions as "Did your husband say it was OK for you to work those hours?" or "Who is going to stay home with your children?" It also meant that, in order to gather all relevant information concerning the personal characteristics known to be related to insurance sales success for both men and women, they would explain the nature of the job and offer all candidates the opportunity to discuss any of their previous life experiences, not just their paid work experiences, that might have called for skills and interests similar to those needed for job success.
3. To provide all persons selected, even those with some product knowledge because of their previous inside sales office experience, with the full sales training that company policy specified for new sales representatives.
4. To equalize the financial backing available to all sales representatives.
5. To provide equal supervisory support, especially in the areas of prospecting for customers and closing sales.

6. To expect women to achieve the same sales results expected of men of comparable status.
7. To meet with all their sales representatives to explain the new, uniform ground rules.

The women attending the meetings, in turn, had agreed:

1. To apply the standard approaches to selling to customers' needs that they would be taught.
2. To *ask* for advice and help from their managers whenever they felt it might be beneficial.
3. To alert their managers whenever they felt they were being unfairly excluded or overlooked.
4. To encourage all sales representatives, especially the other women, to follow a similar course of action.

Top management has been monitoring the situation closely and the national and regional sales managers keep focusing attention on the matter during regular management meetings. The sales volume achieved by women has already improved considerably, although, of course, not all of the individual women have been able to make the grade. But, then, not all the men do either.

Similar leveling-up experiences based on a problem-solving approach are reported by other companies. Some have also learned that it makes sense to invest some *extra* time and effort in organizational support for women when they are moving into especially hostile or nonreceptive environments. A company selling highly sophisticated business products encouraged its female and minority sales representatives to discuss with management some of the problems they were encountering in the field. In this case the problems centered on the difficulty some customers had in believing that these "unusual" sales representatives really knew what they were talking about. Extra emphasis on readily expressed product knowledge coupled with role-playing rehearsals of various kinds of interactions with customers served to build the self-confidence of these relatively inexperienced sales representatives and to help them to make their competence more evident to their customers.

The improvements in sales results have been gratifying and have more than justified management's patience. The division sales manager commented: "It would have been most unfair for us to blame the women and the minority representatives for their customers' initial uncertainty about them. A little extra time and effort were plainly needed. By now everyone agrees they really know their business.

Sales is a field in which success breeds success, so we don't anticipate further problems."

Other Aspects of Corporate Efforts

Two additional aspects of corporate efforts on behalf of women were
briefly explored during the study: the range of strategies being used
to increase or maintain the representation of women in different job
categories; and the joint or cooperative efforts being undertaken
with other organizations to increase the supply of qualified women.
On both issues the responses were much greater with respect to the
managerial and professional job categories, further highlighting the
great unevenness of corporate efforts to date—at least as they are
known at corporate headquarters.

For these job levels, almost all of the companies affirmed their
primary reliance on the two most obvious strategies for increasing
the representation of women—hiring more women directly into the
jobs or else upgrading, transfering, or promoting more women into
them. But a considerable number of companies also noted some use
of other approaches. Among those mentioned most frequently
were:

1. Retaining women who previously would have been terminated. For example, companies are now providing maternity
   leaves as an alternative to termination and are encouraging
   women who marry to continue working.
2. Reevaluating existing jobs and combining titles or classifications. For example, companies have reclassified some of their
   executive secretaries as administrative assistants. Also, some
   companies noted that, in order to match the definitions used
   by the Census, some clerical supervisors have been reclassified as managers.
3. Rehiring women who had terminated their employment. For
   example, companies are encouraging managerial and professional women who left to marry or to have children to come
   back to work.

Most of the companies needing to increase the representation of
women in their higher-level white collar jobs also report undertak-
ing some joint or cooperative efforts to increase the available supply
of qualified women. Collaboration with four-year colleges and uni-

versities and contacts with professional associations are most frequently mentioned.

General Opinions About Corporate Efforts to Improve Job Opportunities

Given the results-oriented thrust of the legal challenge they face, most of the very large companies responding to the survey are understandably cautious in describing their overall success in improving job opportunities for women. Many say their efforts have been somewhat successful (45 percent) or have yielded a mixed bag in terms of success (24 percent, many of them companies from male-intensive industries). Only 10 percent consider their efforts very successful, and only 6 percent say they have been either somewhat or very unsuccessful. An additional 8 percent indicate it is too early to tell—while some regard their effort as too complex to be evaluated yet, others candidly admit little effort has yet been made. Seven percent did not report on the success of their efforts.

The most common comment with respect to the overall success of their corporate efforts is that, although there already is improvement in the company's overall EEO-1 statistics, a considerably longer period of time will be required to achieve good representation of women at the higher levels of responsibility. In some cases this is attributed to legitimate job experience requirements or to the lack of personnel turnover at higher organization levels, but some respondents also note that it will take time to break down the "typical stereotyped negative attitudes" male managers have about women. On the other hand, a number of the companies say that many more women are being promoted to much higher-level jobs than ever before in the company's history. The most common explanations regarding any overall lack of success deal with the effect of the recession and the lack of qualified female candidates for engineering jobs or for "physical labor" jobs.

Four out of five of the companies volunteered that they have gained some important benefits from their efforts to improve the job opportunities they provide to women. As Table 7–2 indicates, most companies noted benefits that go far beyond complying with governmental laws and regulations. Their comments most frequently center on more appropriate human resource utilization and changed employee attitudes, but there is also mention of improved personnel policies and practices, changed management perceptions, and

Table 7–2 Primary Benefits to the Company from Efforts to Improve Job Opportunities for Women

Comments from Companies	In Female-Intensive Industries	In Male-Intensive Industries
More Appropriate Human Resource Utilization		
Better utilization of the talents available within the organization	28%	12%
Women constitute a previously untapped source of competent employees for many jobs	19	33
Better talent employed or promoted when women compete with men for positions	10	2
Women have proved effective, high caliber, successful employees; productivity is good	8	4
Economics due to promoting from within compared with hiring	3	—
Lower turnover	—	3
Other	2	1
Changed Employee Attitudes		
Improved morale, especially among the women	13	8
Improved morale of all employees	2	—
Greater motivation to improve performance and prepare for promotion; having successful role models has encouraged others to try	7	6
More confidence in personnel function; greater credibility due to correcting past inequities	1	3
Other	1	2
Improved Compliance Posture		
Reduced chance of lawsuits	6	11
Better EEO statistics	4	—
Successful compliance reviews; retained contracts	7	3
Other	1	1

Table 7-2 (continued)

Comments from Companies	In Female-Intensive Industries	In Male-Intensive Industries
Improved Personnel Policies and Practices		
More open, objective personnel practices for all	—	5
Greater internal movement; more emphasis on training and development; more emphasis on career planning and counseling	3	3
Changed Management Perceptions		
Myths about "women's work" dispelled; awareness of women's potential for high-ranking positions	5	3
A learning process regarding personnel function	1	1
Improved Community Relations		
Community approval of efforts	3	3
Appropriate response to social change and needs	—	2
Other	1	1
Total number of companies	(107)	(158)

improved community relations. The following quotation captures the flavor of many of the comments:

> *As a corporate program, there has been an overall upgrading of the work force. Objective criteria for employment decisions have become practice, hence all persons are considered for positions on the basis of merit. Previously untapped human resources are now available. Healthy competition for advancement exists. Legal pressures from the compliance agency have been relieved.*

Some of the companies said they have been especially surprised by the remarkably competent performance of women on some nontraditional jobs and also by the rapid acceleration in the number of women expressing interest in career opportunities—and willing to put the time and effort into enhancing their qualifications to advance—once there were a few successful role models. One commentator may have mixed his similes and metaphors a bit, but he certainly got the point across when he wrote: "Getting started was like trying to move a dead elephant with a toothpick. But those first few women were so darned competent they uncorked the whole system."

Generally speaking, companies volunteered far fewer negatives about their efforts to improve job opportunities for women. Twenty-eight percent did not respond at all and, as Table 7–3 shows, among those who did, the most common comment was "None." Some did say there had been a negative reaction from some male employees, but they also indicated it had certainly not been an overwhelming problem. Lack of interest on the part of women in the proferred job opportunities was viewed as a special problem by companies in male-intensive industries; there were also complaints about high recruiting and training costs from these industries. Higher turnover was apparently a problem on some nontraditional jobs. This led to unexpected frustration on the part of line managers when they could not maintain the EEO results they thought they had achieved. The recession, with its massive layoffs based on seniority in some blue collar jobs, also produced some unexpected pitfalls.

The Impact on the Organization

Most of the companies report that equal employment opportunity considerations (for minorities as well as women) have had real impact on their personnel policies and practices. Thirty-nine percent say this impact has been very significant, and an additional 36 per-

Table 7-3 Primary Disadvantages to the Company from Efforts to Improve Job Opportunities for Women

Comments from Companies	In Female-Intensive Industries	In Male-Intensive Industries
None	12%	8%
Male Employee Reactions		
Some believe "reverse discrimination" has occurred	11	—
Resentment by those expecting promotions	4	7
Resistance; difficult to overcome stereotypes	4	6
Other	4	1
Female Employee and Applicant Reactions		
Lack of interest among present female employees	—	6
Lack of qualified applicants	1	3
Some employees have unrealistic aspirations	2	2
Unwillingness of women to move	3	2
Disbelief or disillusionment due to slow progress	—	2
Other	1	1

Table 7-3 (continued)

Comments from Companies	In Female-Intensive Industries	In Male-Intensive Industries
Costs and Personnel Turnover		
Increased recruiting and training costs	3	6
Higher turnover on some nontraditional jobs	6	3
Increased operating or facilities costs	—	2
High costs of paperwork, controls, administration	3	2
Considerable effort for small results	—	2
Other	1	1
Management Problems		
Improper selection of women for some jobs	1	3
Failure to support women who were promoted encouraged their failure	2	1
Top management slow to accept idea; tokenism	3	1
Other	1	1
Community Reactions		
Adverse publicity	—	1
Total number of companies	(107)	(158)

cent categorize the impact as moderate. Only 14 percent say the
impact has been slight or unimportant, while 11 percent say it is too
early to tell or do not answer.

Generally speaking, the comments suggest that, due to EEO
concerns, thoroughgoing reviews and reassessments of personnel
policies and practices have been undertaken resulting in:

1. The modification or elimination of many outmoded or unnecessary procedures and practices;
2. The introduction of new procedures and practices, especially
   with respect to the recruiting of college graduates and also to
   the operation of the internal labor market;
3. The standardization and wider dissemination of information
   about all personnel procedures, policies and practices;
4. Centralized planning, monitoring and control of the impact
   of these procedures, policies and practices on a quantitative
   basis, at least for managerial and professional employees.

There is considerably greater stress on the consistent application
of clearly defined personnel policies, including the equal employment opportunity policy, and much greater attention to appropriate
personnel record keeping, not only with respect to individuals but
also with respect to the various groups protected by law. In most
cases the companies indicate these changes have been of real value
to all company employees—not just to minorities and women—
and also to management.

At the same time, the workload of the personnel department has
increased very significantly, and the nature of its relationship to the
rest of the organization has changed. Comments such as these indicate the scope of the challenge the EEO effort has posed:

"EEO considerations have broadly resulted in a more purposeful
and professional personnel practice."
"EEO requires more management capability both within the per-
sonnel department and throughout the organization."
"EEO is a good management tool."
"EEO is now one of three corporate goals."

Of course, not all companies view the EEO challenge quite so
favorably. Most real dissenters probably did not respond to the
questionnaire at all, but this partially dissenting view was expressed
by a major company in a male-intensive industry: "Government has
forced a structural system of employment practices on the private

sector. Although there are some benefits, implementation has been costly and disruptive."

Advice on Avoiding Problems

The following guidance was offered to senior personnel executives with respect to how to help their companies avoid unnecessary problems in this area:

1. Clear-cut top management commitment and continuing active, strong support are essential.
2. Proper organization of the effort is crucial. Insist on line and staff involvement and accountability from top to bottom.
3. A managed, overall accountability system is necessary.
4. Emphasize quality; tell managers they must expect a good job and a full job from both women and men.
5. Be realistic and recognize that you must take action *now*. Do it voluntarily or your company will be in for a tough time.
6. Develop a long-term approach, not a short-run "crash" solution. Be sure to think through the potential problems that may occur, for their effects may prove hard to overcome.
7. Make sure the first woman in a nontraditional area is very competent and will be a strong role model. A failure is very hard to overcome.
8. Explain the effort to everyone and enlist their active cooperation.
9. Expect and overcome male-manager resistance.
10. Encourage the women to think through their own career goals and how the company can help them to achieve them.

Some Experiences with Improving Women's Opportunities in Managerial and Professional Jobs

Out of the total of 195 examples of successful experiences in improving job opportunities for women, 102 deal with the officials and managers category. But only 37 focus exclusively on officials and managers; the other 65 also cover professional employees. Similarly, there are 94 examples that deal with professional employees. Beyond the 65 that cover the officials and managers category, too, there are also 29 that deal exclusively with professionals. Thus, two-thirds of all the successful experiences reported relate to those two job categories, and many relate to *both* of them.

Generally speaking, there are two kinds of jobs at the lowest levels of the management hierarchies in business organizations. Some of the jobs are for first-line supervisors; but many more are for "individual contributors"—staff specialists such as assistant engineers or beginning market analysts. These individual contributors are usually college graduates and some of them, especially those with technical degrees, are likely to be considered professional employees. But most will simply be considered relatively low-level administrators or managers.

In the early stages of a company's efforts to increase the representation of women in both the professional and managerial categories, most of the women will be employed as individual contributors. Any substantial movement of more women into the higher echelons of management—where the managers of managers are— is likely to occur several years later, for in very large companies almost all of these key managerial jobs are traditionally filled by promotion from the lower-level professional or managerial ranks. Very little is known about moving sizable numbers of women into higher managerial levels; thus far, only exceptional individual women have "made it."

Most of the success stories companies provided deal with increasing the number of women who were individual contributors. Only a few focused on bringing more women into first-line supervisory roles in plants and in retail stores, and an even smaller number dealt with bringing in experienced managers or senior professionals. In the majority of cases the women were relatively recent college graduates. In most instances they were recruited from outside the company, but in many cases qualified women were also being promoted from within, primarily out of the office-and-clerical category.

Success generally was equated with an increased number of qualified women employed in managerial or professional titles during the past two or three years. In some cases, these were the first women ever employed as managers or professionals in the firms. Success was attributed mainly to six factors:

1. Clear top commitment from management to improve job opportunities for women;
2. Accountability of line managers for EEO results;
3. Increased influence over both the staffing process and its

outcomes by the corporate personnel department and the EEO staff;

4. Ability to recruit an ample supply of qualified women, both externally and internally;
5. Training line managers to interview and select qualified women for the available jobs and to identify likely female candidates for further development;
6. Ensuring that the women, as well as the men, with promotion potential acquire the knowledge and skills needed to qualify for higher-level jobs.

Companies have found these factors crucial to successful efforts on behalf of women throughout the organization. Because hiring inexperienced women who are college graduates, hiring women to be supervisors, hiring women who are seasoned professionals and managers, and upgrading women from office and from plant jobs pose somewhat different problems, they are discussed separately.

Hiring Inexperienced College Graduates

This was the principal strategy being used by companies that were successful in increasing the representation of women in professional and managerial roles. Although most of these companies were also upgrading women into such jobs, many reported that a considerably larger number of the women employed were being attracted into entry-level positions for college graduates from outside sources. And—just as with the men—some, but by no means all, of the women hired were regarded as being on "fast tracks" or were enrolled in formal training programs leading toward higher-level managerial roles.

External recruiting represents a continuation of the traditional method for filling openings in these categories.[5] In a few instances the external recruiting of women was adopted as an alternative following a disappointing effort to upgrade women already in the company. Such a switch was reported, for example, by a retail chain, but even then it constituted a return to the previous standard practice of recruiting externally for all managerial candidates.

Campus Recruiting

Among the companies selected for follow-up interviews, campus recruiting is almost always centrally planned and implemented, and it has been a primary method for locating especially promising managerial and professional employees for at least a decade. Despite some optimistic projections of the supply of female candidates on the campus, translating a potential supply into actual candidates qualified for specific openings appears to demand energetic and innovative recruiting activity.

Expanding the range of campus contacts to include women's colleges and women's organizations at coeducational colleges is a first step, and one that has had varying results. Some companies report the majority of female recruits come from their traditional source for men—coeducational colleges. Women's colleges, they say, are not yet geared to business, either in curriculum or in guidance. But others have found women's colleges an arena for recruiting high-quality talent. A supermarket chain conducted a very successful recruiting campaign at a cross section of women's college campuses. And a nondurable goods manufacturer has been pleased with the updated skills, managerial qualifications, poise and motivation of older women contacted through the placement offices of selected women's colleges. Perhaps this apparent disagreement stems from considering women's colleges as a homogeneous group, or from attempting to generalize after too short a period.

What many recruiters seem to believe, however, is that the precise selection of colleges to contact is less significant than an open-minded approach. This viewpoint was expressed by the personnel director of a large bank: "Six or seven years ago we applied a strict cost-benefit test to recruiting, sending our recruiters only to those campuses where experience showed the best results per man-hour of recruiting time. This led to concentration on a few universities. Now we no longer apply that test. We are willing to expend more time, enlarge our recruiting staff, and not rule out any possible source of qualified female or minority candidates." More important still, many recruiting directors say, are the qualifications of recruiters, their interviewing skill, and their ability to present the realities of an entry job within the context of career development. Recruiters' qualifications assume particular importance in screening female applicants who may have less exposure than male applicants to the industry or the occupation. As one recruiter said: "The women may be reluctant to ask the questions men ask unhesitantly, for fear of displaying ignorance or uncertainty."

Because most recruiters are still men, some companies seek to improve recruiters' skills by providing intensive training in the questions to ask and not to ask when interviewing women, in the analysis of job functions and requirements, in the background factors beyond directly relevant education and work experience that should be considered, and in the career paths radiating from an entry job. In addition, several report adding women to the recruiting staff. Of particular interest are examples reported where the female recruiters are "on loan" to the personnel department for limited periods. They are drawn from a range of management and professional areas and, accordingly, can help to bridge the gap that sometimes occurs between centralized recruiting and local selection.

Several personnel directors also emphasized that skillful recruiters would be relatively ineffective "if they come on campus at the last moment just to interview applicants who have signed up for an interview." A major factor in attracting potential female candidates, according to many, are prerecruitment activities designed to heighten interest on the part of campus women in nontraditional industries and occupations. These include:

1. Advance meetings with deans, placement officers, and faculty members;
2. Meetings with women's associations, on campus and elsewhere;
3. Participation in educational-guidance and career-counseling sessions;
4. Financial support for business and science clubs at selected colleges;
5. Providing grants for scholarships to women majoring in engineering or other fields where they are in short supply;
6. Lending company employees as visiting lecturers, or to assist in curriculum development at selected women's colleges;
7. Providing opportunities for student visits to company facilities;
8. Offering more thorough business and industry familiarization opportunities to college women through work-study programs or summer internships.

Although stimulated by the goal of attracting women (and minorities), improved skill and closer contact between employers and college campuses have actually benefited the total recruiting effort. According to one personnel director: "Not all men are as knowledgeable about career options as we often assume. And college curriculum and guidance services are often out of step with current business practices and opportunities."

The ultimate test of a recruiting strategy, however, is the proportion and quality of recruits that are hired. Attracting a pool of applicants is only the first step. The next is screening before referral to a hiring agent, and it is equally important.

In the initial screening on campus, and in some cases a second screening by corporate personnel representatives, the major emphasis is on the degree level, the major field or more specific course credits, and academic standing. Secondarily, attention is given to interests and to personal characteristics as revealed during one or more interviews. With only few exceptions, it now seems that customary standards are applied uniformly to male and female candidates. According to a director of professional recruiting:

> *Whatever predisposition some recruiters may have had to modify educational requirements for women proved impossible, unnecessary or inadvisable. You can't recruit a liberal arts graduate for an engineering assignment. And if you know how to recruit, you can find women with the appropriate credentials for a growing variety of functions—including marketing, finance, computer science, and even geology and geophysics. Besides, we have enough trouble persuading some managers to hire women without sending them women who are clearly less qualified for their specific jobs than the available men.*

This view was echoed widely. Many personnel directors consider maintaining all truly valid requirements the best way to diminish male resistance. And it was frequently noted that academic standing is not a problem because women who elect nontraditional major fields of study tend to rank well toward the top of their class.

The problem areas for recruiting are engineering and some other scientific disciplines, where women continue in short supply, and those industries that have a "negative" image as being dirty, stodgy, or almost exclusively male working environments. Recruiting women engineers, for example, is generally intensely competitive. Therefore companies give equal, if not more, attention to activities calculated to increase the future supply.[6]

But some shortages are more apparent than real. A shortage of women with MBAs for instance, has evaporated for some firms that have found they need place less emphasis on the MBA degree as a prerequisite for their management positions. They have learned that carefully selected bachelor-level graduates—perhaps with undergraduate degrees in business administration or liberal arts degrees with a major in economics—can also learn to do the jobs, and that they may not even require a longer training period. As a railroad personnel manager says: "We have learned that much of our preference for MBAs was founded on the expectation that they would progress more rapidly—and that expectation became self-fulfilling." Similarly, a retail chain relaxed its requirements for potential store managers; it no longer demands a business major from either men or women, with no discernible negative effect. But such changes in basic screening criteria apparently are few.

On-campus screening eliminates clearly unqualified candidates, leaving men and women who meet the company's basic require-ments in a pool from which the line manager will make the final selection. Many companies report that by involving line managers more directly in setting the necessary screening standards for spe-cific jobs, by placing more controls over the manner in which final hiring decisions are reached, and by monitoring hiring results for women and other protected groups, a closer congruence between screening results and final hiring results is achieved.

In general, resistance by male managers has been less of a prob-lem than anticipated. Some companies still find particular "trouble spots," but more often the report is that many male managers have made "a rapid attitudinal turn around." Several directors of recruit-ing noted that all qualified female candidates referred are now promptly hired. As one personnel director says: "The shoe already is on the other foot. We used to devote our time just to persuading managers to consider women. Now they are after us to produce more candidates."

Although examples of national campus recruitng programs were more numerous among our survey respondents, some companies say they handle college recruiting locally or regionally. The concen-tration of most of the professional and managerial jobs in the orga-nization within a limited geographic area was frequently cited as one of the reasons. But a prominent durable goods manufacturer that operates nationwide also prefers a local recruiting approach—when it is coupled with strong central support and guidance—and has had good success in hiring inexperienced female professionals in this manner. Each local plant manager is given both the responsibil-ity and the necessary time and dollar resources to carry out all recruiting efforts for his unit.

According to this company's personnel director, one of the keys to the success the local line managers have had in recruiting women for beginning jobs as systems analysts, lawyers, accountants and for many less technical individual contributor roles as well, is that the company president is a prominent figure in the civil rights field. His commitment is well known externally and it is backed up organizà-tionally in many ways. The formal statement of EEO policy is bol-stered by clear guidelines, centralized monitoring—"hand done but nonetheless effective"—and ongoing managerial education and dis-cussion of EEO results at all management levels.

This personnel director stressed, however, that when college recruiting is decentralized, it, as well as the actual hiring, must be monitored. At first all local managers were required to report to the corporate personnel department the recruiting sources used, the number of female applicants, and the number hired. As results began to show in hiring data, the focus shifted to the percentage employed. The 1977 EEO program statement still regulates recruit-ing, stipulating that each unit continue to maintain contact with at least one female-oriented (and one minority) college in the locality. But each local manager now determines the mix of colleges and other referral sources to be used.

Passive Recruiting

In some of the largest and best-known companies, passive recruit-ing—hiring by reviewing unsolicited applications—has been the custom for entry-level individual contributor jobs in nontechnical areas. Interestingly enough, passive techniques are also reported to have successfully recruited women for some clearly nontraditional roles, such as engineers and airline pilots. But even for these jobs, passive recruiting is most likely to work for the larger, better-known employers.

A nondurable goods manufacturing company notes that the re-sumes received from women frequently need to be analyzed for skills and abilities relevant to a wide range of jobs available within the company, rather than merely being considered for the specific kind of job requested. Many women with liberal arts degrees, for example, apply for a customer-service job—a type of position this company does not have. An analysis of the applicant's background and interests may lead to considering her for jobs in public rela-tions, consumer affairs, government affairs, personnel, market re-search, business development, trade research, or other classifica-tions that are available.

Assignment and Training after Hiring

Assigning women to specific managerial and professional positions apparently proceeds in the same manner used for men, apart from a few companies that report assigning women to managers "who are open to women." Most managerial recruits, male or female, are assigned directly to a job. Training other than general orientation is usually informal and in relation to the specific work assignment.

Although some companies report that women are dispersed throughout the company equally with men, in male-intensive industries the women are often concentrated in "softer" fields—public relations, personnel and the like—and are more likely to be working at corporate headquarters. Fewer women work in plants or at construction sites, probably partly because there are fewer women in engineering and technical occupations, but also, as frequently reported, because plant personnel are less receptive to women.

A few companies, banks and insurance companies in particular, recruit both male and female trainees for structured management-training programs. Customarily, the training period varies with the college education of the trainee. The general pattern in one large bank, for example, has been three years of training for most college graduates, but half that time for those with graduate degrees in business. This pattern still prevails, so that now that women comprise about one third of the trainees, and relatively few have graduate business degrees, the overall average of the time for training is now closer to three years.

Another bank traditionally confined recruiting to the MBA graduates of a few prestigious universities, who were to be trained as commercial lending officers. Only a few bachelor's degree graduates were accepted. To recruit more women and minority trainees, recruiting contacts have been broadened and a larger proportion of each year's trainees are bachelor-level graduates chosen for their apparent high potential. Traditionally, trainee starting salaries varied with the academic degree level. MBAs are still paid more than those with only a bachelor's degree, but consideration is also given to relevant experience. The increasing number of trainees without an MBA has led to a revised evaluation system. Instead of receiving annual salary increments, all trainees are now appraised frequently to determine how many months remain before they will qualify for officer status, and their compensation is adjusted accordingly. As in the past, however, each trainee is hired for a specific lending department and, after completing the core training program, goes on to specialized training.

The bank's personnel and EEO officers consider the more flexible approach to recruiting and training beneficial to both male and female trainees and to the bank's ability to develop future officers. As the EEO officer says: "We now look at more than the degree and evaluate trainees on a performance basis. Although it may appear on the surface that the bank has assumed more of the cost of training, this is not the case. Some with only the bachelor's degree quickly catch up or overtake those with graduate degrees."

Few problems are reported in integrating newly hired women into management and professional categories and, for the most part, those that are reported are a function of male failure to accept female colleagues, rather than a reflection of any general deficiencies in female capability or performance. In a few companies in male-intensive industries, higher turnover rates for women have been experienced. Some of this is attributed to the company's lack of experience in evaluating female candidates, but there are also reports of some pirating due to the relative shortage of women with certain skills.

Hiring Women to Be First-Line Supervisors

A restaurant chain provides another example of successful local recruiting of women by line managers, in this case as candidates for field-unit supervision. Again, a written EEO plan followed by continuing discussion of corporate goals at regular management meetings, and careful evaluation of both the numbers and the performance of the women hired, are seen as key elements. Initially some area supervisors focused on recruiting recent college graduates, a focus that soon proved unsatisfactory. Eagerness to make a good numerical showing resulted in faulty selection: many of the women hired were insufficiently mature to manage a work crew. They were often unable to meet the demands of the work, the long hours, weekend assignments, and the stress. Subsequent management sessions on EEO matters emphasized the desirability of allowing sufficient lead time for recruiting to permit more careful selection. Rather than a college degree, selection was to be based on knowledge of the food industry or on supervisory ability. Line managers' suggestions for appropriate qualifications include: restaurant work of any type as evidence of familiarity with the stress, the hours, and the working conditions; retail experience of any kind with sufficient customer contact; or other work or life experiences that would indicate a readiness for a supervisory role. Parents or teachers, for example, because of their experience in directing young people, or home economists for their technical knowledge, were considered possible candidates. Local employment agencies are now the principal referral sources, and the emphasis on selection has enabled the company not only to hire but to retain and promote women to restaurant management.

Several other retailers have found it helpful to conduct "generalized" recruiting, presenting to women's groups the opportunities for management in these fields as a stimulus to career interest. They also do so by participating in back-to-work programs for housewives, and in mid-career counseling programs sponsored by community organizations or community colleges. These activities may produce only a few immediate applicants, but the continuing "trickle" of resumes received does provide a source for future supervisory and managerial openings.

Hiring Experienced Managers and Professionals

Many companies report that they rarely recruit experienced managers or professionals, preferring to hire inexperienced individuals whom they can then develop for more responsible roles within the organization. A durable goods manufacturing company in a male-intensive industry has, however, elected to recruit experienced females to fill certain openings at corporate headquarters that call for a high level of professional expertise. An ongoing relationship has been established with several recruiting agencies that specialize in professional and managerial women, and considerable attention has been given to making sure the agency personnel not only understand the jobs to be filled but also the company's philosophy and atmosphere and the longer range opportunities available.

By disregarding the industries in which individuals have been working and concentrating instead on carefully evaluating their very specialized professional competence, the company has found it can locate well-qualified women for many of its jobs and then "sell" them to the line managers on an individualized basis. Furthermore, because so many of these women were previously employed in the generally lower-paying female-intensive industries, they often regard the salaries being offered as especially attractive. It has proven important to select women with good self-confidence and demonstrated persistence in the face of obstacles. Even at its corporate headquarters this company is still a very masculine world and, while this is not intentional, some women might not find the atmosphere comfortable. A nucleus of very competent, experienced professional women has now been employed at corporate headquarters as economists, financial analysts, accountants, public affairs managers, and personnel specialists. As they gain the necessary industry experience, many are being viewed as clear contenders for further promotions, including possible high-level managerial roles.

Upgrading Women into Professional and Managerial Roles

About 30 percent of the companies reporting successful efforts in the management and professional categories indicate upgrading was the only strategy being used. Many more say they use both upgrading and external hiring. Thus far, however, at least among the examples selected for further study, relatively few women have moved from nonexempt jobs to positions as managers or professionals. More significant than numbers, according to personnel directors, EEO officers, and other reporting executives, are the numerous modifications in personnel policies and procedures that have been made to stimulate and facilitate such upgrading.

In some instances the modifications made are characterized as "only attitudinal—extending to women the advancement opportunities men enjoy," or "just a natural expansion of our commitment to internal development." But in others the changes reported are structural—"new internal mechanisms to identify and develop employees, stimulated by the goal of upgrading opportunities for women, but benefiting both men and women."

The internal development of human resources is so integral to the managerial philosophy of some companies that it is characterized as the organization's single overriding personnel policy. Now that such companies recognize that this policy must extend to all employees, regardless of such irrelevant considerations as race or sex, they are not only placing special emphasis on upgrading female employees but are finding that, in doing so, the advantages they have always valued still accrue. For example, the personnel director of a durable goods manufacturing company in which most key executives have come up through the ranks says: "Upgrading offers the benefit of dealing with known quantities, people who are already adjusted to the company environment, who understand our business and our policies." Another personnel director comments: "We are a very fluid organization. External recruiting may look easier, but new recruits are untested and, in any event, they, too, have to be developed inside the company." However, some companies that prefer upgrading say they have been forced at least temporarily to turn to external recruiting because so few of the women on the payroll have responded to their upgrading efforts.

In some cases upgrading is adopted as a strategy only because external recruiting efforts have been unsuccessful. For example, an engineering-oriented firm decided "to take a hard look inside for women with management potential to compensate for the small numbers of female engineers available." Again, an apparel manufacturer, unable to recruit women with managerial experience, turned to in-house employees "with surprisingly satisfactory results." And for some firms upgrading was the only option during the recession when external recruiting was radically curtailed for cost reasons.

Many companies that use both upgrading and external hiring seem to have added upgrading as a strategy because they view it as a necessary adjunct. As one EEO officer says: "We could not in good conscience mount an intensive recruiting effort directed at women outside the firm and ignore our long-service clerical workers." And others, who were skeptical of the outcome of an upgrading effort because of the low educational level of the majority of their female employees, say they were impelled to make the effort to avoid damaging employee morale and to lessen the risks of complaints alleging discriminatory treatment.

Upgrading White Collar Workers

Opening career opportunities to female office workers, and then translating "opportunity" into actual transfers and promotions, is reported to "take a lot of effort and a close, critical look at the company's inner workings." Upgrading clerical workers, it becomes apparent, confronts a range of issues in the management of human resources that have only recently become of major concern to many businesses. Among these issues are whether promotion should be a

reward for loyalty, length of service, and superior job performance—or should be in recognition of future potential, and, if the
latter, whether the emphasis should be on general "potential" or on
how to identify, assess, and develop the potential to perform specific kinds of higher level jobs. These problems are brought into
sharper focus in considering the development of clerical workers
because many of them have some college education and promoting
them often means crossing some long-established, sex-related de-
marcation lines.

Recalling the wide differences in typical male-female employment patterns in different industries, the varying levels of technolog-
ical development in goods-producing and service industries, and
the uneven impact of underlying economic forces on the growth of
employment in various parts of the economy, it becomes under-
standable that the upgrading of women into managerial and professional roles from clerical positions has been receiving quite different
emphasis in different kinds of companies. Thus, one corporate personnel director in a male-intensive high-technology manufacturing
industry summarizes his company's upgrading strategy for female
clerical workers by saying: "It's a low-keyed informal effort—not a
program." But the personnel director of a major bank enumerates
all the following internal staffing system mechanisms that are being
used to facilitate such upgrading:

1. A computerized skills data bank;
2. Identification of employees with satisfactory records remaining in grade beyond the average time span;
3. Submission of requisitions for any openings unfilled within
   the department to allow companywide internal search;
4. Job posting of a range of exempt positions;
5. A system for employee transfer and promotion requests;
6. A "hot line" for employees who believe they are in dead-end
   jobs or are being held back;
7. A liberal, well-publicized tuition-refund program;
8. Analysis of "job families" to create new career paths;
9. Individual career counseling on request;
10. Group career seminars.

When so many activities are being undertaken simultaneously,
the specific contribution of any particular part of the upgrading
system becomes difficult to evaluate. But, for now, the bank's basic
concern is not with which *one* activity helps the most, but rather

with a good faith effort, through a *combination* of activities, to stimulate appropriate internal flows of qualified women into its professional and managerial jobs.

Comparisons of White Collar Upgrading with External Recruiting

Some of the more provocative comments come from companies that are able to compare the results of clerical upgrading with those from external recruiting because both strategies have been applied. A company that successfully recruits women on the campus for retail store managers reports a disappointing experience with a special program to stimulate transfers from clerical jobs in the headquarters office to store-management training. Despite provision of a no-obligation trial period, tours of the store facilities, the offer of vocational testing by an outside psychologist, and a full exposition of career opportunities, few women responded and the program was cancelled. Personnel executives attribute the lack of response to the dramatic differences between the office and store environments, and also to differences in the hours of work. They are hopeful that the presence of female store managers recruited on college campuses will result in an attitudinal change among clerical employees that will permit reinstating the upgrading program in the near future.

A very large company manufacturing nondurables reports successful external recruiting and also successful upgrading of clerical women into professional positions at corporate headquarters. Thus far there have been no differences in retention or performance between the two groups "of sufficient importance to trigger an analytic study." But what has been learned in regard to promoting clerical workers is that to achieve success rates equal to those achieved with external recruiting requires more care in selection, more counseling, and more support from the personnel department staff. The internal candidates are almost all college graduates and, so far as objective criteria can predict, should be equal to the external recruits. Moreover, they are on the average ten years older and have the supposed advantage of eight to ten years' experience with the company.

But what seemed to be an advantage can be a handicap. The transition from a clerical or secretarial job to a professional one is complicated by less ready acceptance by male colleagues. "They sometimes expect her to bring her typewriter along or to take notes at all departmental meetings." Under this pressure, she may revert to a subordinate role and find it difficult to maintain an independent stance and sell her viewpoint. The personnel department finds it difficult to identify those women best able to make the transition because "unlike new hires, the ability to adjust seems to be unrelated to basic qualifications nor does counseling seem to be of much help."

Another company representative in a male-intensive industry warns that when a secretary is promoted "you must make sure that it's not just giving her a new title." He contrasted the clear success in one instance where a secretary was promoted to purchasing agent—a promotion that involved a change of department—with the disappointing experience of upgrading a secretary to become an administrative assistant to the same executive. No new secretary was hired and there was no real change in her functions.

Several companies report that they are becoming increasingly alert to signs that promoted clerical women are being exploited, and are issuing memos to the effect that notetaking and post-meeting cleanup are not of necessity women's tasks. They are also watching for any indications that these women are excluded from meetings, trips, or other job-related activities. But some also note that women are beginning to act more assertively and to handle such problems on their own. As for the future outlook for promotions from clerical positions, one EEO officer says: "Once such promotions are perceived as a normal progression and not as experimental or special programs, there will be less resistance and also less acceptance of subordination."

Rapid Advancement for Some Clerical Employees

A limited number of former clerical employees have been placed on informal "fast tracks" leading to higher-level jobs or enrolled in formal management trainee programs. A railroad's first woman management trainee was "an underutilized woman clerical employee, a college graduate pursuing an advanced degree in economics on her own time." And some women without college degrees, but with demonstrated superior ability, have also been invited into management-training programs. For example, several banks report internal searches for trainees, accepting college graduates or those with years of banking experience or a combination of experience and specific banking course completions.

In many companies rapid advancement depends on technical educational achievement, so some companies now are using counseling as a way to stimulate more participation by high-potential employees in financially assisted degree programs or advanced education. But a number of personnel specialists believe that "fast track" advancements for clerical women are likely to prove a temporary phenomenon because so many of these opportunities are now directly accessible to outstanding young women obtaining appropriate college degrees.

Upgrading Blue Collar Women to Production Supervision

Examples of successful efforts to improve opportunities for women in plant management or first-line production supervision were relatively few, but they also suggest a wide range of possible techniques. In the course of a review of all women employees, a nondurable goods manufacturer identified a plant manager's office assistant who was described by the manager as "completely able to take over in my absence." Because she had only a high school diploma, the company secured a place for her in a university-run intensive management program, normally open only to college graduates. She now supervises a predominantly male blue-collar force of 150 workers and is enrolled in a college degree program at night.

Some companies are seeking ways to upgrade blue collar female employees to first-line supervision by extending their plant job-posting systems to cover those positions. Results thus far are varied and inconclusive. One company reports that a sizable proportion of the women initially putting in bids to be considered for such jobs decide, in the end, to turn the promotions down. Whether they have merely been testing the company's willingness to make them an offer or whether they change their minds based on fuller information about the job or on the reaction of their coworkers is not yet clear.

Several personnel managers commented that first-line supervision is always a difficult level to fill, even with qualified men. Skilled workers eligible for promotion are not always eager to become the boss of their coworkers and wish to avoid the stress, the possible longer hours, and additional responsibilities of supervision. The same considerations affect women; some respondents believe they affect women even more because women are culturally conditioned to avoid the role of boss even when they would only supervise women.

Given the perceived obstacles, the few examples of success in promoting blue collar women take on increased significance. But, again, there is no single "best way." One company uses an entirely informal, individualized approach; one uses a standard university-administered training program; and one has used an on-the-job "internship" program that has proven beneficial for both men and women candidates for plant supervision.

Endnotes

1. Two companies, both in retailing, noted that women are adequately represented at all levels in all applicable EEO-1 job categories. They indicated that this reflected the nature of the business and that no special effort on behalf of women had been required.
2. This result may be influenced by the fact that the questionnaires were filled out at corporate headquarters, where little may be known about how the staffing of blue collar jobs is handled. There was much less response throughout the questionnaire regarding the nature of the efforts being made to improve job opportunities for women in the blue collar job categories. But, given the limited progress that seems to have been made in the blue collar categories, it may indeed be true that most companies have given less emphasis to increasing the representation of women in their blue collar job categories.
3. Allen R. Janger, *The Personnel Function: Changing Objectives and Organization*, Conference Board Report 712, 1977.
4. See, for example, Ruth Gilbert Shaeffer, *Staffing Systems-Managerial and Professional Jobs*, Conference Board Report 558, 1972.
5. Ibid.
6. In some cases companies are participating in career discussions in the community to influence parents, teachers, guidance counselors, and junior and senior high school students. As one recruiter notes, "Once they are in college, it may already be too late for them to pick up the full math and science background so many of our jobs require."

Appendix A

COMPARISONS OF EMPLOYMENT PATTERNS BY SIZE OF COMPANY

The following sets of 1970-1975 male-female employment statistics, by occupational category in various broad industry groups, have been used:

1. *Census and Current Population Survey (CPS) data.* This information covers companies of all sizes, including very small firms.

2. *EEOC data.* This information was submitted to the Equal Employment Opportunity Commission (EEOC) by employers with 100 or more employees (or 50 or more employees if they were government contractors). It is the data called for on the EEO-1 form.

3. *CB survey data.* This is EEO-1 form information that was submitted directly to the Conference Board by 111 very large companies. The same firms are represented in both the 1970 and 1975 data. These corporations probably are not typical of all the very large companies in their industries. Nonetheless, they are important because they account for a significant share of the total employment.

Table A7–1 **Representation of Women in Higher-Level Occupations by Size of Company, 1970[a] (percent)**

Occupational Category, by Industry Group	All Companies (Census)	Companies With 50–100 or More Employees (EEOC)	Some Very Large Corporations (CB Survey)
Female Managers			
Durable goods manufacturing	5%	2%	1%
Nondurable goods manufacturing	9	5	3
Transportation	9	3	5
Communications	15	35	NA
Electric and gas utilities	4	2	2
Retail trade	21	24	22
Banking	19	13	17
Insurance	17	11	6
Female Professional and Technical Workers (combined)			
Durable goods manufacturing	7%	6%	4%
Nondurable goods manufacturing	21	14	14
Transportation	9	5	4
Communications	17	16	NA
Electric and gas utilities	4	4	4
Retail trade	28	29	17
Banking	31	23	24
Insurance	29	24	31
Female Sales Workers[b]			
Durable goods manufacturing	6%	8%	1%
Nondurable goods manufacturing	13	10	3
Insurance	12	5	1
Female Craft Workers[c]			
Durable goods manufacturing	5%	3%	1%
Nondurable goods manufacturing	11	20	2
Transportation	1	d	d
Communications	4	1	NA
Electric and gas utilities	1	d	d

SOURCES: *U.S. Census of Population*, EEOC. CB Survey.

[a] The occupational categories in the Census are not precisely comparable with the EEO-1 Form categories. Also, the very large corporations are probably not typical.
[b] In industries where this is an important higher-level job category.
[c] In industries where this is an important job category.
[d] Less than .5 percent.

Table A7-2 Representation of Women in Higher-Level Occupations by Size of Company, 1970 and 1975[a] (percent)

Occupational Category by Industry Group	All Companies (Census/CPS)		Companies With 50–100 or More Employees (EEOC)		Some Very Large Corporations (CB Survey)	
	1970	1975	1970	1975	1970	1975
Female Managers						
Durable goods manufacturing	5%	6%	2%	4%	1%	2%
Nondurable goods manufacturing	9	10	5	8	3	6
Transportation	9	11	3	5	5	4
Communications	15	27	35	32	NA	NA
Electric and gas utilities	4	3	2	3	2	3
Retail trade	21	24	24	28	22	34
Banking	19	29	13	25	17	30
Insurance	17	18	11	17	6	10
Female Professional and Technical Workers (combined)						
Durable goods manufacturing	7%	8%	6%	8%	4%	7%
Nondurable goods manufacturing	21	24	14	19	14	20
Transportation	9	10	5	6	4	5
Communications	17	19	16	27	NA	NA
Electric and gas utilities	4	7	4	7	4	7
Retail trade	28	33	29	36	17	35
Banking	31	39	23	30	24	32
Insurance	29	29	24	37	31	46

Table A7-2 (continued)

Occupational Category by Industry Group	All Companies (Census/CPS)		Companies With 50–100 or More Employees (EEOC)		Some Very Large Corporations (CB Survey)	
	1970	1975	1970	1975	1970	1975
Female Sales Workers[b]						
Durable goods manufacturing	6%	8%	8%	15%	1%	4%
Nondurable goods manufacturing	13	16	10	16	3	7
Insurance	12	15	5	7	1	3
Female Craft Workers[c]						
Durable goods manufacturing	5%	4%	3%	4%	1%	2%
Nondurable goods manufacturing	11	11	20	16	2	2
Transportation	1	d	d	d	d	d
Communications	4	5	1	7	NA	NA
Electric and gas utilities	1	d	d	d	d	d

SOURCES: *U.S. Census of Population, Current Population Survey,* EEOC. CB Survey

[a] The occupational categories in the Census and Current Population Survey are not precisely comparable with the EEO-1 Form categories. Also, the very large corporations are probably not typical.
[b] In industries where this is an important higher-level job category.
[c] In industries where this is an important job category.
[d] Less than .5 percent.

Appendix B

ABOUT THE STUDY

In 1974, The Conference Board began a program to study the efforts of major organizations to change the relative status of working women. The goals of this study program are to focus attention on this complex problem, and to provide experience-based, results-oriented information for key executives involved in improving their organization's efforts to provide equal employment opportunity for women.

Our first research project has been limited to studying corporate efforts to increase the representation of women in relatively broad occupational categories where they have previously been underutilized.

The results of this first study were presented in two reports. Conference Board Report 744, *Improving Job Opportunities for Women, A Chartbook Focusing on the Progress in Business* (1978) shows the 1970-1975 changes in male-female occupational patterns in the corporate sector in considerable detail. Report 755, *Corporate Experiences in Improving Women's Job Opportunities* (1979) focused on the nature of the change process as viewed from a corporate perspective.

A Methodological Note

By the time we began to plan this study most major corporations were well aware of the potential legal and financial liabilities they faced in the area of employment discrimination, and some reported experiences in which their previous efforts to cooperate in research projects or information-sharing meetings about such matters had turned out to have serious compliance or public relations implications for them. In keeping with the Board's policy of confidentiality, the research project was designed to enable major companies to share useful information about their efforts to improve the job opportunities they provide to women anonymously.

The research design that was ultimately worked out consisted of three main parts:

1. *The comparison of 1970 and 1975 male-female employment statistics both by industry and by occupational category.* The statistics used were from several government sources as well as from very large corporations surveyed by mail. The figures do not provide information with respect to any company's compliance with the EEO laws and regulations, but they have enabled us to analyze by sex the existing employment patterns in various settings and to assess the net effects by 1975 of corporate efforts to improve women's job opportunities in various occupational categories, including certain clearly nontraditional jobs.

2. *The analysis of data collected by means of a 32-page mailed questionnaire covering corporate experiences with, and perspectives on, the change process.* In addition to yielding some of the figures mentioned above, the purposes of this aspect of the research were:
   a. To identify the major job categories at all organization levels for which companies have found efforts to improve opportunities for women to be necessary, and to learn where the greatest emphasis has been placed;
   b. To describe changes in staffing strategies and approaches that companies have tried in order to increase the representation of women in different job categories, with special emphasis on those they have found either especially effective or especially inappropriate;
   c. To determine whether any joint or collaborative efforts have been undertaken with unions, other employers, schools or other institutions that influence the supply of women who are qualified for various occupational roles;
   d. To identify some of the special factors, both within the company and in its environment, that have been found to influence the success of corporate efforts to improve job opportunities for women;
   e. To identify some of the perceived consequences, both positive and negative, of such corporate efforts;

    f. To determine whether any changes in compensation, benefit or layoff and recall practices have had the direct effect of changing the employment patterns of women in various job categories

3. *Almost 200 confidential telephone and on-site interviews dealing with examples of successful experiences.* These experiences have been analyzed and summarized by job categories. (Because even reports of "success stories" in this area have sometimes had unfortunate legal consequences, the only companies mentioned by name in the reports were those operating under published agreements with administrative agencies or court decrees.)

All told, 1,015 companies were contacted in the mailed survey. They were drawn from among the largest companies in the following broad industry categories: mining; construction; manufacturing; transportation; communications; gas and electric utilities; retailing; wholesale trade; banking; insurance. For those industry categories covered by the *Fortune* 1300 lists, the basic sample was largely drawn from this frame. But some other lists of the largest companies by industry were also used. In addition, we were fortunate enough to obtain the cooperation of some industry associations in encouraging their largest members to respond.

Compared with most Conference Board surveys of corporate policies and practices, the overall response rate to this survey was somewhat low, probably due not only to the sensitivity of the topic but also to the length of the questionnaire. However, the quality of most responses was high.

The question of the "purity" of the sample was not deemed of primary importance because there were many reasons why the respondents were not likely to be typical. As this was viewed as an exploratory study, it was considered more important to obtain sufficient responses to permit impressionistic analyses of data about very broad categories and not to attempt to find statistically significant differences between groups.

Responses to some of the general questions were cross-tabulated to determine whether there might be important differences in the perspectives of these large corporations by industry; whether they are national, regional or local organizations; by the number of employees; or by their particular compliance or enforcement experiences. A few such differences have been noted. Given the small size of the subsamples, the impressionistic nature of the data, and the known lack of typicality of the companies, it has not seemed appropriate to apply rigorous statistical tests.

The breakdown by industry of the companies providing usable responses in various parts of the survey effort is shown in the table on the next page. There is no assurance that these companies are typical of all the very large companies in these industries; nonetheless, their data and their comments on this key topic must be regarded as important, for they employ millions of American men and women.

The Respondents

The findings in this report reflect the perceptions, opinions and attitudes of those in the personnel function at corporate headquarters and do not necessarily fully cover what has been happening at all of the many hundreds of establishments in the responding corporations. The questionnaires were addressed to the senior personnel executives of the companies, and they were asked to respond personally or to turn the matter over to someone else on the corporate staff, such as an affirmative action officer or the EEO coordinator, who might be even more knowledgeable than they about this topic. It was made plain that they were expected to draw upon their existing fund of knowledge about what had been going on in the company and not to conduct an internal survey of all locations. Similarly, the initial follow-up interviews were with headquarters' personnel executives or staff members, although in some cases additional on-site interviews with line managers or local personnel staff members were arranged. Generally speaking, the women whose improved job assignments were being discussed were not interviewed, but a considerable number of them were observed at work.

In designing the questionnaire, the EEO-1 job category of "service workers" was inadvertently omitted in a number of questions. The employment statistics gathered do cover this category, but no data are available about corporate perspectives on efforts to improve job opportunities for women by moving them into these jobs. While this oversight is regrettable, it is not likely to prove important from a practical point of view. Few jobs in this category pay well enough and command enough status in the hierarchy of the organization to be categorized as "higher level."

Table B7-1 Very Large Corporations Responding to The Conference Board Survey

Industry Group	Providing Usable Questionnaires		Providing Some Information About Nontraditional Jobs		Providing Usable Matched EEO-1 Data For 1970 and 1975	
	Number	Percent	Number	Percent	Number	Percent
Durable goods manufacturing	44	17	33	16	14	
Nondurable goods manufacturing	50	19	39	19	23	
Transportation	21	8	16	8	b	
Electric and gas utilities	60	23	58	28	32	
Retail trade	14	5	9	4	b	
Banking	27	10	11	5	10	
Insurance	37	14	30	15	16	
Other (e.g., mining, construction, communications, wholesale trade)[a]	12	4	11	5	b	
Total	265	100%	207	100%		c
Male-intensive industries	158	60	134	65	73	
Female-intensive industries	107	40	73	35	38	
Total	265	100%	207	100%		c

[a] These industries are grouped together as "other" because of the limited number of responses from each.
[b] Less than 10 companies.
[c] Because of their known lack of typicality, the 111 companies have not been combined into an overall sample.

Chapter 8

CONCLUSIONS

by Phyllis A. Wallace

We end this volume on a cautious note. The preceding chapters repeat the theme that, despite the increase in the number and proportion of working women, the types of jobs that women hold and the income disparities that women experience have not changed significantly. Major determinants of the labor market status of women during the decade of the 1980s will be the economic environment, the stance of labor unions on aggressive unionization of women, strategies for facilitating effective change in employing organizations, and the environment for implementing administrative and legal decisions on employment discrimination. The interaction of these variables may produce a short-term setback, maintenance of the status quo, or incremental improvements in the status of women workers. By the end of the decade approximately 55 percent of working women will be in the 25-to-44-age group as compared with only 44 percent in 1979. This cohort from the postwar baby boom population is well educated, has high job expectations, and is increasingly aware of its legal right to participate fully in all work settings.

Economic Environment

There is consensus that the American economy will be driven by the need to improve its sagging productivity. While some sectors will be accelerating introduction of technology that may displace workers, other sectors in the service industries will be generating more jobs. How will women workers fare in the "restructured economy" and increasingly segmented labor markets described in a recent issue of *Business Week*?[1] Will there be a differential in male/

215

female preparation for a restructured economy? Are there data on female enrollments in science and engineering in high schools, colleges, and graduate schools? Do these support an optimistic or pessimistic view? A recent study shows that at all three degree levels, the engineering field maintained the lowest percentage of degrees earned by women. For 1974–1975, women earned 2.2 percent of all the bachelor's degrees awarded in engineering, 2.4 percent of all master's degrees, and 2.1 percent of all doctoral degrees.[2]

To the extent that there is a healthy, less inflationary economic environment, it will be beneficial for women and all workers. If the economy experiences many of the shortcomings of the late 1970s, it will be more difficult for women workers to achieve a reduction in the earnings gap or a trade-off of costly fringe benefits for wages. Will women bear the brunt of higher unemployment or layoffs in the public sector, especially of public school teachers, social workers, and others in typically female occupations?

The Role of Unions

A large proportion of employed women work in the largely non-unionized clerical and service occupations. In May 1977 only 15 percent of the women wage and salary workers in clerical occupations were represented by unions. Because the usual weekly earnings of full-time wage and salary women workers in the clerical occupations were 21 percent greater than those of such workers who were not represented by unions ($192 per week versus $159 per week), one might conclude that these traditionally hard-to-organize, female-dominated occupations offer great potential for expanding the declining membership of unions. The recently organized Local 925 of the Service Employees International Union (SEIU), Boston office workers, represents such a trend.

However, unions are presently facing a major challenge to their survival and organizational drives may not have much priority. A recent article in *The New York Times* stated:[2]

> *Confronted with management demands for wage cuts, Washington's desire to reduce federal regulations, and what is widely described as a fundamental rewriting of labor programs that date back to the New Deal [labor] neither understands the workplace trends nor when it does see trends, is it able to come up with imaginative strategies to counter them.*

However, the action of Working Women, a national organization of women who work in offices, may be a catalyst for greater unionization.

Organizational Changes

In the preceding chapter Ruth Shaeffer and Edith Lynton discussed the strategies that large corporations have used to improve women's job opportunities. Many of these activities have now been incorporated into their personnel policies and practices. But how effectively does management respond to the changing role of women workers in the smaller companies? An executive from such a private firm, who attended the MIT Symposium on "Women in the Workplace" (see Chapter 1) responded in this manner:

First, with respect to assisting supervisors, we believe that the salient objective of EEO Staff Groups should be to establish training and consulting strategies that will provide the supervisors with the necessary information and management expertise to effectively manage their own EEO affairs in their respective work areas.

Second, we believe that EEO Staff Groups must first work to assure that the top-of-the-house commitment to EEO (this assumes there is a commitment) is translated into demonstrable accountability systems. Without accountability, without systems to monitor and measure affirmative action efforts at the supervisory level, well-intentioned training and consulting programs by Staff Groups will have little or no chance for success.

Third, we believe that because of the evidence that the real impetus for affirmative action has shifted from the Staff Groups to the Line Groups, the need for the training of Line Managers is no longer a question of why, but is now a question of how.

Fourth, we believe that EEO training activities carried out by staff people for Line Managers should be integrated into traditional pre-existing management training programs. This rationale is based on the knowledge that management failure rather than intentional discrimination is very often the cause of many discrimination incidents.

Fifth, and last, we believe that although training and consulting activities established for supervisors are important, similar efforts directed to middle level executives are just as important if not more so. The reality of management accountability systems, as well as human nature, is that First Line Supervisors will tend to model the behavior of their immediate authority figure—The Boss. So it is, that if the Boss is not a role model or is reluctant to set limits on the behavior of his or her subordinates, then EEO problems and discrimination incidents will continue.

The executive concluded that his company had been successful in improvement of employment opportunities for women by approaching the problem as a management problem. Such internal company strategies are not ordinarily discussed with outsiders, and it may be that the company discussed here is not representative of all segments of American industry.

Legal Environment

The strong emphasis on deregulation that is supported by the Reagan administration may weaken the influence of the Equal Employment Opportunity Commission and the Office of Federal Contract Compliance Programs. In the short run there may be some erosion in the status of women in the workplace. However, the major decision in the Supreme Court on equal pay (*Gunther* v. *Washington Co.*, see Chapter 1) may provide women workers with the support they need to pursue other litigation and for those who are represented by unions to bargain more forcefully on wage issues.

By 1990 women workers may have improved their status. The increasing presence of women in the labor market will be affected significantly by those determinants of their labor market status discussed above. Also, women workers will have had an additional decade of work experience, many in nontraditional occupations. They may have demonstrated how well they perform in a myriad of demanding, complex, sometimes challenging, sometimes dull jobs. Whether they bring the work ethic to the workplace with a continuing vengeance remains to be seen.[4]

Endnotes

1. "America's Restructured Economy," *Business Week*, June 1, 1981.
2. Leo J. Eiden, "Trends in Female Degree Recipients," *American Education* 12, 9 (November 1976).
3. William Servum, "Where Are the Pickets of Yesterday?" *The New York Times*, May 31, 1981, p. F1.
4. Peter F. Drucker, "Working Women: Unmaking the 19th Century," *The Wall Street Journal*, July 6, 1981.

Appendix

EEOC GUIDELINES ON DISCRIMINATION BECAUSE OF SEX

Authority: Sec. 713(b), 78 Stat. 265, 42 U.S.C. 2000e-12.
Source: 37 FR 6836. April 5, 1972, unless otherwise noted.

§ 1604.1   General principles

(a) References to "employer" or "employers" in this Part 1604 state principles that are applicable not only to employers but also to labor organizations and to employment agencies insofar as their action or inaction may adversely affect employment opportunities.

219

(b) To the extent that the views expressed in prior Commission pronouncements are inconsistent with the views expressed herein, such prior views are hereby overruled.

(c) The Commission will continue to consider particular problems relating to sex discrimination on a case-by-case basis.

§ 1604.2 Sex as a bona fide occupational qualification

(a) The commission believes that the bona fide occupational qualification exception as to sex should be intepreted narrowly. Label—"Men's jobs" and "Women's jobs"—tend to deny employment opportunities unnecessarily to one sex or the other.

(1) The Commission will find that the following situations do not warrant the application of the bona fide occupational qualification exception:

(i) The refusal to hire a women because of her sex based on assumptions of the comparative employment characteristics of women in general. For example, the assumption that the turnover rate among women is higher than among men.

(ii) The refusal to hire an individual based on stereotyped characterizations of the sexes. Such stereotypes include, for example, that men are less capable of assembling intricate equipment: that women are less capable of aggressive salesmanship. The principle of nondiscrimination requires that individuals be considered on the basis of individual capacities and not on the basis of any characteristics generally attributed to the group.

(iii) The refusal to hire an individual because of the preferences of co-workers, the employer, clients or customers except as covered specifically in paragraph (a)(2) of this section.

(2) Where it is necessary for the purpose of authenticity or genuineness, the Commission will consider sex to be a bona fide occupational qualification, e.g., an actor or actress.

(b) Effect of sex-oriented State employment legislation.

(1) Many States have enacted laws or promulgated administrative regulations with respect to the employment of females. Among these laws are those which prohibit or limit the employment of females, e.g., the employment of females in certain occupations, in jobs requiring the lifting or carrying of weights exceeding certain prescribed limits, during certain hours of the night, for more than a specified number of hours per day or per week, and for certain periods of time before and after childbirth. The Commission has found that such laws and regulations do not take into account the capacities, preferences, and abilities of individual females and, therefore, discriminate on the basis of sex. The Commission has concluded that such laws and regulations conflict with and are superseded by title VII of the Civil Rights Act of 1964. Accordingly, such laws will not be considered a defense to an otherwise established unlawful employment practice

or as a basis for the application of the bona fide occupational qualification exception.

(2) The Commission has concluded that State laws and regulations which discriminate on the basis of sex with regard to the employment of minors are in conflict with and are superseded by title VII to the extent that such laws are more restrictive for one sex. Accordingly, restrictions on the employment of minors of one sex over and above those imposed on minors of the other sex will not be considered a defense to an otherwise established unlawful employment practice or as a basis for the application of the bona fide occupational qualification exception.

(3) A number of States require that minimum wage and premium pay for overtime be provided for female employees. An employer will be deemed to have engaged in an unlawful employment practice if:

(i) It refuses to hire or otherwise adversely affects the employment opportunities of female applicants or employees in order to avoid the payment of minimum wages or overtime pay required by State law; or

(ii) It does not provide the same benefits for male employees.

(4) As to other kinds of sex-oriented State employment laws, such as those requiring special rest and meal periods or physical facilities for women, provision of these benefits to one sex only will be a violation of title VII. An employer will be deemed to have engaged in an unlawful employment practice if:

(i) It refuses to hire or otherwise adversely affects the employment opportunities of female applicants or employees in order to avoid the provision of such benefits; or

(ii) It does not provide the same benefits for male employees. If the employer can prove that business necessity precludes providing these benefits to both men and women, then the State law is in conflict with and superseded by title VII as to this employer. In this situation, the employer shall not provide such benefits to members of either sex.

(5) Some States require that separate restrooms be provided for employees of each sex. An employer will be deemed to have engaged in an unlawful employment practice if it refuses to hire or otherwise adversely affects the employment opportunities of applicants or employees in order to avoid the provision of such restrooms for persons of that sex.

§ 1604.3   Separate lines of progression and seniority systems

(a) It is an unlawful employment practice to classify a job as "male" or "female" or to maintain separate lines of progression or separate seniority lists based on sex where this would adversely affect any employee unless sex is a bona fide occupational qualification for that job. Accordingly, employment practices are unlawful which arbitrarily classify jobs so that:

(1) A female is prohibited from applying for a job labeled "male," or for a job in a "male" line of progression; and vice versa.

(2) A male scheduled for layoff is prohibited from displacing a less senior female on a "female" seniority list; and vice versa.

(b) A Seniority system or line of progression which distinguishes between "light" and "heavy" jobs constitutes an unlawful employment practice if it operates as a disguised form of classification by sex, or creates unreasonable obstacles to the advancement by members of either sex into jobs which members of that sex would reasonably be expected to perform.

§ 1604.4   *Discrimination against married women*

(a) The Commission has determined that an employer's rule which forbids or restricts the employment of married women and which is not applicable to married men is a discrimination based on sex prohibited by title VII of the Civil Rights Act. It does not seem to us relevant that the rule is not directed against all females, but only against married females, for so long as sex is a factor in the application of the rule, such application involves a discrimination based on sex.

(b) It may be that under certain circumstances, such a rule could be justified within the meaning of section 703(e)(1) of title VII. We express no opinion on this question at this time except to point out that sex as a bona fide occupational qualification must be justified in terms of the peculiar requirements of the particular job and not on the basis of a general principle such as the desirability of spreading work.

§ 1604.5   *Job opportunities advertising*

It is a violation of title VII for a help-wanted advertisement to indicate a preference, limitation, specification, or discrimination based on sex unless sex is a bona fide occupational qualification for the particular job involved. The placement of an advertisement in columns classified by publishers on the basis of sex, such as columns headed "Male" or "Female," will be considered an expression of a preference, limitation, specification, or discrimination based on sex.

§ 1604.6   *Employment agencies*

(a) Section 703(b) of the Civil Rights Act specifically states that it shall be unlawful for an employment agency to discriminate against any individual because of sex. The Commission has determined that private employment agencies which deal exclusively with one sex are engaged in an unlawful employment practice, except to the extent that such agencies limit their services to furnishing employees for particular jobs for which sex is a bona fide occupational qualification.

(b) An employment agency that receives a job order containing an unlawful sex specification will share responsibility with the employer placing the job order if the agency fills the order knowing that the sex specification is not based upon a bona fide occupational qualification. However, an employment agency will not be deemed to be in violation of the law, regardless of the determination as to the employer, if the agency does not have reason to believe that the employer's claim of bona fide occupations qualification is without substance and the agency makes and maintains a written record available to the Commission of each such job order. Such record shall include the name of the employer, the description of the job and the basis for the employer's claim of bona fide occupational qualification.

(c) It is the responsibility of employment agencies to keep informed of opinions and decisions of the Commission on sex discrimination.

§ 1604.7   *Pre-employment inquiries as to sex*

A pre-employment inquiry may ask "Male........., Female.........."; or "Mr. Mrs. Miss," provided that the inquiry is made in good faith for a nondiscriminatory purpose. Any pre-employment inquiry in connection with prospective employment which expresses directly or indirectly any limitation, specification, or discrimination as to sex shall be unlawful unless based upon a bona fide occupational qualification.

§ 1604.8   *Relationship of title VII to the Equal Pay Act*

(a) The employee coverage of the prohibitions against discrimination based on sex contained in title VII is coextensive with that of the other prohibitions contained in title VII and is not limited by section 703(h) to those employees covered by the Fair Labor Standards Act.

(b) By virtue of section 703(h), a defense based on the Equal Pay Act may be raised in a proceeding under title VII.

(c) Where such a defense is raised the Commission will give appropriate consideration to the interpretations of the Administrator, Wage and Hour Division, Department of Labor, but will not be bound thereby.

§ 1604.9   *Fringe benefits*

(a) "Fringe benefits," as used herein, includes medical, hospital, accident, life insurance and retirement benefits; profit-sharing and bonus plans; leave; and other terms, conditions, and privileges of employment.

(b) It shall be an unlawful employment practice for an employer to discriminate between men and women with regard to fringe benefits.

(c) Where an employer conditions benefits available to employees and their spouses and families on whether the employee is the "head of the household" or "principal wage earner" in the family unit, the benefits tend to be available only to male employees and their families. Due to the fact that such conditioning discriminatorily affects the rights of women employees, and that "head of household" or "principal wage earner" status bears no relationship to job performance, benefits which are so conditioned will be found a prima facie violation of the prohibitions against sex discrimination contained in the act.

(d) It shall be an unlawful employment practice for an employer to make available benefits for the wives and families of male employees where the same benefits are not made available for the husbands and families of female employees; or to make available benefits for the wives of male employees which are not made available for female employees; or to make available benefits to the husbands of female employees which are not made available for male employees. An example of such an unlawful employment practice is a situation in which wives of male employees receive maternity benefits while female employees receive no such benefits.

(e) It shall not be a defense under title VIII to a charge of sex discrimination in benefits that the cost of such benefits is greater with respect to one sex than the other.

(f) It shall be an unlawful employment practice for an employer to have a pension or retirement plan which establishes different optional or compulsory retirement ages based on sex, or which differentiates in benefits on the basis of sex. A statement of the General Counsel of September 13, 1968, providing for a phasing out of differentials with regard to optional retirement age for certain incumbent employees is hereby withdrawn.

§ 1604.10 Employment policies relating to pregnancy and childbirth

(a) A written or unwritten employment policy or practice which excludes from employment applicants or employees because of pregnancy, childbirth or related medical conditions is in prima facie violation of Title VII.

(b) Disabilities caused or contributed to by pregnancy, childbirth, or related medical conditions, for all job-related purposes, shall be treated the same as disabilities caused or contributed to by other medical conditions, under any health or disability insurance or sick leave plan available in connection with employment. Written or unwritten employment policies and practices involving matters such as the commencement and duration of leave, the availability of extensions, the accrual of seniority and other benefits and privileges, reinstatement, and payment under any health or disability insurance or sick leave plan, formal or informal, shall be applied to disability due to pregnancy, childbirth or related medical conditions on the same terms and conditions as they are applied to other disabilities. Health insurance benefits for abortion, except where the life of the mother would be endangered if the fetus were carried to term or where medical complications have arisen from an abortion, are not required to be paid by an employer; nothing herein, however, precludes an employer from providing abortion benefits or otherwise affects bargaining agreements in regard to abortion.

(c) Where the termination of an employee who is temporarily disabled is caused by an employment policy under which insufficient or no leave is available, such a termination violates the Act if it has a disparate impact on employees of one sex and is not justified by business necessity.

(d)(1) Any fringe benefit program, or fund, or insurance program which is in effect on October 31, 1978, which does not treat women affected by pregnancy, childbirth, or related medical conditions the same as other persons not so affected but similar in their ability or inability to work, must be in compliance with the provisions of § *1604.10(b)* by April 29, 1979. In order to come into compliance with the provisions of 1604.10(b), there can be no reduction of benefits or compensation which were in effect on October 31, 1978, before October 31, 1979 or the expiration of a collective bargaining agreement in effect on October 31, 1978, whichever is later.

(2) Any fringe benefit program implemented after October 31, 1978, must comply with the provisions of 1604.10(b) upon implementation.

[44FR 23805, Apr. 20, 1979]

§ 1604.11   Sexual harassment

(a) Harassment on the basis of sex is a violation of Sec. 703 of Title VII.[1] Unwelcome sexual advances, requests for sexual favors, and other verbal or physical conduct of a sexual nature constitute sexual harassment when (1) submission to such conduct is made either explicitly or implicitly a term or condition of an individual's employment, (2) submission to or rejection of such conduct by an individual is used as the basis for employment decisions affecting such individual, or (3) such conduct has the purpose or effect of substantially interfering with an individual's work performance or creating an intimidating, hostile, or offensive working environment.

(b) In determining whether alleged conduct constitutes sexual harass-

---

[1]The principles involved here continue to apply to race, color, religion or national origin.

ment, the Commission will look at the record as a whole and at the totality
of the circumstances, such as the nature of the sexual advances and the
context in which the alleged incidents occurred. The determination of the
legality of a particular action will be made from the facts, on a case by case
basis.

(c) Applying general Title VII principles, an employer, employment
agency, joint apprenticeship committee or labor organization (hereinafter
collectively referred to as "employer") is responsible for its acts and those
of its agents and supervisory employees with respect to sexual harassment
regardless of whether the specific acts complained of were authorized or
even forbidden by the employer and regardless of whether the employer
knew or should have known of their occurrence. The Commission will
examine the circumstances of the particular employment relationship and
the job functions performed by the individual in determining whether an
individual acts in either a supervisory or agency capacity.

(d) With respect to persons other than those mentioned in paragraph (c)
of this section, an employer is responsible for acts of sexual harassment in
the workplace where the employer, or its agents or supervisory employees, knows or should have known of the conduct. An employer may
rebut apparent liability for such acts by showing that it took immediate and
appropriate corrective action.

(e) Prevention is the best tool for the elimination of sexual harassment.
An employer should take all steps necessary to prevent sexual harassment
from occurring, such as affirmatively raising the subject, expressing strong
disapproval, developing appropriate sanctions, informing employees of
their right to raise and how to raise the issue of harassment under Title VII,
and developing methods to sensitize all concerned.

[45 FR 25025, Apr. 11, 1980]

Appendix

Questions and Answers on the Pregnancy Discrimination Act, Pub. L.
95-555, 92 STAT. 2076 (1978)

INTRODUCTION

On October 31, 1978, President Carter signed into law the *Pregnancy
Discrimination Act* (Pub. L. 95-955). The Act is an amendment to Title VII
of the Civil Rights Act of 1964 which prohibits, among other things, discrimination in employment on the basis of sex. The *Pregnancy Discrimination Act* makes it clear that "because of sex" or "on the basis of sex", as used
in Title VII, includes "because of or on the basis of pregnancy, childbirth
or related medical conditions." Therefore, Title VII prohibits discrimination in employment against women affected by pregnancy or related conditions.

The basic principle of the Act is that women affected by pregnancy and related conditions must be treated the same as other applicants and employees on the basis of their ability or inability to work. A woman is therefore protected against such practices as being fired, or refused a job or promotion, merely because she is pregnant or has had an abortion. She usually cannot be forced to go on leave as long as she can still work. If other employees who take disability leave are entitled to get their jobs back when they are able to work again, so are women who have been unable to work because of the pregnancy.

In the area of fringe benefits, such as disability benefits, sick leave and health insurance, the same principle applies. A woman unable to work for pregnancy-related reasons is entitled to disability benefits or sick leave on the same basis as employees unable to work for other medical reasons. Also, any health insurance provided must cover expenses for pregnancy-related conditions on the same basis as expenses for other medical conditions. However, health insurance for expenses arising from abortion is not required except where the life of the mother would be endangered if the fetus were carried to term, or where medical complications have arisen from an abortion.

Some questions and answers about the *Pregnancy Discrimination Act* follow. Although the questions and answers often use only the term "employer," the Act—and those questions and answers—apply also to unions and other entities covered by Title VII.

1. Q. What is the effective date of the Pregnancy Discrimination Act?

A. The Act became effective on October 31, 1978, except that with respect to fringe benefit programs in effect on that date, the Act will take effect 180 days thereafter, that is, April 29, 1979.

To the extent that Title VII already required employers to treat persons affected by pregnancy-related conditions the same as persons affected by other medical conditions, the Act does not change employee rights arising prior to October 31, 1978, or April 29, 1979. Most employment practices relating to pregnancy, childbirth and related conditions—whether concerning fringe benefits or other practices—were already controlled by Title VII prior to this Act. For example, Title VII has always prohibited an employer from firing, or refusing to hire or promote, a woman because of her pregnancy or related conditions, and from failing to accord a women on pregnancy-related leave the same seniority retention and accrual accorded those on other disability leaves.

2. Q. If an employer had a sick leave policy in effect on October 31, 1978, by what date must the employer bring its policy into compliance with the Act?

A. With respect to payment of benefits, an employer has until April 29, 1979, to bring into compliance any fringe benefit or insurance program, including a sick leave policy, which was in effect on October 31, 1978.

However, any such policy or program created after October 31, 1978, must be in compliance when created.

With respect to all aspects of sick leave policy other than payment of benefits, such as the terms governing retention and accrual of seniority. credit for vacation, and resumption of former job on return from sick leave, equality of treatment was required by Title VII without the Amendment.

3. Q. Must an employer provide benefits for pregnancy-related conditions to an employee whose pregnancy begins prior to April 29, 1979, and continues beyond that date?

A. As of April 29, 1979, the effective date of the Act's requirements, an employer must provide the same benefits for pregnancy-related conditions as it provides for other conditions, regardless of when the pregnancy began. Thus, disability benefits must be paid for all absences on or after April 29, 1979, resulting from pregnancy-related temporary disabilities to the same extent as are paid for absences resulting from other temporary disabilities. For example, if an employee gives birth before April 29, 1979, but is still unable to work on or after that date, she is entitled to the same disability benefits available to other employees. Similarly, medical insurance benefits must be paid for pregnancy-related expenses incurred on or after April 29, 1979.

If an employer requires an employee to be employed for a predetermined period prior to being eligible for insurance coverage, the period prior to April 29, 1979, during which a pregnant employee has been employed must be credited toward the eligibility waiting period on the same basis as any other employee.

As to any programs instituted for the first time after October 31, 1978, coverage for pregnancy-related conditions must be provided in the same manner as for other medical conditions.

4. Q. Would the answer to the preceding question be the same if the employee became pregnant prior to October 31, 1978?

A. Yes.

5. Q. If, for pregnancy-related reasons, an employee is unable to perform the functions of her job, does the employer have to provide her an alternative job?

A. An employer is required to treat an employee temporarily unable to perform the functions of her job because of her pregnancy-related condition in the same manner as it treats other temporarily disabled employees, whether by providing modified tasks, alternative assignments, disability leaves, leaves without pay, etc. For example, a woman's primary job function may be the operation of a machine, and, incidental to that function, she may carry materials to and from the machine. If other employees temporarily unable to lift are relieved of these functions, pregnant employees also unable to lift must be temporarily relieved of the function.

6. Q. What procedures may an employer use to determine whether to

place on leave as unable to work a pregnant employee who claims she is able to work or deny leave to a pregnant employee who claims that she is disabled from work?

A. An employer may not single out pregnancy-related conditions for special procedures for determining an employee's ability to work. However, an employer may use any procedure used to determine the ability of all employees to work. For example, if an employer requires its employees to submit a doctor's statement concerning their inability to work before granting leave or paying sick benefits, the employer may require employees affected by pregnancy-related conditions to submit such statement. Similarly, if an employer allows its employees to obtain doctor's statements from their personal physicians for absences due to other disabilities or return dates from other disabilities, it must accept doctor's statements from personal physicians for absences and return dates connected with pregnancy-related disabilities.

7. Q. Can an employer have a rule which prohibits an employee from returning to work for a predetermined length of time after childbirth?

A. No.

8. Q. If an employee has been absent from work as a result of a pregnancy-related condition and recovers, may her employer require her to remain on leave until after her baby is born?

A. No. An employee must be permitted to work at all times during pregnancy when she is able to perform her job.

9. Q. Must an employer hold open the job of an employee who is absent on leave because she is temporarily disabled by pregnancy-related conditions?

A. Unless the employee on leave has informed the employer that she does not intend to return to work, her job must be held open for her return on the same basis as jobs are held open for employees on sick or disability leave for other reasons.

10. Q. May an employer's policy concerning the accrual and crediting of seniority during absences for medical conditions be different for employees affected by pregnancy-related conditions than for other employees?

A. No. An employer's seniority policy must be the same for employees absent for pregnancy-related reasons as for those absent for other medical reasons.

11. Q. For purposes of calculating such matters as vacations and pay increases, may an employer credit time spent on leave for pregnancy-related reasons differently than time spent on leave for other reasons?

A. No. An employer's policy with respect to crediting time for the purpose of calculating such matters as vacations and pay increases cannot treat employees on leave for pregnancy-related reasons less favorably than employees on leave for other reasons. For example, if employees on leave for medical reasons are credited with the time spent on leave when computing entitlement to vacation or pay raises, an employee on leave for pregnancy-related disability is entitled to the same kind of time credit.

12. Q. Must an employer hire a woman who is medically unable, because of a pregnancy-related condition, to perform a necessary function of a job?

A. An employer cannot refuse to hire a woman because of her pregnancy-related condition so long as she is able to perform the major functions necessary to the job. Nor can an employer refuse to hire her because of its preferences against pregnant workers or the preferences of co-workers, clients, or customers.

13. Q. May an employer limit disability benefits for pregnancy-related conditions to married employees?

A. No.

14. Q. If an employer has an all female workforce or job classification, must benefits be provided for pregnancy-related conditions?

A. Yes. If benefits are provided for other conditions, they must also be provided for pregnancy-related conditions.

15. Q. For what length of time must an employer who provides income maintenance benefits for temporary disabilities provide such benefits for pregnancy-related disabilities?

A. Benefits should be provided for as long as the employee is unable to work for medical reasons unless some other limitation is set for all other temporary disabilities in which case pregnancy-related disabilities should be treated the same as other temporary disabilities.

16. Q. Must an employer who provides benefits for long-term or permanent disabilities provide such benefits for pregnancy-related conditions?

A. Yes. Benefits for long-term or permanent disabilities resulting from pregnancy-related conditions must be provided to the same extent that such benefits are provided for other conditions which result in long-term or permanent disability.

17. Q. If an employer provides benefits to employees on leave, such as installment purchase disability insurance, payment of premiums for health, life or other insurance, continued payments into pension, saving or profit sharing plans, must the same benefits be provided for those on leave for pregnancy-related conditions?

A. Yes, the employer must provide the same benefits for those on leave for pregnancy-related conditions as for those on leave for other reasons.

18. Q. Can an employee who is absent due to a pregnancy-related disability be required to exhaust vacation benefits before receiving sick leave pay or disability benefits?

A. No. If employees who are absent because of other disabling causes receive sick leave pay or disability benefits without any requirement that they first exhaust vacation benefits, the employer cannot impose this requirement on an employee absent for a pregnancy-related cause.

18.(A). Q. Must an employer grant leave to a female employee for childcare purposes after she is medically able to return to work following leave necessitated by pregnancy, childbirth or related medical conditions?

A. While leave for childcare purposes is not covered by the Pregnancy Discrimination Act, ordinary Title VII principles would require that leave for childcare purposes be granted on the same basis as leave which is granted to employees for other non-medical reasons. For example, if an employer allows its employees to take leave without pay or accrued annual leave for travel or education which is not job related, the same type of leave must be granted to those who wish to remain on leave for infant care, even though they are medically able to return to work.

19. Q. If state law requires an employer to provide disability insurance for a specified period before and after childbirth, does compliance with the state law fulfill the employer's obligation under the Pregnancy Discrimination Act?

A. Not necessarily. It is an employer's obligation to treat employees temporarily disabled by pregnancy in the same manner as employees affected by other temporary disabilities. Therefore, any restrictions imposed by state law on benefits for pregnancy-related disabilities, but not for other disabilities, do not excuse the employer from treating the individuals in both groups of employees the same. If, for example, a state law requires an employer to pay a maximum of 26 weeks benefits for disabilities other than pregnancy-related ones but only six weeks for pregnancy-related disabilities, the employer must provide benefits for the additional weeks to an employee disabled by pregnancy-related conditions, up to the maximum provided other disabled employees.

20. Q. If a State or local government provides its own employees income maintenance benefits for disabilities, may it provide different benefits for disabilities arising from pregnancy-related conditions than for disabilities arising from other conditions?

A. No. State and local governments, as employers, are subject to the Pregnancy Discrimination Act in the same way as private employers and must bring their employment practices and programs into compliance with the Act, including disability and health insurance programs.

21. Q. Must an employer provide health insurance coverage for the medical expenses of pregnancy-related conditions of the spouses of male employees? Of the dependents of all employees?

A. Where an employer provides no coverage for dependents, the employer is not required to institute such coverage. However, if an employer's insurance program covers the medical expenses of spouses of female employees, then it must equally cover the medical expenses of spouses of male employees, including those arising from pregnancy-related conditions.

But the insurance does not have to cover the pregnancy-related conditions of other dependents as long as it excludes the pregnancy-related conditions of the dependents of male and female employees equally.

22. Q. Must an employer provide the same level of health insurance coverage for the pregnancy-related medical conditions of the spouses of male employees as it provides for its female employees?

A. No. It is not necessary to provide the same level of coverage for the pregnancy-related medical conditions of spouses of male employees as for female employees. However, where the employer provides coverage for the medical conditions of the spouses of its employees, then the level of coverage for pregnancy-related medical conditions of the spouses of male employees must be the same as the level of coverage for all other medical conditions of the spouses of female employees. For example, if the employer covers employees for 100 percent of reasonable and customary expenses sustained for a medical condition, but only covers dependent spouses for 50 percent of reasonable and customary expenses for their medical conditions, the pregnancy-related expenses of the male employee's spouse must be covered at the 50 percent level.

23. Q. May an employer offer optional dependent coverage which excludes pregnancy-related medical conditions or offers less coverage for pregnancy-related medical conditions where the total premium for the optional coverage is paid by the employee?

A. No. Pregnancy-related medical conditions must be treated the same as other medical conditions under any health or disability insurance or sick leave plan *available in connection with employment,* regardless of who pays the premiums.

24. Q. Where an employer provides its employees a choice among several health insurance plans, must coverage for pregnancy-related conditions be offered in all of the plans?

A. Yes. Each of the plans must cover pregnancy-related conditions. For example, an employee with a single coverage policy cannot be forced to purchase a more expensive family coverage policy in order to receive coverage for her own pregnancy-related condition.

25. Q. On what basis should an employee be reimbursed for medical expenses arising from pregnancy, childbirth or related conditions?

A. Pregnancy-related expenses should be reimbursed in the same manner as are expenses incurred for other medical conditions. Therefore, whether a plan reimburses the employees on a fixed basis, or a percentage of reasonable and customary charge basis, the same basis should be used for reimbursement of expenses incurred for pregnancy-related conditions. Furthermore, if medical costs for pregnancy-related conditions increase, reevaluation of the reimbursement level should be conducted in the same manner as are cost reevaluations of increases for other medical conditions.

Coverage provided by a health insurance program for other conditions must be provided for pregnancy-related conditions. For example, if a plan provides major medical coverage, pregnancy-related conditions must be so covered. Similarly, if a plan covers the cost of a private room for other conditions, the plan must cover the cost of a private room for pregnancy-related conditions. Finally, where a health insurance plan covers office visits to physicians, pre-natal and post-natal visits must be included in such coverage.

26. Q. May an employer limit payment of costs for pregnancy-related medical conditions to a specified dollar amount set forth in an insurance policy, collective bargaining agreement or other statement of benefits to which an employee is entitled?

A. The amounts payable for the costs incurred for pregnancy-related conditions can be limited only to the same extent as are costs for other conditions. Maximum recoverable dollar amounts may be specified for pregnancy-related conditions if such amounts are similarly specified for other conditions, and so long as the specified amounts in all instances cover the same proportion of actual costs. If, in addition to the scheduled amount for other procedures, additional costs are paid for, either directly or indirectly, by the employer, such additional payments must also be paid for pregnancy-related procedures.

27. Q. May an employer impose a different deductible for payment of costs for pregnancy-related medical conditions than for costs of other medical conditions?

A. No. Neither an additional deductible, an increase in the usual deductible, nor a larger deductible can be imposed for coverage for pregnancy-related medical costs, whether as a condition for inclusion of pregnancy-related costs in the policy or for payment of the costs when incurred. Thus, if pregnancy-related costs are the first incurred under the policy, the employee is required to pay only the same deductible as would otherwise be required had other medical costs been the first incurred. Once this deductible has been paid, no additional deductible can be required for other medical procedures. If the usual deductible has already been paid for other medical procedures, no additional deductible can be required when pregnancy-related costs are later incurred.

28. Q. If a health insurance plan excludes the payment of benefits for any conditions existing at the time the insured's coverage becomes effective (pre-existing condition clause), can benefits be denied for medical costs arising from a pregnancy existing at the time the coverage became effective?

Yes. However, such benefits cannot be denied unless the pre-existing condition clause also excludes benefits for other pre-existing conditions in the same way.

29. Q. If an employer's insurance plan provides benefits after the insured's employment has ended (i.e., extended benefits) for costs connected with pregnancy and delivery where conception occurred while the

insured was working for the employer, but not for the costs of any other medical condition which began prior to termination of employment, may an employer (a) continue to pay these extended benefits for pregnancy-related medical conditions but not for other medical conditions, or (b) terminate these benefits for pregnancy-related conditions?

A. Where a health insurance plan currently provides extended benefits for other medical conditions on a less favorable basis than for pregnancy-related medical conditions, extended benefits must be provided for other medical conditions on the same basis as for pregnancy-related medical conditions. Therefore, an employer can neither continue to provide less benefits for other medical conditions nor reduce benefits currently paid for pregnancy-related medical conditions.

30. Q. Where an employer's health insurance plan currently requires total disability as a prerequisite for payment of extended benefits for other medical conditions but not for pregnancy-related costs, may the employer now require total disability for payment of benefits for pregnancy-related medical conditions as well?

A. Since extended benefits cannot be reduced in order to come into compliance with the Act, a more stringent prerequisite for payment of extended benefits for pregnancy-related medical conditions, such as a requirement for total disability, cannot be imposed. Thus, in this instance, in order to comply with the Act, the employer must treat other medical conditions as pregnancy-related conditions are treated.

31. Q. Can the added cost of bringing benefit plans into compliance with the Act be apportioned between the employer and employee?

A. The added cost, if any, can be apportioned between the employer and employee in the same proportion that the cost of the fringe benefit plan was apportioned on October 31, 1978, if that apportionment was nondiscriminatory. If the costs were not apportioned on October 31, 1978, they may not be apportioned in order to come into compliance with the Act. However, in no circumstance may male or female employees be required to pay unequal apportionments on the basis of sex or pregnancy.

32. Q. In order to come into compliance with the Act, may an employer reduce benefits or compensation?

A. In order to come into compliance with the Act, benefits or compensation which an employer was paying on October 31, 1978 cannot be reduced before October 31, 1979 or before the expiration of a collective bargaining agreement in effect on October 31, 1978, whichever is later.

Where an employer has not been in compliance with the Act by the times specified in the Act, and attempts to reduce benefits, or compensation, the employer may be required to remedy its practices in accord with ordinary Title VII remedial principles.

33. Q. Can an employer self-insure benefits for pregnancy-related conditions if it does not self-insure benefits for other medical conditions?

A. Yes, so long as the benefits are the same. In measuring whether benefits are the same, factors other than the dollar coverage paid should be considered. Such factors include the range of choice of physicians and hospitals, and the processing and promptness of payment of claims.

34. Q. Can an employer discharge, refuse to hire or otherwise discriminate against a woman because she has had an abortion?

A. No. An employer cannot discriminate in its employment practices against a woman who has had an abortion.

35. Q. Is an employer required to provide fringe benefits for abortions if fringe benefits are provided for other medical conditions?

A. All fringe benefits other than health insurance, such as sick leave, which are provided for other medical conditions, must be provided for abortions. Health insurance, however, need be provided for abortions only where the life of the woman would be endangered if the fetus were carried to term or where medical complications arise from an abortion.

36. Q. If complications arise during the course of an abortion, as for instance excessive hemorrhaging, must an employer's health insurance plan cover the additional cost due to the complications of the abortion?

A. Yes. The plan is required to pay those additional costs attributable to the complications of the abortion. However, the employer is not required to pay for the abortion itself, except where the life of the mother would be endangered if the fetus were carried to term.

37. Q. May an employer elect to provide insurance coverage for abortions?

A. Yes. The Act specifically provides that an employer is not precluded from providing benefits for abortions whether directly or through a collective bargaining agreement, but if an employer decides to cover the costs of abortion, the employer must do so in the same manner and to the same degree as it covers other medical conditions.

[44 FR 23805, Apr. 20, 1979]

INDEX